ACQUAINTANCE RAPE:

Assessment, Treatment, and Prevention

Edited by
Thomas L. Jackson, PhD

Professional Resource Press
Sarasota, Florida

Published by Professional Resource Press
(An imprint of Professional Resource Exchange, Inc.)
Post Office Box 15560
Sarasota, FL 34277-1560

The copy editor for this book was Patricia Rockwood, the managing editor was Debra Fink, the production coordinator was Laurie Girsch, and the cover was created by Jami's Graphic Design.

Library of Congress Cataloging-in-Publication Data

Acquaintance rape : assessment, treatment, and prevention /
    edited by Thomas L. Jackson.
        p.   cm.
    Includes bibliographical references and index.
    ISBN 0-943158-99-0 (hardbound : alk. paper)
    1. Acquaintance rape--United States. 2. Acquaintance rape--United States--Prevention. 3. Rape victims--Services for--United States.
I. Jackson, Thomas L., date.
HV6561.A268   1996
362.88'3'0973--dc20   95-23831
                                                       CIP

Acknowledgements

Many individuals and institutions have contributed to the completion of this edited book and are owed significant gratitude. I would like to express my appreciation first and foremost to the contributors of this book. Their professional dedication, tireless efforts on the part of acquaintance rape victims, and patience with the process of integrating and publishing their work are truly appreciated. I am also indebted to those individuals who assisted with the editing and proofing of the chapters included herein. They include Patricia Petretic-Jackson, PhD and Laura Pitman, MBA from the University of Arkansas, and Debra Fink, Laurie Girsch, and the staff at Professional Resource Press.

Resource support for this edited book came from the Marie Wilson Howells Fund at the University of Arkansas. This endowment, dedicated to mental health research, was invaluable in the completion of this volume. Further, I am extremely grateful for the flexibility, patience, and support of the publisher, Lawrence G. Ritt, PhD, President of Professional Resource Press.

Finally, I, and I'm sure all of the contributors, want to give our heartfelt thanks to our loved ones for their continuing support, encouragement, stimulation, and inspiration.

Editor and Contributors

Kenneth K. Berry, PhD, received his doctorate in psychology from Texas Christian University. He has served on the faculty at Indiana University Medical School in Indianapolis, the University of Nebraska College of Medicine, the University of Queensland in Australia, and the University of Hartford. He is currently the Dean of Faculty at the Chicago School of Professional Psychology. A Diplomate of the American Board of Professional Psychology in Clinical Psychology, Dr. Berry's research interests include forensic and professional issues in clinical psychology. Dr. Berry can be contacted at the Chicago School of Professional Psychology, 806 S. Plymouth Court, Chicago, IL 60605.

Barry R. Burkhart, PhD, ABPP, is currently a Professor of Psychology at Auburn University. A Diplomate of the American Board of Professional Psychology in Clinical Psychology, Dr. Burkhart's research and clinical interests include assessment and treatment of perpetrators and victims of sexual assault. He is widely published and highly respected for his expertise in sexual violence literature. Dr. Burkhart has been a featured speaker at numerous national and international symposia and is a consultant to law enforcement, universities, and several other national groups. Dr. Burkhart can be contacted at The Department of Psychology, Auburn University, Auburn, AL 36849.

Kelly Carroll, PhD, is currently the Clinical Director of the Atlanta Rehabilitation Institute. She served on the Steering Committee for the Sexual Harassment Working Party of Cambridge University while attending as a visiting scholar and has presented numerous workshops and papers in the areas of sexual assault and harassment. Dr. Carroll received her PhD from the University of Arkansas in 1993 and may be reached at the Atlanta Rehabilitation Institute, 1450 S. Johnson Ferry Road, Atlanta, GA 30319-4316.

Mary Ellen Fromuth, PhD, is currently an Associate Professor of Psychology at Middle Tennessee State University. Her training is in clinical psychology with an emphasis on childhood. Her primary research interest is in child sexual abuse with a focus on epidemiological factors, male victims, and long-term correlates. Dr. Fromuth may be contacted through the Psychology Department, Box 436, Middle Tennessee State University, Murfreesboro, TN 37132.

Christine A. Gidycz, PhD, is an Associate Professor of Psychology at Ohio University in Athens, Ohio. She has authored numerous papers in the area of sexual victimization. Specific research interests include the traumatic impact of sexual assault, sexual revictimization, and sexual assault prevention. Dr. Gidycz may be contacted at the Department of Psychology, Porter Hall, Ohio University, Athens, OH 45701.

Thomas L. Jackson, PhD, is a Professor and the Director of Clinical Training in the Department of Psychology at the University of Arkansas. He has directed two American Psychological Association-accredited clinical psychology doctoral programs, and has chaired the Boards of Examiners in Psychology in two different states. His research and clinical interests include the areas of sexual assault and violence and have resulted in over 40 articles, chapters, and books, and consultation and paper presentations to over 60 regional, national, and international groups. Dr. Jackson is Associate Editor of *Innovations in Clinical Practice: A Source Book,* and can be contacted at the Psychology Department, 216 Memorial Hall, University of Arkansas, Fayetteville, AR 72701.

Melissa J. Layman, MS, is currently a doctoral student in child clinical psychology at Ohio University. She has coauthored several articles on sexual assault and revictimization, and is particularly interested in differences between acknowledged and unacknowledged rape victims. She will complete her graduate training next year as an intern at the Columbus Children's Hospital in Columbus, Ohio. Ms. Layman may be contacted at the Department of Psychology, Porter Hall, Ohio University, Athens, OH 45701.

Andrea Parrot, PhD, is an Associate Professor in the Department of Human Service Studies at Cornell University and co-founder and chair of the Cornell Coalition Advocating Rape Education. She is a nationally recognized expert on acquaintance rape and sexually assertive communication. She has authored numerous texts and articles involving acquaintance rape, and is in great demand for consultations and paper presentations. Dr. Parrot may be contacted at the Department of Human Service Studies N 132 MVR Hall, Cornell University, Ithaca, NY 14853.

Patricia Petretic-Jackson, PhD, is currently an Associate Professor in Clinical Psychology at the University of Arkansas. She completed her doctoral work in developmental psychology at Bowling Green State University and post-doctoral lateral retraining in clinical psychology at the University of South Dakota. Prior to her present position, she was on the faculty at the University of South Dakota. Her primary research and clinical activities involve the assessment and treatment of victims of interpersonal and family violence. She has been actively involved in prevention and professional in-service educational programming in the area of acquaintance rape prevention for the last decade. Dr. Petretic-Jackson may be contacted at the Department of Psychology, 216 Memorial Hall, University of Arkansas-Fayetteville, Fayetteville, AR 72701.

Linda J. Skinner, PhD, received her doctorate in clinical psychology from the University of Alabama. After serving as a faculty member of the Department of Psychiatry, College of Physicians and Surgeons, Columbia University and most recently the Department of Clinical Psychology at the University of Hartford, she joined the Department of Psychology faculty at the University of Arkansas. She continues to be actively involved in research on sexual abuse, victimization, and aggression, as well as legal, ethical, professional, and gender issues in clinical psychology. Dr. Skinner may be contacted at the Department of Psychology, University of Arkansas, 216 Memorial Hall, Fayetteville, AR 72701.

Susan C. Tobin, PhD, is currently a licensed psychologist in the state of California. She is a Counselor at the Psychological Counseling Center and also a part-time instructor in the Department of Psychology at California State University, Chico. She currently teaches the Psychology of Women and has counseled, as well as researched, the issue of childhood trauma in adults, including rape trauma. She received her PhD from the University of Missouri-Columbia. Dr. Tobin may be contacted at the Psychological Counseling Center, California State University, Chico, CA 95926.

Table of Contents

ACQUAINTANCE RAPE:

Assessment, Treatment, and Prevention

1

Introduction:
The Definition, Incidence,
and Scope of Acquaintance Rape
and Sexual Assault

Thomas L. Jackson
and
Patricia A. Petretic-Jackson

This edited volume is designed to present the reader with the most salient issues involved in a trauma of epidemic proportions - the crime of acquaintance rape. The contributors to this book represent the best, most prolific researchers, clinicians, and consultants in the field today. All of the chapters are felt to be informative, instructional, and representative of the most current, state-of-the-art knowledge and techniques relevant to the various aspects of acquaintance rape.

There are a number of important reasons why this book was undertaken. The first reason involves the consequences or "cost" of rape. The human suffering that results from the perpetration of sexual assaults is essentially immeasurable. Koss et al. (1994), suggest "Long term reactions in women who are physically assaulted and threatened by male partners include fear, anxiety, fatigue, sleeping and eating disturbances, intense startle reactions, nightmares, and physical complaints" (p. 80). The well-documented symptoms that result from rape can be debilitating and long lasting. We believe that rape represents the most severe invasion of privacy an individual can suffer. In some ways, as will be documented in later chapters, acquaintance rape represents an even greater invasion of privacy and betrayal of trust than the "classic" or stranger rape - resulting in significant trauma to the "self" or "spirit" as well as the body of the victim (Katz, 1991; Kilpatrick et al., 1988; Koss et al., 1988; Roth, Wayland, & Woolsey, 1990). The victim of acquaintance rape must cope with the trauma associated with her* own response to victimization. Compounding this is the concomitant societal denial of her rape as a "real" victimization because of her preexisting relationship with her assailant. The implicit assumption is that, because the victim and perpetrator were acquainted, the rape could have been prevented or was not really rape at all, it was instead consensual sex. Having to contend with both sets of processes may make the journey from "victim" to "survivor" all the more perilous for the victim of acquaintance rape.

The second reason for the existence of that text involves the actual content that is presented within the chapters. This book diverges from previous works on the topic of acquaintance rape in that it represents a strong clinical orientation. Its primary purpose is to facilitate the clinician's professional growth as a knowledgeable practitioner in conceptualizing, assessing, treat-

---

*The term victim will be used to indicate someone who has been forced to have sexual experiences against his or her will or without his or her consent. Some professionals working with sexual assault victims prefer to use the term "survivor." However, although victims may have survived physically, the victimization experience is likely to interrupt their psychological state and interfere with interpersonal relationships. Therefore, they are still being emotionally victimized by the sexual assault. Until victims are able to place the blame for their victimization with the assailants (where it belongs), and put the assault in perspective in their lives, they are still being victimized by the assault. Because many victims of sexual assault do not seek help, and because all victims experience some level of trauma after the assault, the term "victim," rather than "survivor," will be used.

ing, and educating members of the community about acquaintance rape. At the same time, the chapters in this volume represent the successful integration of current empirical findings with experience-based recommendations for clinical interventions.

The third reason for this book's existence relates to the social-historical context in which it is written. It is an issue of "timing." A quick search of *Newspaper Abstracts*, a database which summarizes coverage of 25 national and regional newspapers, reveals that over 10,000 articles have been published over the past 6 years on the topic of rape. Clearly, the time is now "right." The topic of acquaintance rape is now salient. Rape has traditionally been a taboo topic of discussion in our patriarchical society, as it has been in many others. Although rape is an event which occurs at an alarming rate, particularly in the case of acquaintance rape, it is most often minimized or denied by the perpetrator and the community. As Bechofer and Parrot (1991) have noted, "The bottom line is that acquaintance rape is viewed by most people as something other than 'real rape'" (p. 13). For the victim of acquaintance rape, the conflict generated between her traumatic experience and the negation of her assault as a legitimate crime and relabeling the assault experience as "her problem" by the larger social community may result in a kind of "cognitive-emotional paralysis" (Koss & Burkhart, 1989, p. 32). Oftentimes the victim will minimize or deny the experience as "true rape." Although most women who are raped by acquaintances will view themselves as victims, they tend not to perceive themselves as legitimate crime victims (Estrich, 1987). Those who identify their assault as rape rarely tell anyone about their experience out of fear that they will not be believed or will be blamed for "leading the man on" and precipitating their own rape. Thus it is not surprising that help seeking from medical, legal, or mental health service providers is rare in victims of acquaintance rape (Koss, 1985). The rape becomes a "dirty little secret" shared only by the woman and her perpetrator. The resulting "invisibility" of acquaintance rape victims led Koss (1985) to refer to acquaintance rape as "hidden rape."

Our reluctance to address the topic of acquaintance rape has been challenged by several high-profile, public cases and a number of significant research reports involving the issue of rape and sexual harassment that have recently captured the public's attention. With regard to public cases, the media's presentation of the issues associated with sexual assault and other forms of sexually coercive and harassing behaviors has increased significantly the visibility of the issue of acquaintance rape for the general public. Several high-profile rape cases have recently been tried within the judicial system as well as within the court of public opinion. Consider the press surrounding the acquaintance rape conviction of Mike Tyson and the acquaintance rape acquittal of William Kennedy Smith. As Mike Tyson was released from incarceration after 3 years confinement, the discussion continued to revolve around whether he actually committed the offense he was convicted of, and if so, whether 3 years of confinement was sufficient to make up for the crime.

In their investigation of public attributions made in the William Kennedy Smith case, Cowan and Curtis (1994) found that the political affiliation and ethnicity of college males strongly predicted male college students beliefs regarding whether rape had actually occurred. Journalistic attention can represent a double-edged sword, however. White and Sorenson (1992) report an apparent stifling effect on rape reporting in the county associated with the trial following Smith's acquittal.

There has also been spirited public debate ensuing from a jury verdict of guilty in a rape case in which, at the request of the victim, the defendant interrupted the assault to put on a condom. Several sexual assault cases have also gained notoriety, among them the disclosure of the Navy "Tailhook Incident" and the congressional investigations of alleged sexual impropriety by government officials including Clarence Thomas and Robert Packwood.

Witness also the apparent use of rape as a wartime instrument of subjugation and degradation in Bosnia from 1993 to 1995 as evidence that sexual assault and rape can represent an overpowering force in conquest. Further, a recent report on the incidence of sexual harassment in high schools found that an astounding 85% of high school females report having been victimized (American Association of University Women [AAUW], 1993). Finally, there was an initial increase, then subsequent apparent decrease in reports of sexual harassment following the disclosures by Anita Hill during the hearings involving now Supreme Court Justice Clarence Thomas. It appears from the above that, although increased public attention has been focused on acquaintance rape, women still have mixed feelings about reporting victimization to legal authorities. However, as will be discussed next, at least with regard to psychotherapy, women believe that it is no longer necessary to keep the "dirty little sexual secrets" hidden. They identify sexual victimization for what it is. As such, it becomes a more salient issue for the clinical practitioner.

Recent research has suggested that between 50% and 90% of females represented in various clinical samples report a history of rape and/or other forms of sexual assault (Bryer et al., 1987; Jacobson & Richardson, 1987; Root, 1991; Saunders et al., 1989; Stone & Archer, 1990). Thus, clinicians have undoubtedly treated a number of victims of acquaintance rape in their practice. In the small but growing number of cases where women present for treatment immediately following their rape and acknowledge their status as legitimate rape victims, issues relating to case conceptualization and to selection of assessment and treatment alternatives may be clear for the practitioner. However, when faced with the much more prevalent cases of "hidden" victims of acquaintance rape - women who sometimes present for treatment years following the assaultive incident - the clinician may not readily identify the issue of rape as salient in contributing to the client's presenting distress and/or psychopathology. In part, this failure to consider the role of assault in presenting client concerns may be due to the client's own inability to recognize the relationship of a prior assault to her presenting problems. A victim of acquaintance rape often not only fails to acknowledge her assault as a legitimate victimization, but also most often is a delayed treatment seeker. Thus, understanding her presenting symptomatology, which may be consistent with a clinical picture of posttraumatic stress disorder (Foa, Rothbaum, & Steketee, 1993; Hanson, 1990; Resnick & Newton, 1992), appears problematic to both the client and her therapist. With the change in social climate in recent years, there appears to be a greater likelihood that a woman who has experienced rape by an acquaintance will recognize her post-assault distress as reality-based, as being due to her assault experience, and as a legitimate concern which brings her to therapy.

This book is organized to provide the practitioner with information regarding several different issues concerning acquaintance rape. The present chapter by Thomas Jackson and Patricia Petretic-Jackson will outline the organization of the book and present definitional issues involving the continuum of sexual assault. Additionally, this chapter will provide the most recent incidence and prevalence data for rape and sexual assault, and detail additional factors which must be considered when dealing with acquaintance rape.

The second chapter in this book was written by Christine Gidycz and Melissa Layman, two outstanding researchers and scholars in the field today. This chapter addresses many of the factors that allow rape to continue at an unabated pace in today's society, such as societal issues, situational circumstances, mistaken perceptions, blame factors, and our culture's responses to victims and perpetrators alike.

The third chapter in this book addresses the characteristics of rapists, as well as many assessment and therapeutic issues involved in dealing with perpetrators. It has been written by Linda Skinner and Kenneth Berry, scholars exceedingly knowledgeable and well published in the areas of assault and, specifically, perpetrator issues and processes. Besides reviewing the empirical literature on salient perpetrator characteristics and traits, these authors also provide the reader with a variety of empirically supported therapeutic interventions and orientations. Of special note in this chapter is the presentation of the complex and sensitive legal and ethical issues involved in dealing with perpetrators.

The fourth and fifth chapters deal with victims of sexual assault and rape. Particular attention is focused on responses of acquaintance rape victims although much of this information is applicable to a wider set of assault victims as well. The fourth chapter, by Patricia Petretic-Jackson and Susan Tobin, is designed to provide a comprehensive listing of the range of emotional, behavioral, and cognitive sequelae present in victims of acquaintance rape. Both authors are experienced clinicians and excellent researchers in this area. Similarities and differences between acknowledged and unacknowledged victims in terms of symptom presentation are discussed, and specific examples of symptom expression are provided. Additionally, the authors provide suggestions for assessing specific components of many of the most common symptoms exhibited.

Barry Burkhart and Mary Ellen Fromuth co-authored the fifth chapter, which focuses on assessment and treatment issues. These contributors have developed a national reputation for their work in victimization. This chapter presents their comprehensive therapeutic model for dealing with acquaintance rape victims. Their poignant presentation of case histories and the underlying "working through" involved in therapy is extremely sensitive and informative.

The sixth and seventh chapters of this book address education and prevention of rape. The sixth chapter, co-authored by Kelly Carroll and Thomas Jackson, presents a basic core program for rape education and prevention programs, as well as several additional specialized program components. The chapter is designed to familiarize the practitioner with the myriad issues that are involved with acquaintance rape and its discussion in public forums.

Chapter 7, written by Andrea Parrot, summarizes a significant component of rape education and treatment programs - sexually assertive communication training. The content of this chapter has applicability beyond the scope of educational programs and can be successfully integrated into couples therapy and work with sexual assault victims and perpetrators. Dr. Parrot is *the* recognized expert in this area and presents her work in an informative and instructive manner, using appropriate examples and exercises.

A final, brief summary chapter by the Editor will attempt to consolidate the previously presented material and reiterate the importance of providing quality services in this most difficult area of acquaintance rape.

The remainder of this first chapter will present definitional issues and incidence figures involving rape and sexual assault. It will also provide the reader with a sense of the seriousness with which the crime of rape and its treatment must be addressed.

RAPE: DEFINITIONS, INCIDENCE, AND IMPACT

DEFINITIONAL ISSUES

Although the legal definition of rape may vary as a function of state jurisdiction, the salient dimensions remain relatively constant. The three major components of the legal definition of rape include (a) carnal knowledge of a person, which is defined as sexual penetration; (b) lack of consent to this carnal knowledge; and (c) use of force or the threat of force to accomplish the act. This legal definition, despite its simplicity, does not always correspond to the social definition of rape - the definition used by victims, offenders, jurists, and citizens. The research definition of rape, that is, how rape is defined in the context of psychological and social investigations of rape, varies along several dimensions (Muehlenhard et al., 1992). These dimensions include the sexual behaviors specified, the criteria used to establish nonconsent (e.g., victim's behavior, victim's state of mind), the individuals specified (e.g., gender, age, and victim-perpetrator relationship), and who makes the determination of whether a sexual assault has occurred (e.g., researcher vs. victim). Critics of rape research have generally challenged research criteria as being too broad in scope and have further challenged the various definitions employed by specific researchers. However, their criticisms of inflated rates are unfounded because in the vast majority of research studies, the criteria used to determine rape victimization are consistent with the statutes of most North American jurisdictions. Critics have also incorrectly assumed that responses in sexual victimization surveys included instances of nonrape from the spectrum of other sexual victimizations, such as psychological coercion, within the reported rape incidence figures. In reality, criteria for research studies of rape have employed criteria as, or more conservative than, the comparable legal criteria. The research definition of rape commonly restricts it to an act of nonconsensual intercourse involving the use of physical force. Subjects are typically asked if they have experienced being "physically forced to have sexual intercourse against their will."

A more extensive defense of date rape incidence and prevalence figures is provided by Koss (1992). Most recently, Koss (1993) presented a review of commonly used research methods in which she addressed the definitions underlying the studies, the questions used to elicit reports of assault, and other methodological issues. Based on her review, Koss (1993) also included specific recommendations for the design of future studies of rape prevalence so that the true scope of rape can be determined.

Although an act of acquaintance rape may meet the criteria for the legal definition of rape, several factors serve to confound legal and social responsibility issues. First, the degree of relatedness in the victim/offender relationship is closer than the lay public believes exists in a "real rape." When members of the community hear that the victim and offender were dating partners or even marital partners, their first impulse is to question the validity of the charge of rape. In the case of intimate relationships, as in dating relationships, there is a possibility for consensual sex to occur, which is unlikely in the case of strangers. Secondly, victim self-blame appears to be greater in cases of acquaintance rape than in cases of stranger rape. The victim who has been assaulted by an acquaintance is less likely to blame the perpetrator of her assault, a person she had previously trusted, and consequently assumes more personal responsibility for the assault. She may minimize or deny the assault as being such, often failing to view herself as a legitimate crime victim. Society tends to exacerbate this problem, redefining the rape as "the victim's problem." The inequity with which stranger and acquaintance rapes are viewed is similarly present within the legal system as prosecuting attorneys are less likely to take cases involving acquaintance rape to court, and when they do, are less likely to obtain verdicts of guilty. In light of the finding that over 80% of rape victims know their assailant, the legal, societal, and personal reluctance to view acquaintance rape as "real rape" compounds the tragedy for the victim (Koss, 1988).

In contrast to both rape and acquaintance rape, sexual assault is viewed as a less severe crime. It is typically defined as being touched, held, or fondled against one's will. Although legal definitions of rape and sexual assault have some utility for the prosecution of offenders, they lack clinical meaning, that is, a relevance within a clinical context. The legal definitions employ a dichotomy, wherein a woman is classified as being or not being a sexual assault victim. Victimization status is conferred on the basis of the act itself, not the trauma exhibited by the victim. A much improved definitional system would permit the use of a continuum of sexually assaultive behaviors, with rape being one endpoint (Koss, Gidycz, & Wisniewski, 1987). This classification approach would then allow for a range of sexual assault victimizations to be recognized. Such an approach would also add legitimacy to the trauma suffered by many women who, while having been assaulted and having experienced traumatic responses to this event, do not meet all the required criteria for a legal definition of rape. Conceptualizing sexually assaultive/coercive behaviors on a continuum appears to have considerable clinical utility. Typically, when researchers and clinicians have offered a variant of the continuum approach to the definition of sexual assault, sexual harassment falls at one endpoint. Behaviors of increasing assaultive severity - coercive sexual interactions, sexual assault - fall at various points between harassment/street hassling and the other endpoint of rape/incest. However, in determining the "severity" or "intensity" of sexually assaultive behaviors, it is important to consider that "any assessment of the 'toxicity' of an act of [sexual] victimization must take into account its wider social consequences as well as the life circumstances of the victim" (Leidig, 1992, p. 149).

INCIDENCE FIGURES

The U.S. Department of Justice regularly gathers crime statistics in two ways. First, the Uniform Crime Reports represent an annual compilation of the number of crimes that have been formally reported to law enforcement agencies. The 1995 Uniform Crime Reports estimated that there were approximately 102,000 reported rapes in 1994 in the United States (Federal Bureau of Investigation, 1995). While this 1994 estimate represents a 4% decrease over 1993 levels, it nevertheless represents an 8% increase in the 5 years since 1989, a 21% increase in the 10 years since 1984, and an 85% increase in the 20 years since 1974.

The second process by which the Department of Justice collects reports of criminal activity is through the National Crime Victimization Survey. The National Crime Victimization Survey recently was modified to include behavior-specific wording regarding sexual violence. Using this method of questioning, women were found to report in excess of 500,000 annual rapes and sexual assaults to interviewers for 1992-1993 (Bachman & Saltzman, 1995).

While the aforementioned statistics are useful, it is important to note that rape is the most underreported of all violent crimes. It is estimated that rape actually occurs between 2.5 and 10 times as often as it is reported. Based on the Uniform Crime Reports figure of 102,000 reported rapes, this translates to a possible incidence of over 1 million rapes in the United States during 1994. Similarly, the incidence figure suggested by the National Crime Victimization Survey, while lower than some estimates, is felt to finally represent a more accurate portrayal of the true scope of the current problem of rape and sexual assault in the United States.

It is believed that many sexual assaults are not reported due to victims' fears of retribution, embarrassment, denial, mislabeling of the event, or insensitive treatment and revictimization by legal and health care professionals. The figures provided do not permit a distinction to be made between the rates of rape perpetrated by strangers and those perpetrated by acquaintances of the victims. However, although social science research indicates that significantly more women are raped by acquaintances, findings from studies investigating nonreported rapes suggest that the reporting rate for acquaintance rape (approximately 5%) is considerably lower than that for stranger rape (Koss et al., 1987).

Other well-established statistics involving acquaintance rape propose (a) at least one-half of all women will be sexually assaulted at some time in their lives; (b) fully three-quarters of the rape victims will know their offenders; (c) one woman in five reports that at some time in her dating history, she has been physically forced, against her will, to have sex - she has been raped; and (d) three-quarters of males report that a dating partner had said no to sex "when she really meant yes." At the very least, this last finding suggests extraordinarily poor communication among the majority of dating partners; at worst it can result in sexual assault and rape (Koss et al., 1987; Sandberg, Petretic-Jackson, & Jackson, 1987). Clearly, the numbers of victims of sexual harassment, assault, and rape are staggering. The serious impact of rape makes these incidence figures even more distressing.

IMPACT OF
ACQUAINTANCE RAPE

All of the clinician contributors in this book have had victims walk into their offices and report, "I've lost the last 10-15 years of my life because of an assault." Victims report having "lived in a fog," not being able to maintain intimate relationships, and not being able to feel "clean" since the assault. Secondary victims (spouses, family, and friends of the victim) suffer as well. Perpetrators and their friends, teammates, fraternity brothers, and families also bear great costs and embarrassment. Clearly there are no winners when miscommunication or psychopathology leads to acquaintance rape. The costs are overwhelming and long lasting.

It is the intent of this edited volume to present important information that can be used to provide primary and secondary prevention efforts as well as valuable assessment and treatment techniques to deal with this most serious problem.

REFERENCES

American Association of University Women. (1993). *Hostile Hallways: The AAUW Survey on Sexual Harassment in America's Schools*. Washington, DC: Author.

Bachman, R., & Saltzman, L. E. (1995). *Violence Against Women: Estimates from the Redesigned Survey* [Special Report]. Washington, DC: Bureau of Justice Statistics.

Bechofer, L., & Parrot, A. (1991). What is acquaintance rape? In A. Parrot & L. Bechofer (Eds.), *Acquaintance Rape: The Hidden Crime* (pp. 9-25). New York: Wiley.

Bryer, J. B., Nelson, B. A., Miller, J. B., & Kroll, P. A. (1987). Childhood sexual and physical abuse as factors in adult psychiatric illnesses. *American Journal of Psychiatry, 114,* 1426-1430.

Cowan, G., & Curtis, S. R. (1994). Predictors of rape occurrence and victim blame in the William Kennedy Smith case. *Journal of Applied Social Psychology, 24,* 12-20.

Estrich, S. (1987). *Real Rape: How the Legal System Victimizes Women Who Say No.* Cambridge, MA: Harvard University Press.

Federal Bureau of Investigation. (1995). *Uniform Crime Reports.* Washington, DC: U.S. Department of Justice.

Foa, E. B., Rothbaum, B. O., & Steketee, G. S. (1993). Treatment of rape victims. *Journal of Interpersonal Violence, 8,* 256-276.

Hanson, R. K. (1990). The psychological impact of sexual assault on women and children: A review. *Annals of Sex Research, 3,* 187-232.

Jacobson, A., & Richardson, B. (1987). Assault experiences of 100 psychiatric inpatients: Evidence of the need for routine inquiry. *American Journal of Psychiatry, 144,* 908-913.

Katz, B. L. (1991). The psychological impact of stranger versus non-stranger rape on victims' recovery. In A. Parrot & L. Bechofer (Eds.), *Acquaintance Rape: The Hidden Crime* (pp. 251-269). New York: Wiley.

Kilpatrick, D. G., Best, C. L., Saunders, B. E., & Veronen, L. J. (1988). Rape in marriage and in dating relationships: How bad is it for mental health? *Annals of the New York Academy of Sciences, 528,* 335-344.

Koss, M. P. (1985). The hidden rape victim: Personality, attitudinal, and situational characteristics. *Psychology of Women Quarterly, 9,* 193-212.

Koss, M. P. (1988). Hidden rape: Sexual aggression and victimization in a national sample of students in higher education. In A. W. Burgess (Ed.), *Rape and Sexual Assault* (Vol. 2, pp. 3-25). New York: Garland.

Koss, M. P. (1992). Defending date rape. *Journal of Interpersonal Violence, 7,* 122-126.

Koss, M. P. (1993). Detecting the scope of rape: A review of prevalence research methods. *Journal of Interpersonal Violence, 8,* 199-222.

Koss, M. P., & Burkhart, B. R. (1989). A conceptual analysis of rape victimization: Long-term effects and implications for treatment. *Psychology of Women Quarterly, 13,* 27-40.

Koss, M. P., Dinero, T. E., Seibel, C. A., & Cox, S. (1988). Stranger and acquaintance rape: Are there differences in the victim's experience? *Psychology of Women Quarterly, 12*(1), 1-24.

Koss, M. P., Gidycz, C., & Wisniewski, N. (1987). The scope of rape: Incidence and prevalence of sexual aggression and victimization in a national sample of higher education students. *Journal of Clinical and Consulting Psychology, 55,* 162-171.

Koss, M. P., Goodman, L. A., Browne, A., Fitzgerald, L. F., Keita, G. P., & Russo, N. F. (1994). *No Safe Haven: Male Violence Against Women at Home, at Work, and in the Community.* Washington, DC: American Psychological Association.

Leidig, M. W. (1992). The continuum of violence against women: Psychological and physical consequences. *Journal of American College Health, 40,* 149-155.

Muehlenhard, C. L., Powch, I. G., Phelps, J. L., & Gust, L. M. (1992). Definitions of rape: Scientific and political implications. *Journal of Social Issues, 48,* 23-44.

Resnick, H. S., & Newton, T. (1992). Assessment and treatment of post-traumatic stress disorder in adult survivors of sexual assault. In D. W. Foy (Ed.), *Treating PTSD: Cognitive-Behavioral Strategies* (pp. 99-126). New York: Guilford.

Root, M. (1991). Persistent disordered eating as a gender-specific, post-traumatic stress response to sexual assault. *Psychotherapy, 28,* 96-102.

Roth, S., Wayland, K., & Woolsey, M. (1990). Victimization history and victim-assailant relationship as factors in recovery from sexual assault. *Journal of Traumatic Stress, 3,* 169-180.

Sandberg, G., Petretic-Jackson, P., & Jackson, T. (1987). College students' attitudes regarding sexual coercion and aggression: Developing educational and preventive strategies. *Journal of College Student Personnel, 28,* 302-311.

Saunders, B. E., Kilpatrick, D. G., Resnick, H. S., & Tidwell, R. P. (1989). Brief screening for lifetime history of criminal victimization at mental health intake: A preliminary study. *Journal of Interpersonal Violence, 4,* 267-277.

Stone, G., & Archer, J. (1990). College and university counseling centers in the 1990s: Challenges and limits. *Counseling Psychologist, 18,* 539-607.

White, J. W., & Sorenson, S. B. (1992). A sociocultural view of sexual assault: From discrepancy to diversity. *Journal of Social Issues, 48,* 187-195.

2

The Crime of
Acquaintance Rape*

Christine A. Gidycz
and
Melissa J. Layman

This chapter provides an overview of the crime of acquaintance rape. It also presents the associated societal and individual correlates of acquaintance rape as well as a number of cultural and environmental components that contribute to maintaining the distressing prevalence of this crime. A final goal of this chapter is to provide the theoretical and empirically derived underpinnings of the subsequent chapters involving perpetrators, victims, and the general public.

In 1987, a national survey of sexual victimization was conducted on college campuses throughout the United States. Statistics from this study revealed that one out of four women were victims of rape or attempted rape at some time after the age of 14 (M. P. Koss, Gidycz, & Wisniewski, 1987). A recent nation-

*The authors gratefully acknowledge the assistance of Mary P. Koss, PhD, on the initial draft of this chapter.

wide survey of adult women in the general population found that one out of eight women had been raped in their lifetimes (National Victim Center, 1992). Although parents, educators, and administrators often warn young women to "be careful of strangers" or to "not walk alone at night," as an attempt to prevent young women from being raped, these well-meaning warnings often do not go far enough. Statistics would suggest that parents and educators also need to warn their daughters and students about the nice-looking, well-dressed, middle-class young men that they meet in their classes, at bars, or at parties. Statistics reveal that in the national study on college campuses, 84% of the women raped knew their attackers and 57% of the rapes occurred on dates (M. P. Koss et al., 1987). Similarly, in the National Victim Center (1992) study, 75% of women were raped by acquaintances.

Despite the fact that rape of any type is a crime, only 8% of acquaintance rape victims ever report the assault to the police, and as many as 50% of acquaintance rape victims never tell anyone about the assault, not even their closest family members and friends (M. P. Koss, 1988). It is, therefore, a serious crime which is grossly underreported and often not talked about with anyone. Furthermore, it unfortunately is a crime that seems to have far-reaching consequences for its victims. Studies have demonstrated that rapid recovery does not characterize the majority of victims. Acquaintance rape victims often experience anxiety, depression, relationship and sexual difficulties, physical symptoms, and increased medical utilization for a substantial amount of time after an assault (see reviews of the literature by Gidycz & M. P. Koss, 1991; M. P. Koss, 1993; M. P. Koss et al., 1994; M. P. Koss & Harvey, 1991; Resick, 1993). Acquaintance rape is, therefore, a crime where victims often suffer in silence, and offenders go unpunished. It is also a crime that appears to be pervasive in our society.

In the pages that follow, it will be shown that there are various societal factors, situational factors (including victim and offender situational characteristics), and characteristics of our legal system surrounding the acquaintance rape issue that contribute to the continuation of this crime. It is important to keep in mind that acquaintance rape is a multidetermined crime. The primary cause of rape is the rapist, but there is no simple answer to the question "Why do men rape?" It is the thesis of this chapter that no one factor contributes in isolation to the continuation of this crime; rather, many variables interact in a complex manner. As suggested by M. P. Koss et al. (1994), "Violence is so pervasive that it cannot be explained as solely the product of individual psychopathology or faulty communication" (p. 3). The multiple classes of influences that determine the expression of sexually assaultive behavior will be discussed next.

SOCIETAL FACTORS: THE INITIAL IMPETUS FOR ACQUAINTANCE RAPE

GENDER INEQUALITY

Violence towards women has been viewed as a manifestation of gender inequality and as a mechanism for the subordination of women. Thus, it has been suggested that in order to understand violence towards women, one must examine the legal, economic, and physical power inequalities between men and women (M. P. Koss et al., 1994). The fact that one out of four women are subjected to this crime is not surprising given that the United States is a society which continues to be demeaning to women in many respects. It is a society that often fosters dominance of men over women and ultimately violence against women, a society where women's needs are not given high priority.

Economic statistics provide some compelling evidence for the differential power of men over women. For example, in 1991 the mean income for a male college graduate was $50,747, while the mean income for a female college graduate was $33,144. Thus, in an educated sample of men and women, females earn only 65% of what males earn. Figures are equally

bleak for women with less than a high school education. The
average income of a man with an eighth grade education in
1991 was $19,632, while the average income level of a woman
with a comparable educational status was $12,570 (United States
Department of Commerce, 1993). These statistics provide some
direct evidence for the continued power differential in our society between men and women. Other statistics provide more
compelling evidence for our society's continued, open degradation of women.

In 1985, the Pornography Commission appointed by the
Surgeon General reported that pornography industry revenues
had grown from a few million dollars annually in the 1960s to
between 7 to 10 billion dollars per year at the time of the
Commission's report. Although some of the money comes from
narcotics, gambling, and prostitution, the federal commission
reported that several billions of dollars each year come from
the sale of men's magazines, hard-core films, videocassettes,
peep shows, cable television, and dial-a-porn (United States
Department of Justice, 1988). These statistics are particularly
alarming for a couple of reasons. First, the Commission also
reported that despite laws that prohibit initial sale of this material to children, adolescents comprise the largest category of
consumers of pornography in the United States. Second, the
Commission concluded that there has been a dramatic change
in the content of pornography over the years; that is, the content has "deteriorated rapidly." Although it was concluded that
in the 1960s only a small fraction of the pornographic material
centered on degradation, subordination, and violence, in 1985
the Commission concluded the following: "Extremely explicit
depictions of sadomasochism, torture, racism, rape, child sexual
abuse, bestiality, and many other incidents of degradation, subordination, humiliation, and victimization - especially of
women - pervade today's pornography" (United States Department of Justice, 1988, p. 5).

Finally, the Commission concluded that both sexually violent material (i.e., material that involves the sexualization of
violence), and material that involves nonviolent sexual activity
(which includes degradation and humiliation), affect our soci-

ety in many significant ways. The social effects of this material seem to be directly and indirectly related to the continuation of the crime of rape.

THE PERPETUATION
OF THE CRIME OF RAPE

There is a substantial amount of empirical evidence that suggests that there is a relationship between societal factors that demean women and the rates of rape. For example, Donnerstein (1980) assessed the effects of aggressive erotica on violence against women in a laboratory setting. He found that male subjects who had viewed an aggressive pornographic film increased their aggressive behavior toward a female confederate to a higher level than the men who viewed a nonaggressive film. Other laboratory investigators have found comparable effects of pornographic material on the aggressive behavior of men who viewed this material, especially when the female presented in the material affronted, insulted, or provoked the man (see Linz, Wilson, & Donnerstein, 1992).

Furthermore, some researchers have extended this research to specifically address the relationship between pornographic material and the frequency of rape. For example, Jaffee and Straus (1987) surveyed pornographic consumption, as measured by sex magazine readership, in 41 states throughout the country. These researchers found that sex magazine readership was positively related to the rate of reported rape. Additionally, rates of attempted and completed rape increased (although lesser sexual crimes decreased) subsequent to heightened availability of sadistic pornography in Denmark, England, Sweden, United States, Australia, and New Zealand (Court, 1976). Finally, other researchers have specifically studied self-reported sexual aggression among a national sample of college males who primarily assaulted acquaintances. These researchers found that the more serious the self-reported sexual aggression, the more likely the men were to be involved in peer groups that reinforced highly sexualized views of women as well as to have frequently viewed violent and degrading pornography (M. P. Koss & Dinero, 1989).

A survey by Fritner and Rubinson (1993) supported the notion that peer groups that endorse highly sexualized views of women, in this case fraternities and male student/athletes, are overrepresented among accused sexual assailants. It is, therefore, likely that the modeling of sexual aggression in pornography contributes to the link between pornography and sexual aggression. It seems equally likely that societal practices which foster demeaning practices towards women affect the rate of rape indirectly through the fostering of the acceptance of rape myths and attitudes that condone violence toward women. Chapter 3 of this book expands on these and other issues related to perpetrator characteristics, assessment, and treatment.

THE ACCEPTANCE OF RAPE MYTHS

Societal practices that continue to foster the notion that men are dominant, as well as practices that openly allow sexually violent material to reach the hands of young people, serve to perpetuate "rape myths" (United States Department of Justice, 1988). Following are some examples of rape myths:

> It's OK for a guy to force a woman to have sex if she gets him sexually excited.
> In the majority of rapes, the victim is promiscuous or has a bad reputation.
> A woman who goes to the home or apartment of a man implies that she is willing to have sex (Burt, 1980, p. 223).

Research evidence suggests that these rape myths permeate our society. For example, Goodchilds et al. (1988) asked adolescents to indicate the circumstances under which it would be okay for a guy to hold a girl down and force her to have sexual intercourse. Alarmingly, 49% of the boys and 58% of the girls indicated that it would be okay for a guy to force a girl to have sex if she gets him sexually excited. Studies with adult samples have found equally disturbing results. For example, Burt (1980) assessed approximately 600 adults, and over half of the sample agreed with the statement that rapes are reported as rape only because the woman was trying to get back at a man she was angry with or trying to cover up an illegitimate pregnancy. The social control model of rape (e.g., Weiss & Borges, 1975) suggests that these rape supportive beliefs prevalent in our society are particularly problematic because they facilitate sexually aggressive behavior. Specifically, these beliefs allow the sexually aggressive male to avoid defining the use of force or threat of force to obtain sexual intercourse as rape. Rather, force is seen as a normal and acceptable way to obtain sexual intercourse with a woman.

Currently, there is an expanding body of research which suggests that these rape myths are directly related to sexually aggressive activity in men. Sexually aggressive men endorse rape myths to a greater extent than nonsexually aggressive men (M. P. Koss et al., 1985; Muehlenhard & Linton, 1987). For example, M. P. Koss et al. (1985) assessed the presence of rape myths in a sample that contained nonsexually aggressive men as well as men who had perpetrated sexually aggressive acts against acquaintances. They found that the more sexually aggressive the man had been, "the more likely he was to attribute adversarial qualities to interpersonal relationships, to accept sex-role stereotypes, to believe myths about rape, to feel that rape prevention is the woman's responsibility and to view as normal an intermingling of aggression and sexuality" (p. 989). Furthermore, sexually aggressive men have been found to report significantly lower levels of empathy for victims than men who have not been sexually aggressive (Rice et al., 1994). Finally, other researchers (e.g., M. P. Koss & Dinero, 1989; M. P. Koss et al., 1985; Malamuth, 1986) have found that men who are sexually aggressive are likely to condone attitudes that are accepting of violence toward women. Findings such as these have led some researchers to conclude, "rape can be regarded as a logical and psychological extension of a dominant ideology that degrades women and justifies coercive sexuality" (Lottes, 1988, pp. 194-195). Chapter 6 of the present book provides a more extensive presentation of rape myths and the manner in which they can be confronted.

SITUATIONAL VARIABLES:
RELEASERS OF
SEXUAL AGGRESSION

Although societal factors obviously contribute to the continuation of acquaintance rape, there are situational variables surrounding the assault that also contribute to its perpetuation.

VICTIM'S VANTAGE POINT

From the victim's perspective, acquaintance rape often occurs in the context of an ongoing intimate relationship. For example, in the national study of sexual victimization on college campuses, M. P. Koss (1988) found that 57% of the women who were victimized were assaulted by dates. Furthermore, a substantial number of the victims had engaged in prior intercourse with the offender and a substantial number of victims were using alcohol (45%) at the time of the assault. This finding was also supported by Fritner and Rubinson (1993). Compared to stranger rape victims, acquaintance rape victims have been found to perceive the assault and its impact differently. Specifically, M. P. Koss et al. (1988) noted that assaults by acquaintances were perceived by the victims as being less violent than assaults by strangers. Assaults by strangers, for example, were more likely than assaults by acquaintances to involve threats of bodily harm, hitting, slapping, and display or use of weapons (M. P. Koss et al., 1988; Ullman & Seigel, 1993).

These situational variables surrounding the acquaintance rape are important in that they most likely interact with societal factors to contribute to the perpetuation of rape. It has been found, for example, that the majority of rape victims do not conceptualize the experience as such (M. P. Koss et al., 1988; Layman, Gidycz, & Lynn, in press). Of particular importance to the crime of acquaintance rape is that acquaintance rape victims are less likely than stranger rape victims to conceptualize the experience as rape. For example, M. P. Koss et al. (1988) found that while 55% of stranger rape victims conceptualized the assault as rape, only 23% of acquaintance rape victims conceptualized the assault as such. There could be various reasons why many acquaintance rape victims do not acknowledge the assault as rape. For example, because acquaintance rapes are less violent, they may violate the victims' as well as society's stereotypical notion of what a rape entails. Furthermore, because the assault occurred in a trusting and intimate relationship, this may also serve to disqualify the assault as rape for the victim. For example, Shotland and Goodstein (1992) found that subjects were significantly less likely to define a vignette event as rape if a high level of precedent sexual activity was established for the couple. Finally, because society tends to blame acquaintance rape victims for the assault and to be less likely to view these assaults as "real rapes" (compared to stranger rapes), it may be that some victims deny the experience to avoid dealing with stigmatization or the hostile reactions of others.

When victims do not conceptualize the experience as rape, it may increase the probability that these types of assaults continue. Unlike stranger rapes, which tend to occur only once, victims of acquaintance rapes are likely to be assaulted on multiple occasions by the same person. Research has suggested that 44% of acquaintance rape victims, compared to only .8% of stranger rape victims, are likely to be assaulted more than once by the same offender (M. P. Koss et al., 1988). Unfortunately, there may still be strong disincentives to construe and report the experience as rape. Claims of rape may be met with a host of negative outcomes including disbelief, blame, unsupportive behavior, and aversive publicity (see National Victim Center, 1992; Roth, Wayland, & Woolsey, 1990). Until policy and societal changes occur, it is likely that a subgroup of victims will fail to label assaults that meet the legal definition of rape as "true" rape (Layman et al., in press). See Chapter 4 of this text by Petretic-Jackson and Tobin for more in-depth coverage of victim identification, attitudes, and assessment.

OFFENDER'S VANTAGE POINT

Similar to the response of acquaintance rape victims, many men who sexually assault women they know report that these experiences occurred on dates (61%). Furthermore, many of the offenders have had prior sexual involvement with their victims. Finally, a substantial number of the offenders (73%) in the national study of sexual victimization acknowledged that they were drinking and/or using other drugs at the time of the assault (M. P. Koss, 1988). Other researchers have corroborated M. P. Koss's findings that alcohol is associated with sexually aggressive behavior (Fritner & Rubinson, 1993; Levine & Kanin, 1987; B. Miller & Marshall, 1987; Muehlenhard & Linton, 1987; Sorenson & Brown, 1990).

As previously mentioned, men who are sexually aggressive tend to be predisposed to behave in a violent manner toward women as they tend to have incorporated many of society's rape myths as well as attitudes that condone violence toward women. Thus, some men come to an acquaintance rape situation already believing that "Women say 'No' when they really mean 'Yes' " or "Sometimes the only way a man can get a cold woman turned on is to use force." Because a woman may have consented to sex in the past, the man erroneously assumes that he is entitled to the sexual relations despite the woman's protestations. The fact that the man is likely to be drinking may serve multiple functions in sexual assaults: (a) as a disinhibitor for the man, (b) as an excuse for his behavior after the fact, and (c) as a strategy to reduce victim resistance (Richardson & Hammock, 1991).

These situational variables, as well as attitudes that accept violence toward women, most likely contribute to the offender's failure to conceptualize these experiences as rape. In the national study of sexual victimization it was found that only 16% of the men who indicated that they had perpetrated an assault which met the legal definition of rape perceived the experience to be rape. Given these findings it is tragic, but not surprising, that offenders in the national study of sexual victimization were more likely to feel "proud" after the assault than scared, angry, or depressed. Furthermore, it is equally troubling that 47% of the offenders in this study indicated that they expected to engage in a similar assault at some future time (M. P. Koss, 1988). Again, Chapter 3 presents additional information regarding perpetrator characteristics.

SEXUAL MISCOMMUNICATION

A number of researchers (Abbey, 1991; Berkowitz, 1992; Lundberg-Love & Geffner, 1989; Muehlenhard, 1989; Sawyer, Desmond, & Lucke, 1993) have discussed the importance of sexual miscommunication in the perpetuation of acquaintance rape. As several authors describe, the societal expectations about dating relationships form sexual scripts that may lead to sexual assault (for reviews see M. P. Koss et al., 1994; M. P. Koss & Harvey, 1991). For example, our society expects the man to be the initiator of sexual activity and the woman to be the resister, even if she is interested in sexual activity. This may contribute to the widespread belief on the part of males that "No" does not actually mean "No."

Many people feel uncomfortable discussing sexual intentions and desires. As a result, they attempt to infer sexual intent from indirect and nonverbal cues, a strategy that is bound to produce frequent errors (Abbey, 1991). It appears that men tend to interpret a woman's friendly behavior in a more sexual-ized way than she intends (Abbey, 1987; Bostwick & DeLucia, 1992). More than two-thirds of the students in one survey be-lieved that on various occasions their friendliness had been per-ceived as a sexual invitation (Abbey, 1987).

Research has begun to clarify the types of cues that men are likely to misperceive. For example, it has been demonstrated that nonverbal cues such as touching, eye contact, and close interpersonal distance as well as "seductive" clothing were in-terpreted as signs of sexual interest more often by men than women (Abbey et al., 1987; Abbey & Melby, 1986). Abbey et al. (1987) suggested that because our society does not encourage open and honest communication about sex it is difficult to re-solve these misperceptions. Such misperception can and does result in date rape. For example, a man who has interpreted certain cues to mean that a woman wants to have sex with him and later learns that she is not interested may become angry. He may feel justified in forcing her to have sex because he feels led on; he may not take her objections seriously (Check & Malamuth, 1983); or he may perceive refusal as a threat to his manhood (Beneke, 1982).

For a detailed explication of sexually assertive communication training, a technique designed to counteract some of the aforementioned misperceptions and miscommunications, the reader is referred to Chapter 7 in this book.

POSTASSAULT FACTORS: THE NEGLECTED VICTIMS

Whether a victim conceptualizes an assault as rape, acquaintance rape is undeniably traumatic. Empirical evidence suggests that acquaintance rape victims are no less traumatized than stranger-rape victims (M. P. Koss et al., 1988). Specifically, after an assault, fearfulness and anxiety are often initial reactions. As with stranger rapes, feelings of shock, anger, and confusion are often reported to occur both during and immediately after the assault (M. P. Koss, 1988). Additionally, victims of acquaintance rape often experience feelings of depression, suicidal ideation, relationship and sexual difficulties, and physical problems for a substantial amount of time after an assault (Gidycz & M. P. Koss, 1989; Kilpatrick et al., 1985; M. P. Koss, P. G. Koss, & Woodruff, 1991). Empirical studies have suggested that only 25% of rape victims were free of significant psychological symptoms 1 year after the assault (Kilpatrick, Resick, & Veronen, 1981).

A rape experience, like other types of victimization, also violates beliefs that have been confirmed over many years. Janoff-Bulman (1985a) contends that people tend to believe that they are invulnerable; that is, although individuals acknowledge that victimizations and disasters strike other people, they believe that "It can't happen to me." Therefore, prior to a victimization experience the rape victim is likely to believe that she is less likely than others to encounter a negative event such as a sexual assault. However, after the assault, the victim who has been raped by someone she knows often feels intensely vulnerable. Because she has been assaulted by someone she knows and most likely has trusted, the breakdown of safety and security seems to be particularly acute (Janoff-Bulman, 1985b). Unlike the stranger-rape victim who may have intimate friends to provide support for her, the acquaintance rape victim may feel that "No one can be trusted." Sommerfeldt, Burkhart, and Mandoki (1989) interviewed 189 acquaintance rape victims and found that approximately half of them stated that after the assault, they exhibited more cautious behavior and a destruction of trust, particularly with regard to males.

Furthermore, Janoff-Bulman (1985a) contends that people try to make sense of their world by regarding events as being controllable and by believing that they are good and worthy people. Specifically, for the acquaintance rape victim, this means that prior to the assault she is likely to believe that she is a good and worthy person and that she can be protected from misfortunes, like a rape, if she engages in precautionary behaviors. However, after an assault, rape victims' beliefs in the predictability and orderliness of their worlds and in their own self-worth are likely to be challenged, leading to feelings of self-blame. These feelings of self-blame may increase victims' failure to label acquaintance rape as "real rape," thereby increasing the likelihood that the crime of acquaintance rape continues.

RAPE VICTIMS' SELF-BLAME: AN INTERNALIZATION OF SOCIETAL ATTITUDES

Empirical evidence has substantiated that self-blame is frequently experienced by victims of sexual assault. Furthermore, some researchers have found that acquaintance rape victims are even more likely to experience self-blame than stranger rape victims (Katz & Burt, 1988). The following description given by an acquaintance rape victim typifies the feelings of self-blame often experienced by acquaintance rape victims: "It was my fault for being in his bedroom with him and for rubbing his back. He was stressed from work and finals. He didn't know that I'm a virgin. I had been a little bit of a 'tease' in our petting before this incident" (Sommerfeldt et al., 1989, p. 1).

As this example illustrates, after an assault victims feel responsible for an acquaintance rape for a number of reasons. Victims may blame themselves because they went to an isolated place with the offender or because they engaged in some type of sexual behavior with the offender at some time in the past. Furthermore, victims may blame themselves because they had been drinking or simply because "they should have known better." Warshaw (1988) interviewed a number of acquaintance rape victims and stated that "Time and time again women spoke about how, before their rapes, they disregarded their own feelings, inner signals that were telling them something was wrong with the guy, the place, or the situation" (p. 58). This discomfort can occur because the man dropped clues about his hostile or demeaning attitudes towards women, but often there are no clear clues from the offender and the feelings come solely from within the victim.

Therefore, unlike the stranger-rape victim who may just have happened to run into a rapist on the streets, the acquaintance rape situation is typically a setting where the victim willingly went somewhere with a "nice" man with whom she may have had an ongoing relationship and ended up getting raped. Because of the setting, the acquaintance rape victim in many instances seems to erroneously accept responsibility for the assault, leading to feelings of self-blame. These feelings of self-blame may contribute to the perpetuation of rape by contributing to the victim's reluctance to report the assault to authorities and the reluctance to seek psychological assistance.

THE PROCESS OF
REPORTING TO AUTHORITIES

DECIDING WHETHER TO REPORT

Rapes of all kinds are grossly underreported. However, research suggests that acquaintance rapes are even less likely than stranger rapes to be reported to the police. M. P. Koss et al. (1988) estimated that while only a small percentage of stranger rape victims (i.e., 29%) ever report the assault to the police, even fewer acquaintance rape victims report their assaults. In the national study of sexual victimization among college students, it was found that only 3% of the victims who were assaulted by acquaintances reported their assaults to the police (M. P. Koss et al., 1988). These findings are also consistent with community studies of adult women (e.g., Russell, 1984). Following is a description of an acquaintance rape victim who decided not to report her assault to the police after talking with the officer:

> I was afraid to tell him the story because there were so many places in it where I felt I could be judged and that I was naïve and stupid. I was really blaming myself. Why did I go with him? Why didn't I drive my own car? Why didn't I scream for his roommate? Why didn't I know that he was this kind of guy? (Warshaw, 1988, pp. 57-58)

As this victim's statement illustrates, feelings of self-blame may be related to the victim's decision not to report the assault. Because the victim may feel that she was responsible for the assault, she may fear stigmatization from others. In fact, in a national study of women, the majority of rape victims indicated that they would be more likely to report a rape if there were laws prohibiting the media from disclosing victims' names and addresses (National Victim Center, 1992). Victims' fears of stigmatization may not be totally unfounded and in fact may be a partial internalization of society's negative views toward acquaintance rape victims. Warshaw (1988) states that society does not blame the victims of most crimes like it blames acquaintance rape victims. Warshaw (1988) contends that society does not blame a mugging victim for carrying a pocketbook, nor a store owner for handing over the money when threatened. However, acquaintance rape victims are often blamed for the assault because they ignored discomfort that they might have felt regarding the offender, because they might have had some prior sexual involvement with the offender, or because they might have been drinking at the time of the assault. Unfortunately, research suggests that these negative attitudes towards acquaintance rape victims are often incorporated into our legal system, resulting in negative consequences for the acquaintance rape victims who do decide to press charges against the offender.

THE PROCESS OF REPORTING

If a woman decides to report an acquaintance rape, the road to conviction and sentencing can be a long process (see, e.g., Estrich, 1987). It has been suggested that to the extent that rapes deviate from the stereotypical view of rape - that is, rape as a sudden, violent attack by a stranger in a deserted public place - officials may be more skeptical of the case and/or spend less time and energy processing it. The probability of reporting, arrest, and conviction are all related to social status and race. The image of a rapist derived from crime statistics is that of a young black urban male, often of lower class status (LaFree, 1989). However, this is incorrect according to general community surveys. Several investigations have found either no significant differences or very small effect sizes for differences in the incidence or prevalence of sexual assault as a function of race, social class, or place of residence (Ageton, 1983; Hall & Flannery, 1984; M. P. Koss et al., 1987; Rouse, 1988).

Obviously, because acquaintance rape victims often are assaulted within an ongoing relationship, where the victim willingly went somewhere with the offender, these assaults deviate substantially from society's myths about rape. Because our legal system has incorporated these inappropriate cultural myths, victims of acquaintance rape can suffer further consequences as they go through the legal process.

Empirical evidence suggests that, although acquaintance rapists may be more likely to be arrested than stranger rapists, probably because they are easier to identify (LaFree, 1981), rape cases that violate stereotypical views of rape are less likely to result in convictions (LaFree, 1980). LaFree (1980) reviewed the court records of 124 adjudicated rape cases and found that victim characteristics were related to the likelihood of a conviction. He found that in cases where the woman was assaulted by a prior acquaintance or relative, convictions were less likely to occur. Furthermore, it was found that a rape that is not reported promptly is less likely to result in a conviction (LaFree, 1980). This is problematic for acquaintance rape victims because so many of them do not conceptualize the assault as such and, therefore, are unlikely to immediately report the event. Finally, LaFree (1980) also found that assaults which involved some type of "misconduct" or carelessness on the part of the victim were less likely to result in convictions. Because acquaintance rape victims are often erroneously open to charges of "misconduct" this further contributes to the low conviction rates for acquaintance rapes. Given that the process of prosecution can be very difficult for some acquaintance rape victims, it is not surprising that some researchers have found that victims whose cases were tried showed heightened psychological symptoms compared to victims whose cases were not tried (Sales, Baum, & Shore, 1984).

In sum, rapes are grossly underreported, and in cases where they are reported they are less likely to result in convictions if they have occurred between acquaintances. The consequence for the victims is that they suffer in silence, while the offenders go unpunished. Furthermore, this allows rape to continue as it perpetuates the myth that acquaintance rape is rare and that, when it does occur, it is likely to happen to a woman with a "bad reputation" or one who was "asking for it." The truth, however, is that all women are potential victims and, contrary to popular myth and media depictions, most victims cannot be differentiated from nonvictims by specific behaviors or attitudes (M. P. Koss & Dinero, 1989). In fact, some researchers (M. P. Koss et al., 1994) suggest that continued search for victim characteristics that might predict violence is no longer useful as reliable factors have not been found which distinguish victims from nonvictims.

OBTAINING SUPPORTIVE SERVICES

In addition to deciding not to press charges, many victims also do not receive crisis services after an assault. Although research has suggested that acquaintance rape victims are no less traumatized than stranger rape victims (see, e.g., Atkeson et al., 1982; Becker et al., 1984; Frank, Turner, & Stewart, 1980; M. P. Koss et al., 1988), they are less likely to seek crisis services (M. P. Koss et al., 1988). M. P. Koss (1988) reported that only 3% of college student acquaintance rape victims sought

crisis services compared to 24% of stranger rape victims. Similarly, Ullman and Siegel (1993) found acquaintance rape victims in the general population significantly less likely than
stranger rape victims to seek support from a friend, relative, or
professional helper. Additionally, although a substantial number of acquaintance rape victims acknowledge feeling that they
need therapy, very few victims actually seek therapy immediately after an assault (M. P. Koss & Burkhart, 1989; M. P. Koss
et al., 1988). Even when victims do seek therapy in the initial
postassault period, empirical support is lacking for its effectiveness (M. P. Koss & Burkhart, 1989). It is possible that one
reason it is difficult to treat the recent rape victim is that after
the initial shock subsides, many victims go through a stage of
denial. Although this denial can be adaptive in that it allows
victims to go back to work or school and to "go on" with their
lives, it is problematic as they may drop out of therapy prema-
turely and perhaps not resolve the trauma. Again, Chapter 4 of
this text provides details regarding the "stages" involved in responding to sexual victimization.

Despite victims' reluctance to seek immediate therapeutic
assistance, many victims ultimately seek therapy during the
years following the assault. Among samples of women raped 1
to 16 years previously, 31% to 48% stated that they eventually
sought psychotherapy (Ellis, Atkeson, & Calhoun, 1982; M. P.
Koss, 1988). Furthermore, although acquaintance rape victims
are less likely than stranger rape victims to seek immediate
crisis services, they are more likely than stranger rape victims
to be delayed treatment seekers (Frank et al., 1988). These
statistics also suggest that over half of victims do not seek psychotherapy. Although it is likely that some of these victims
resolve the trauma on their own or with the help of family and
friends, at least half of all rape victims tell no one about the
assault, not even their most intimate acquaintances (M. P. Koss,
1988). Thus, many victims carry the burden of their assaults
with them, privately, for a long time.

The consequences of not obtaining supportive services may
be potentially devastating for the victims. In order to resolve
the trauma, it is necessary for victims to come to terms with
shattered assumptions and to make successful cognitive reap-

praisals. For example, the victim must be able to answer questions such as "What is the significance of the event?" "What caused it to happen?" and "How can I keep this from happening again?" Victims also need to promote self-enhancement so that self-blame does not get incorporated into their sense of self. Victims can promote a sense of self by redefining the event and construing benefit from the experience. The victim who does not seek support from others, however, will not have the opportunity to develop a positive or, at least strengthening, reinterpretation of her experience. Instead, the victim may incorporate degradation and helplessness into her beliefs and behaviors (Janoff-Bulman, 1985a; M. P. Koss & Burkhart, 1989; Taylor, 1983).

To the extent that a victim sees herself as damaged and unworthy, she may become compromised in her ability to see herself as able, or even willing, to affirm her dignity. Symptomatically, such beliefs could lead to a clinical picture that varies from a constricted, fear-dominated, withdrawn person to a person who acts out her sense of unworthiness and powerlessness by repeated involvement in abusive relationships (M. P. Koss & Burkhart, 1989). Thus, once a victim has been sexually assaulted, if the trauma is not resolved, it may increase the probability that she will be assaulted again. The results of a prospective investigation lend some support to the possibility that unresolved trauma from an early abuse may predict subsequent victimization (Gidycz et al., 1993).

RECOMMENDATIONS

As stated at the onset of this review, acquaintance rape is a complex problem perpetuated in part by societal factors which continue to be degrading toward women. Because it is a multidetermined crime, it is a crime which will require effort from legislators, educators, mental health professionals, and legal officials for its ultimate prevention. Recognizing this fact, in 1991 the American Psychological Association's Committee on Women in Psychology established the first Task Force on Male Violence Against Women to review research and recom-

mend directions for change (Goodman et al., 1993). The Task
Force concluded "by emphasizing that the problem of violence
against women cannot be fully understood, let alone solved, by
focusing exclusively on individual psychology. Only by changing the social and cultural institutions that have given rise to
the problem can a lasting solution be achieved" (Goodman et
al., 1993, p. 1055). Listed are some recommendations suggested
by the literature.

PREVENTION PROGRAMS

The Need for Prevention Programs. Priority must be
given to education and awareness programs for young men and
women. Because research has suggested that young women
between the ages of 16 to 24 (Bureau of Justice Statistics, 1992)
are at the highest risk for a sexual assault, it is important that
discussions of acquaintance rape be incorporated into prevention and education programs for teenagers as well as college-
aged men and women.

Although there are some universities that have a history of
well-designed acquaintance rape prevention programs (e.g., the
University of Florida in Gainesville and the Ohio State University for general student populations, and the University of Arkansas and University of Maine for student/athletes), many high
schools and universities continue to ignore the problem. The
word "ignore" is utilized because, as suggested by Warshaw
(1988), university personnel are most likely aware of the occurrences of acquaintance rape, but choose to keep quiet about
them because of fears of overly negative publicity. With high
school personnel, it has been our experience that administrators either do not believe that acquaintance rape could possibly
be a problem among their students, or they fear negative reactions from parents if the topic is discussed. The failure to discuss these experiences with young men and women can be devastating for young women as they may continue to mistakenly
believe that rape is a rare occurrence that happens to women
who are "asking for it." This belief is likely to increase their
feelings of invulnerability, ultimately placing these young
women at a greater risk for a sexual assault. For men, the

failure of university and high school personnel to discuss the problem ultimately supports their beliefs that what they are doing is really not rape. Thus, by ignoring the problem, administrators and educators ultimately give young men the message that their aggressive behavior toward acquaintances is acceptable.

Content of Prevention Programs. It seems imperative that well-designed prevention programs provide young people with accurate information about the frequency of acquaintance rape as well as a description of high-risk situations. This type of information should help to dispel many of society's rape myths. Young men and women in our classes continue to be amazed that one out of two college women are sexually assaulted and that women are at a much greater risk of being assaulted by an acquaintance than a stranger. In addition, women need to be taught to pay attention to the "little voice" inside of them that may warn them about potential rapists. The concept that it is acceptable for a woman to say "No" to sex and really mean "No" - even if she has had sex with the man in the past - needs to be reinforced. Women need to be told that it is best to go to public places with a man or double-date until they get to know their partner (Warshaw, 1988). Men need to be told that it is never all right to proceed with sex if a woman says "No" or is reluctant. Furthermore, M. P. Koss et al. (1994) suggested that prevention efforts must address issues of alcohol norms and expectations and their relationship to violence. Because research has suggested that victims perceive their resistance and the man's violence as much more extreme than the offenders do, programs also need to emphasize communication between men and women (M. P. Koss, 1988). Men need to be educated to perceive women's behavior and feelings accurately and to communicate clearly with women if they are unsure of the woman's feelings. Finally, research suggests that prevention programs need to be as salient and personally relevant as possible to increase the consciousness-raising impact of the intervention (Gray et al., 1990; Johnson & Russ, 1989). Chapter 6 of this book provides outlines and references for several types of these education and prevention programs.

In sum, an emphasis needs to be placed on the development of prevention programs for young people. However, the implementation of these programs without evaluation of them, which is frequently the case, may be costly. M. P. Koss (1987) suggests that because intimate violence poses more threat to women than other types of criminal violence, funding priorities need to reflect this reality. As this review would indicate, prevention efforts need to continue to be developed, targeted at high-risk groups, and evaluated scientifically. Although little research has been conducted to evaluate the effectiveness of these efforts (Hanson & Gidycz, 1993), several recent studies have been designed to address this issue (Breitenbecker & Gidycz, 1995; Hanson & Gidycz, 1993; Holcomb et al., 1993; Layman, 1995; Pinzone & Gidycz, in press). Basic findings from these studies indicate that these specific prevention programs did in fact raise subjects' awareness of sexual assault issues (Hanson & Gidycz, 1993), increase empathic and egalitarian attitudes toward rape victims (Holcomb et al., 1993; Pinzone & Gidycz, in press), improve ability to accurately label depictions of rape (Pinzone & Gidycz, in press), and reduce the incidence of sexual assault (for women without a victimization history) over the course of the following academic quarter (Hanson & Gidycz, 1993). However, secondary prevention efforts such as those previously described may not be sufficient; coincident primary prevention programs need to be developed and tested. Administrators', educators', and legislatures' support and facilitation of these types of programs is ultimately a commitment to women. It is a statement that acquaintance rape is wrong, and it should ultimately help to dispel some of society's rape myths.

Finally, Benson, Charlton, and Goodhart (1992) recommend an interdisciplinary, comprehensive strategy for colleges and universities to both support victims of acquaintance rape and prevent further occurrences. This system would include educational programs about acquaintance rape, advocacy services for survivors, and an internal judicial system. These authors also advocate distribution of an official institutional policy on the definition, causes, and options available for acquaintance rape; this policy would provide guidelines for filing reports or pressing charges. Institution-wide official attention to acquaintance rape would serve to firmly establish the serious nature of this crime and the college's or university's commitment to existing and potential victims. As studies have found adolescents to be at risk for acquaintance rape as well (Ageton, 1983), extension of these programs and policies to high schools seems warranted.

The Need to Prevent Revictimization. Both retrospective (Wyatt, Guthrie, & Notgrass, 1992; M. P. Koss & Dinero, 1989) and prospective (Gidycz et al., 1993; Gidycz, Hanson, & Layman, 1995) studies indicate that once a woman has been victimized, she is at a much greater risk to be victimized again. This is particularly alarming given that repeatedly victimized women have been found to experience higher unemployment, greater transiency, lower socioeconomic status, more unplanned pregnancies and abortions, more sexual partners, briefer sexual relationships, and increased psychological symptomatology than single incident victims (Briere & Runtz, 1988; Frank et al., 1980; J. Miller et al., 1978; Wyatt et al., 1992). In addition, prospective studies have revealed that greater severity of the initial victimization is associated with a greater likelihood of revictimization (Gidycz et al., 1993; Gidycz et al., 1995; Breitenbecker & Gidycz, 1995). Furthermore, one empirically tested prevention program, found to be effective for women without a history of victimization, was not effective for women with a history of victimization (Hanson & Gidycz, 1993). Unfortunately, program modifications intended to target multiply victimized women failed to reduce their risk of sexual assault (Breitenbecker & Gidycz, in press). This evidence underscores the need for early intervention with victims in order to attempt to break the cycle of victimization. Future research needs to address the processes through which victimization experiences become linked.

The Role of the Legal System. As a recent review indicates, acquaintance rape can be a difficult crime to prosecute and frequently cases "turn on questions of credibility" (Benson et al., 1992, p. 159). There have undeniably been some legal reforms that benefit victims, including the development of victim-advocacy programs, the abolishment of the spousal exemption laws in many states, the adoption of rape shield laws (laws restricting the scope of cross-examination about the victim's prior sexual conduct), and the repeal of prompt reporting requirements and the corroboration requirements (M. P. Koss et al., 1994; Largen, 1988). In addition, in some cities, special sexual assault units have been established within police departments to deal with rape cases (LaFree, 1989). Largen (1988) attempted to assess the effects of these law reforms and suggested that there was an increase in reports of acquaintance rape as well as in reports of cases where there was little corroborating evidence and where the victims had lifestyles that may not conform to jurors' expectations. However, Largen (1988) suggested that the increase in reports may have been due to shifts in social norms prior to the changes in the law rather than these legal changes. Regardless of the ordering of events, both the changes in the social values and the legal reforms are seen as beneficial.

Despite significant changes in some state laws, not all states have made such changes. Efforts to abolish resistance standards were less successful as many states have retained nonconsent as a necessary element of the crime (Largen, 1988). Furthermore, attitude change by individual legal personnel as well as by society cannot be legislated. LaFree (1989) discussed a special sexual offense unit which was established in the police department in a major city. An analysis of the unit revealed that there were no differences in the number of arrests, seriousness of the charge, or felony filings after the establishment of the unit. Research also suggests that some attorneys still prefer less severe sentences for cases where offenders and victims are acquainted with each other (Morris & Jackson, 1989). As suggested by Estrich (1987), many courts still remain suspicious of women victims and protective of male defendants in cases that do not involve weapons or beatings, as well as in cases that involve friends, neighbors, or "pickups."

Although negative societal attitudes toward acquaintance rape victims and unfair treatment of the victims is difficult to change, it must be attempted if incidence figures are to be decreased. Training and education about acquaintance rape must be provided for legal officials, educators, and service providers (Browne, 1993; M. P. Koss, 1993), as well as funding for research evaluating the effectiveness of these training programs. If training programs or the implementation of special units to handle rape cases do not result in fairer treatment of victims, the units and programs need to be modified rather than abolished. Finally, rape reforms are necessary to ensure that decisions about rape cases are made by inquiring into the man's blameworthiness instead of the woman's (Estrich, 1987). The Violence Against Women Act, introduced in 1991, is such an attempt. This Act seeks to equate "violence based on gender" with other forms of violent discrimination, such as hate crimes based on race or religion (Biden, 1993, p. 1060). This Act is also noteworthy for its funding provisions for support services and emphasis on education for the criminal justice system and educational system.

MENTAL HEALTH ISSUES

The Role of the Mental Health Professional. In addition to legal personnel, mental health professionals play a significant role in preventing the revictimization of women. Given the high frequency of sexual assault, mental health professionals should routinely screen for sexual victimization experiences in their female clients. The following sections describe mental health issues in the treatment of rape victims.

Barriers to Treatment. As M. P. Koss (1993) indicated, there are many barriers to immediate treatment for rape victims. For example, it should not be assumed that if sexual assault victims attend therapy after an assault they will discuss the experience with the therapist. Gidycz and M. P. Koss (1989) found that while only 28% of adolescent sexual assault victims sought therapy after an assault, even fewer (7%) discussed the experience with the therapist. They may not have discussed the experience because they were not asked about potential victimization experiences or, if they were asked, they may have denied it. Further, victims may harbor the hope that the experience will just "go away" if they do not think or talk about it.

Because of this difficulty in disclosure, it is important that the therapist be alert to possible revictimization of clients over time. Finally, practitioners need to realize that victims often have difficulty trusting people after an assault and that a therapeutic relationship may take time to develop.

Once a client discloses a victimization to a therapist, it is important that the therapist examine his or her own attitudes toward rape victims and sexual assault. Dye and Roth (1990) found that a therapist's attitudes toward sexual assault had an impact on how he or she conducted therapy with the victim. Specifically, therapists who held negatively prejudiced attitudes toward sexual assault victims were more likely to endorse treatment strategies that blamed the victim for the assault. Obviously, this type of therapy experience is likely to lead to further problems in the self-esteem of victims and does little to prevent their revictimization.

Components of Effective Treatments. It has been suggested that effective treatments must help the rape victim accomplish some important tasks. First, professionals clearly need to establish a supportive, trusting relationship with the victim, which may be an extended and difficult task. This may enable the victim to feel comfortable talking about the experience, which serves to reduce the distress involved and return control of the event to the victim (M. P. Koss & Harvey, 1991).

Second, service providers need to help victims redefine the event (Janoff-Bulman, 1985a; Taylor, 1983) and validate the experience (Browne, 1993). One way to accomplish this is to discourage victims from conceptualizing the rape as an event that they precipitated or something that was their fault. It should be communicated to victims that even if they utilized poor judgment, it does not make them responsible for the assault (M. P. Koss & Harvey, 1991; Warshaw, 1988). Unfortunately, societal perceptions of acquaintance rape as not "real rape" may make this process difficult.

Third, professionals need to help victims find meaning in their lives once again (Janoff-Bulman, 1985a; M. P. Koss et al., 1994; M. P. Koss & Harvey, 1991; Taylor, 1983). In order to facilitate the search for meaning, professionals need to help victims to answer questions such as "What caused the event to happen?" and "What does my life mean now?" (M. P. Koss & Harvey, 1991; Taylor, 1983). Issues of safety, trust, self-esteem, and intimacy are common (M. P. Koss & Harvey, 1991). Additional strategies that promote resolution of victim insecurity and feelings of empowerment include helping the victim to identify strategies to prevent further victimizations and encouraging the victim to seek social support (Browne, 1993; Janoff-Bulman, 1985a; M. P. Koss & Harvey, 1991; Taylor, 1983). Because family and friends are often misinformed about acquaintance rape, it may at times be appropriate to educate victims' significant others about the dynamics of acquaintance rape.

Related to the search for meaning is the concept of the victim's cognitive appraisal of the experience. The link of the victim's conceptualization of the event to her emotional response is increasingly recognized in the literature (M. P. Koss et al., 1994). As M. P. Koss et al. (1994) point out, cognitive appraisals may be influenced by several individual and sociocultural variables. One such variable affecting cognitive appraisals may be individual coping style, and research suggests that victims' methods of coping with sexual assault may need to be a focus for professional services. Santello and Leitenberg (1993) surveyed a sample of rape victims, 96% of whom were acquainted with their attacker, about postassault coping methods. These researchers found that disengagement methods of coping such as problem avoidance, social withdrawal, and self-criticism were used most often to deal with sexual assault experiences. These methods were also associated with increased pathological symptomatology (Santello & Leitenberg, 1993). In contrast, engagement methods of coping, such as social support, emotional expression, and problem-solving, were used to deal with other life stressors (Santello & Leitenberg, 1993). This research emphasizes a possible goal for professionals, namely to consider victims' coping methods in dealing with assault experiences and perhaps facilitate a more engagement-oriented style. It is through this process of helping victims to accomplish these tasks that mental health professionals will be able to help victims recover and grow from these experiences as well as to decrease the likelihood that they will be revictimized.

Finally, many service providers have come to recognize that a diagnosis of Posttraumatic Stress Disorder (PTSD) may be the most appropriate for rape victims (M. P. Koss et al., 1994; M. P. Koss & Harvey, 1991). In the nationwide general population survey, 31% of rape victims (largely acquaintance rape victims) had experienced PTSD at some point in their lives, and 11% met criteria for a current diagnosis of PTSD (National Victim Center, 1992). With this in mind, practitioners need to be alert to frequent PTSD symptoms such as reexperiencing the event, avoidance of stimuli associated with the trauma, and increased arousal (American Psychiatric Association, 1994; M. P. Koss & Harvey, 1991). Treatment of these anxiety symptoms utilizing relaxation, thought stopping, rational thinking, and other methods is an important consideration for service providers treating victims of rape (M. P. Koss & Harvey, 1991).

Treatment Approaches. Individual psychotherapy approaches with rape victims are many and varied. Unfortunately, few studies have been conducted to evaluate the effectiveness of various treatment approaches (M. P. Koss & Harvey, 1991). Treatment evaluation has been limited to behavioral and cognitive-behavioral methods (M. P. Koss et al., 1994), typically aimed at PTSD symptomatology. Two techniques that have been supported by the literature are exposure and anxiety management techniques (M. P. Koss et al., 1994). Exposure techniques serve to reexpose the victim to feared situations or stimuli, either through imagination or real-life confrontation. Anxiety management involves control over, rather than habituation to, fear and anxiety. This is accomplished by explaining the source of rape-related fear, teaching relaxation techniques, training in stress-inoculation methods, and engaging in rational thinking (Foa et al., 1991).

Recent approaches, such as cognitive processing therapy, include aspects of both techniques (M. P. Koss et al., 1994; Resick & Schnicke, 1992). This approach involves an education phase about PTSD and cognitive processing, an exposure phase where the victim's description of the rape and her emotional reactions are elicited, and a cognitive monitoring phase involving detection and restructuring of negative thoughts and beliefs (Koss et al., 1994; Resick & Schnicke, 1992). Victims in a recent study treated with cognitive processing therapy improved significantly from pre- to posttreatment, whereas the comparison sample did not (Resick & Schnicke, 1992). This combined-technique approach seems a promising area for treatment and further study.

To date, no clear differentiation has been made in the preceding approaches and treatment studies regarding the type of rape the victims have suffered. Essentially, all of these studies included both stranger and acquaintance rape victims in their treatment programs. Chapter 5 of this book, while acknowledging and incorporating the preceding technique-oriented styles of treatment, stresses the critical importance of the therapeutic alliance and the accepting and working through, rather than merely accomodating to, the unique trauma of acquaintance rape.

In addition to individual psychotherapy approaches, M. P. Koss and Harvey (1991) present a single-session debriefing for rape victims that includes many of the concepts described herein. This process is hoped to be "an accessible, nonstigmatizing, one-session response to the victimized person that will have a stabilizing influence on long-term response" (M. P. Koss & Harvey, 1991, p. 159). The debriefing includes establishing a supportive relationship, providing immediate emotional support, meeting medical and legal needs, encouraging ventilation about the experience, involving significant others, making practical arrangements, anticipating the future, and providing follow-up (M. P. Koss & Harvey, 1991). While these recommendations are generally provided for the recent rape victim, likely via a rape crisis center, the applicability to victims of acquaintance rape seems a logical extension.

Finally, several authors review group treatment approaches for rape victims (M. P. Koss et al., 1994; M. P. Koss & Harvey, 1991). Advantages of group treatment include reduced isolation, clear support, confirmation of the experience, rejection of self-blame, and shared grief (M. P. Koss & Harvey, 1991, pp. 208-210). Although empirical support for group approaches for rape survivors is lacking, this is a promising area for treatment and warrants further investigation.

CONCLUSION

Estrich (1987) argues that even when women say "Yes" to sex, it is at times misguided to view this as a sign of true consent. She suggests that many women who say "Yes" to acquaintances would say "No" if they could. Feelings of powerlessness as well as fear may prevent women from saying "No." If women sometimes say "Yes" when they really mean "No," Estrich (1987) concludes that, "It doesn't seem so much to ask men and the law to respect the courage of the woman who does say "No" and to take her at her word" (p. 102). Unfortunately, as this review indicates, many men do not take women at their word, ultimately leading to the perpetuation of the crime of rape. Although it is not an easy task to attempt to decrease the frequency of acquaintance rape, it is a necessarily multifaceted task that must be given a high priority by legal officials, legislators, mental health and healthcare professionals, educators, parents, and young men and women.

REFERENCES

Abbey, A. (1987). Perceptions of personal avoidability versus responsibility: How do they differ? *Basic and Applied Social Psychology, 8*, 3-19.

Abbey, A. (1991). Misperception as an antecedent of acquaintance rape: A consequence of ambiguity in communication between women and men. In A. Parrot & L. Bechhofer (Eds.), *Acquaintance Rape: The Hidden Crime* (pp. 96-112). New York: Wiley.

Abbey, A., Cozzarelli, C., McLaughlin, K., & Harnish, R. J. (1987). The effects of clothing and dyad sex composition on perceptions of sexual intent: Do women and men evaluate these cues differently? *Journal of Applied Social Psychology, 17*, 108-126.

Abbey, A., & Melby, C. (1986). The effects of nonverbal cues on gender differences in perceptions of sexual intent. *Sex Roles, 15*, 283-298.

Ageton, S. S. (1983). *Sexual Assault Among Adolescents*. Lexington, MA: Heath.

American Psychiatric Association. (1994). *Diagnostic and Statistical Manual of Mental Disorders* (DSM-IV, 4th ed.). Washington, DC: Author.

Atkeson, B., Calhoun, K. S., Resick, P. A., & Ellis, E. (1982). Victims of rape: Repeated assessment of depressive symptoms. *Journal of Consulting and Clinical Psychology, 50*, 96-102.

Becker, J. V., Skinner, L. J., Abel, G. G., Axelrod, R., & Treacy, F. C. (1984). Depressive symptoms associated with sexual assault. *Journal of Sex and Marital Therapy, 10*, 185-192.

Beneke, T. (1982). *Men Who Rape*. New York: St. Martins'.

Benson, D., Charlton, C., & Goodhart, F. (1992). Acquaintance rape on campus: A literature review. *Journal of American College Health, 40*, 157-165.

Berkowitz, A. (1992). College men as perpetrators of acquaintance rape and sexual assault: A review of recent research. *Journal of the American College Health Association, 40*, 175-181.

Biden, J. R. (1993). Violence against women: The Congressional response. *American Psychologist, 48*, 1059-1061.

Bostwick, T. D., & DeLucia, J. L. (1992). Effects of gender and specific dating behaviors on perceptions of sex willingness and date rape. *Journal of Social and Clinical Psychology, 11*, 14-25.

Breitenbecker, K. A., & Gidycz, C. A. (1995). *An Empirical Evaluation of a Program Designed to Prevent Sexual Revictimization*. Manuscript submitted for review.

Briere, J., & Runtz, M. (1988). Symptomatology associated with childhood sexual victimization in a nonclinical adult sample. *Child Abuse and Neglect, 12*, 51-59.

Browne, A. (1993). Violence against women by male partners: Prevalence, outcomes, and policy implications. *American Psychologist, 48*, 1077-1087.

Bureau of Justice Statistics. (1992). *Criminal Victimization in the United States, 1990*. Washington, DC: U.S. Department of Justice.

Burt, M. (1980). Cultural myths and support for rape. *Journal of Personality and Social Psychology, 38*, 217-230.

Check, J. V. P., & Malamuth, N. M. (1983). Sex role stereotyping and reactions to depictions of stranger versus acquaintance rape. *Journal of Personality and Social Psychology, 45*, 344-356.

Court, J. H. (1976). Pornography and sex crimes: A re-evaluation in light of recent trends around the world. *International Journal of Criminology and Penology, 5*, 129-157.

Donnerstein, E. (1980). Aggressive erotica and violence against women. *Journal of Personality and Social Psychology, 39*, 269-277.

Dye, E., & Roth, S. (1990). Psychotherapists' knowledge about and attitudes toward sexual assault victim clients. *Psychology of Women Quarterly, 14*, 191-212.

Ellis, F., Atkeson, B., & Calhoun, K. S. (1982). Examination of differences between multiple and single incident victims of sexual assault. *Journal of Abnormal Psychology, 91*, 221-224.

Estrich, S. (1987). *Real Rape.* Cambridge, MA: Harvard University Press.

Foa, E. B., Rothbaum, B. O., Riggs, D. S., & Murdock, T. B. (1991). Treatment of posttraumatic stress disorder in rape victims: A comparison between cognitive-behavioral procedures and counseling. *Journal of Counseling and Clinical Psychology, 59,* 715-723.

Frank, E., Anderson, B., Stewart, B. D., Dancu, C., Hughes, C., & West, D. (1988). Efficacy of cognitive behavior therapy and systematic desensitization in the treatment of rape trauma. *Behavior Therapy, 19*, 403-420.

Frank, E., Turner, S. M., & Stewart, B. D. (1980). Initial response to rape: The impact of factors within the rape situation. *Journal of Behavioral Assessment, 2*, 39-53.

Fritner, M. P., & Rubinson, L. (1993). Acquaintance rape: The influence of alcohol, fraternity membership, and sports team membership. *Journal of Sex Education and Therapy, 19*, 272-284.

Gidycz, C. A., Coble, C. N., Latham, L., & Layman, M. J. (1993). Sexual assault experiences in adulthood and prior victimization experiences: A prospective analysis. *Psychology of Women Quarterly, 17,* 151-168.

Gidycz, C. A., Hanson, K. A., & Layman, M. J. (1995). A prospective analysis of the relationship among sexual assault experiences: An extension of previous findings. *Psychology of Women Quarterly, 19,* 5-29.

Gidycz, C. A., & Koss, M. P. (1989). The impact of adolescent sexual victimization: Standardized measures of anxiety, depression, and behavioral deviancy. *Violence and Victims, 4,* 139-149.

Gidycz, C. A., & Koss, M. P. (1991). The effects of acquaintance rape on the female victim. In A. Parrot & L. Bechhofer (Eds.), *Acquaintance Rape: The Hidden Crime* (pp. 270-283). New York: Wiley.

Goodchilds, J. D., Zellman, G. L., Johnson, P. B., & Giarrusso, R. (1988). Adolescents and their perceptions of sexual interactions. In A. W. Burgess (Ed.), *Rape and Sexual Assault: II* (pp. 245-270). New York: Garland.

Goodman, L. A., Koss, M. P., Fitzgerald, L. F., Russo, N. F., & Keita, G. P. (1993). Male violence against women: Current research and future directions. *American Psychologist, 48,* 1054-1058.

Gray, M. D., Lesser, D., Quinn, E., & Bounds, C. (1990). The effectiveness of personalizing acquaintance rape prevention: Programs on perception of vulnerability and on reducing risk-taking behavior. *Journal of College Student Development, 31,* 217-220.

Hall, E. R., & Flannery, P. J. (1984). Prevalence and correlates of sexual assault experiences in adolescents. *Victimology, 9,* 398-406.

Hanson, K. A., & Gidycz, C. A. (1993). An evaluation of a sexual assault prevention program. *Journal of Consulting and Clinical Psychology, 61,* 1046-1052.

Holcomb, D. R., Sarvela, P. D., Sondag, K. A., & Holcomb, L. C. H. (1993). An evaluation of a mixed-gender date rape prevention program. *Journal of American College Health, 41,* 159-164.

Jaffee, D., & Straus, M. A. (1987). Sexual climate and reported rape: A state-level analysis. *Archives of Sexual Behavior, 16,* 107-123.

Janoff-Bulman, R. (1985a). The aftermath of victimization: Rebuilding shattered assumptions. In C. R. Figley (Ed.), *Trauma and Its Wake: The Study and Treatment of Post-Traumatic Stress Disorder* (pp. 15-35). New York: Brunner/Mazel.

Janoff-Bulman, R. (1985b). Criminal vs. non-criminal victimization: Victim's reactions. *Victimology: An International Journal, 10,* 498-511.

Johnson, J. D., & Russ, I. (1989). Effects of salience of consciousness-raising information on perceptions of acquaintance versus stranger rape. *Journal of Applied Social Psychology, 19,* 1182-1197.

Katz, B., & Burt, M. (1988). Self blame in recovery from rape: Help or hindrance. In A. W. Burgess (Ed.), *Sexual Assault* (Vol. II, pp. 151-168). New York: Garland.

Kilpatrick, D. G., Best, C. L., Veronen, L. J., Amick, A. E., Villeponteaux, L. A., & Ruff, G. A. (1985). Mental health correlates of criminal victimization: A random community survey. *Journal of Consulting and Clinical Psychology, 53,* 866-873.

Kilpatrick, D. G., Resick, P. A., & Veronen, L. J. (1981). Effects of a rape-experience: A longitudinal study. *Journal of Social Issues, 37,* 105-120.

Koss, M. P. (1987). *The Women's Mental Health Research Agenda: Violence Against Women.* Paper presented at NIMH - the National Coalition for Woman's Mental Health Conference, The Woman's Mental Health Agenda, Washington, DC.

Koss, M. P. (1988). Hidden rape: Incidence and prevalence of sexual aggression and victimization in a national sample of college students. In A. W. Burgess (Ed.), *Sexual Assault* (Vol. II, pp. 3-26). New York: Garland.

Koss, M. P. (1993). Rape: Scope, impact, interventions, and public policy responses. *American Psychologist, 48,* 1062-1069.

Koss, M. P., & Burkhart, B. R. (1989). A conceptual analysis of rape victimization: Long-term effects and implications for treatment. *Psychology of Women Quarterly, 13,* 27-40.

Koss, M. P., & Dinero, T. E. (1989). Discriminant analysis of risk factors for sexual victimization among a national sample of college women. *Journal of Consulting and Clinical Psychology, 57*, 242-250.

Koss, M. P., Dinero, T. E., Seibel, C. A., & Cox, S. L. (1988). Stranger and acquaintance rape: Are there differences in the victim's exposure? *Psychology of Women Quarterly, 12*(1), 1-24.

Koss, M. P., Gidycz, C. A., & Wisniewski, N. (1987). The scope of rape: Incidence and revalence of sexual aggression and victimization in a national sample of higher education students. *Journal of Consulting and Clinical Psychology, 55*, 162-170.

Koss, M. P., Goodman, L. A., Browne, A., Fitzgerald, L. F., Keita, G. P., & Russo, N. F. (1994). *No Safe Haven: Male Violence Against Women at Home, at Work, and in the Community*. Washington, DC: American Psychological Association.

Koss, M. P., & Harvey, M. R. (1991). *The Rape Victim: Clinical and Community Interventions* (2nd ed.). Newbury Park, CA: Sage.

Koss, M. P., Koss, P. G., & Woodruff, W. J. (1991). Deleterious effects of criminal victimization on women's health and medical utilization. *Archives of Internal Medicine, 151*, 342-357.

Koss, M. P., Leonard, K., Beezley, D. A., & Oros, C. J. (1985). Nonstranger sexual aggression: A discriminant analysis of the psychological characteristics of undetected offenders. *Sex Roles, 12*, 981-982.

LaFree, G. D. (1980). Variables affecting guilty pleas and convictions in rape cases: Toward a social theory of rape processing. *Social Forces, 58*, 833-850.

LaFree, G. D. (1981). Official reactions to source problems: Police decisions in sexual assault cases. *Social Problems, 28*, 582-594.

LaFree, G. D. (1989). *Rape and Criminal Justice: The Social Construction of Sexual Assault*. Belmont, CA: Wadsworth.

Largen, M. A. (1988). Rape-law reform: An analysis. In A. W. Burgess (Ed.), *Sexual Assault* (Vol. II, 271-292). New York: Garland.

Layman, M. J. (1995). *Evaluation of an Acquaintance Rape Awareness Program: Differential Impact on Acknowledged and Unacknowledged Rape Victims*. Unpublished manuscript, Ohio University, Athens, OH.

Layman, M. J., Gidycz, C. A., & Lynn, S. J. (in press). Acknowledged vs. unacknowledged rape victims: Situational factors, post-traumatic stress, and dissociation. *Journal of Abnormal Psychology.*

Levine, E. M., & Kanin, E. J. (1987). Sexual violence among dates and acquaintances: Trends and their implications for marriage and family. *Journal of Family Issues, 2,* 55-65.

Linz, D., Wilson, B. J., & Donnerstein, E. (1992). Sexual violence in the mass media: Legal solutions, warnings, and mitigation through education. *Journal of Social Issues, 48,* 145-172.

Lottes, I. L. (1988). Sexual socialization and attitudes toward rape. In A. W. Burgess (Ed.), *Rape and Sexual Assault: II* (pp. 193-220). New York: Garland.

Lundberg-Love, P., & Geffner, R. (1989). Date rape: Prevalence, risk factors, and a proposed model. In M. A. Pirog-Good & J. E. Stets (Eds.), *Violence in Dating Relationships: Emerging Social Issues* (pp. 169-184). New York: Praeger.

Malamuth, N. M. (1986). Predictions of naturalistic sexual aggression. *Journal of Personality and Social Psychology, 50,* 953-962.

Miller, B., & Marshall, J. C. (1987). Coercive sex on the university campus. *Journal of College Student Personnel, 28,* 38-47.

Miller, J., Moeller, D., Kaufman, A., DiVasto, P., Pathak, D., & Christy, J. (1978). Recidivism among sex assault victims. *American Journal of Psychiatry, 135,* 1103-1104.

Morris, Y., & Jackson, T. (1989, August). *Midwestern Attorneys' Blame Attribution and Sentencing Preferences in Rape.* Paper presented at the meeting of the American Psychological Association, New Orleans, LA.

Muehlenhard, C. L. (1989). Misinterpreted dating behaviors and the risk of date rape. In M. A. Pirog-Good & J. E. Stets (Eds.), *Violence in Dating Relationships: Emerging Social Issues* (pp. 241-256). New York: Praeger.

Muehlenhard, C. L., & Linton, M. A. (1987). Date rape and sexual aggression in the dating situation: Incidence and risk factors. *Journal of Counseling Psychology, 34,* 186-196.

National Victim Center. (1992, April). *Rape in America: A Report to the Nation.* Arlington, VA: Author.

Pinzone, H., & Gidycz, C. A. (in press). *Acquaintance Rape Awareness Program: Effects on Attitudes and Perceptions.* Manuscript submitted for publication.

Resick, P. A. (1993). The psychological impact of rape. *Journal of Interpersonal Violence, 8,* 223-255.

Resick, P. A., & Schnicke, M. K. (1992). Cognitive processing therapy for sexual assault victims. *Journal of Consulting and Clinical Psychology, 60,* 748-756.

Rice, M. E., Chaplin, T. C., Harris, G. T., & Coutts, J. (1994). Empathy for the victim and sexual arousal among rapists and nonrapists. *Journal of Interpersonal Violence, 9,* 435-449.

Richardson, D., & Hammock, G. (1991). The role of alcohol in acquaintance rape. In A. Parrot & L. Bechhofer (Eds.), *Acquaintance Rape: The Hidden Crime* (pp. 83-95). New York: Wiley.

Roth, S., Wayland, K., & Woolsey, M. (1990). Victimization history and victim-assailant relationship as factors in recovery from sexual assault. *Journal of Traumatic Stress, 3,* 169-189.

Rouse, L. P. (1988). Abuse in dating relationships: A comparison of Blacks, Whites, and Hispanics. *Journal of College Student Development, 29,* 312-319.

Russell, D. E. H. (1984). *Sexual Exploitation.* Beverly Hills, CA: Sage.

Sales, E., Baum, M., & Shore, B. (1984). Victim readjustment following assault. *Journal of Social Issues, 40,* 117-136.

Santello, M. D., & Leitenberg, H. (1993). Sexual aggression by an acquaintance: Methods of coping and later psychological adjustment. *Violence and Victims, 8,* 91-104.

Sawyer, R. G., Desmond, S. M., & Lucke, G. M. (1993). Sexual communication and the college student: Implications for date rape. *Health Values, 17,* 11-20.

Shotland, R. L., & Goodstein, L. (1992). Sexual precedence reduces the perceived legitimacy of sexual refusal: An examination of attributions concerning date rape and consensual sex. *Personality and Social Psychology Bulletin, 18,* 756-764.

Sommerfeldt, T. G., Burkhart, B. B., & Mandoki, C. A. (1989, August). *In Her Own Words: Victims' Descriptions of Hid-*

den Rape Effects. Paper presented at the meeting of the American Psychological Association, New Orleans, LA.

Sorenson, S. B., & Brown, V. B. (1990). Interpersonal violence and crisis intervention on the college campus. *New Directions for Student Services, 49,* 57-66.

Taylor, S. (1983). Adjustment to threatening events: A theory of cognitive adaption. *American Psychologist, 38,* 1161-1173.

Ullman, S. E., & Seigel, J. M. (1993). Victim-offender relationship and sexual assault. *Violence and Victims, 8,* 121-134.

United States Department of Commerce. (1993). *Statistical Abstract of the United States.* Washington, DC: U.S. Government Printing Office.

United States Department of Justice. (1988). *Beyond the Pornography Commission: The Federal Response.* Washington DC: U.S. Government Printing Office.

Warshaw, R. (1988). *I Never Called It Rape: The Ms. Report on Recognizing, Fighting, and Surviving Date and Acquaintance Rape.* New York: Harper & Row.

Weiss, K., & Borges, S. (1975). Victimology and rape: The case of the legitimate victim. In L. G. Schultz (Ed.), *Rape Victimolomy* (pp. 91-141). Springfield, IL: Charles C. Thomas.

Wyatt, G., Guthrie, D., & Notgrass, C. (1992). Differential effects of women's child sexual abuse and subsequent sexual revictimization. *Journal of Consulting and Clinical Psychology, 60,* 167-173.

3

The Perpetrators of Date Rape: Assessment and Treatment Issues

Linda J. Skinner
and
Kenneth K. Berry

Research on sexual aggression in dating relationships is in its infancy. This is particularly true when the aggressor is the focus. However, research on self-reported likelihood to commit date rape underscores the critical need for increased knowledge about date rape perpetrators.* Smeaton and Byrne (1987) assessed both self-reported stanger rape proclivity (i.e., "If you were guaranteed that you would not be caught, how likely would you be to rape a woman?" p. 177) and self-reported acquaintance rape proclivity (i.e., "How likely would you be to push the person with whom you participated in this experiment farther than she says she wants to go sexually?" p. 177) in males paired

---

*Although this chapter considers only male perpetrators, the authors are very concerned about sexual aggression in gay and lesbian relationships and in sexual aggression targeted against males in heterosexual relationships and stress the need for research in these areas.

in an experiment with a female confederate. More than twice as many males reported a likelihood of forcing unwanted sex on the woman they knew (71%) than who reported a likelihood of raping a stranger (30%).

Endeavors to understand date rape (DR) perpetrators have focused primarily on factors underlying their sexually aggressive behavior. Such factors include dispositional or personal characteristics, releasers or external factors which increase the likelihood of sexual aggression, and the social factor of peers (Koss et al., 1994). Empirical findings related to these factors will be briefly reviewed in order to lay a foundation for an in-depth discussion of assessment and treatment needs of DR perpetrators. In addition, the ethical issues of informed consent, confidentiality, and duty to warn/protect are considered in relation to clinical work with these men.

DISPOSITIONAL FACTORS: EMPIRICAL FINDINGS

In an attempt to understand the behavior of DR perpetrators, attention has been directed at the following dispositional factors: (a) attitudes and values, (b) personality characteristics, (c) psychopathology, (d) sexuality, and (e) social perception. Each of these is reviewed below.

ATTITUDES AND VALUES

Several attitudes and values are strongly related to dating sexual aggression. Particularly salient characteristics include a traditional male sex role (Check & Malamuth, 1983) or "macho" personality (Smeaton & Byrne, 1987), misogynistic and hostile attitudes toward women (Burkhart & Stanton, 1988; Malamuth, 1986), an acceptance of interpersonal violence (Stets & Pirog-Good, 1989), and an acceptance of myths supportive of rape (Byers, 1988).

Sex role orientation is a primary factor underlying dating sexual aggression. Similarity between the arousal patterns of rapists and highly traditional males has been found (Check &

Malamuth, 1983). Although not related to arousal in consenting intercourse scenes, sex role stereotyping mediates arousal to rape, particularly acquaintance rape, and traditional males are more likely to admit to the possibility of rape. In addition, traditional males report that "leading a man on" can justify rape (Muehlenhard, 1988).

The sexual behavior-sex role orientation relationship generally holds in self-reports of dating behavior, with a higher incidence of verbal and/or physical sexual coercion reported by traditional versus less traditional males (J. L. Bernard, S. L. Bernard, & M. L. Bernard, 1985). However, sex role orientation may not be predictive of the severity of self-reported aggressive sexual behavior (Rapaport & Burkhart, 1984).

An exaggerated, hypermasculine sex role has been found in males reporting a proclivity to commit both rape and date rape (Smeaton & Byrne, 1987). These researchers suggest that fears of inadequate masculinity underlie acquaintance rape, with assault of a desirable female perceived as proof of masculinity. Moreover, "macho" men tend to have comparatively less anger, contempt, disgust, distress, fear, guilt, and shame when imagining themselves committing a violent rape (Mosher & Anderson, 1986). However, compulsive masculinity has not always been found to be related to sexual assault in dating relationships (Stets & Pirog-Good, 1989). In addition, more feminine roles reflecting emotional expressiveness and relationship orientation have been associated with dating sexual aggression (Burke, Stets, & Pirog-Good, 1988). The desire for greater relationship involvement prompts greater activity which, if resisted, can become abusive.

A second particularly salient attitudinal characteristic of DR perpetrators is their general acceptance of violence and aggression. Many males with a history of using a high level of force in dating relationships view force as an acceptable means of obtaining sex from their partners (Fischer, 1992; D. R. Holcomb et al., 1991; Petty & Dawson, 1989). Relatedly, sexual aggressors, including men who report a likelihood of raping, hold attitudes that are supportive of rape. These men have narrow definitions of rape which generally exclude the use of sexual aggression in a dating context (Burt & Albin, 1981) and are less likely to characterize an assailant's behavior as violent (Jenkins

& Dambrot, 1987). Moreover, actual sexual aggression in dating relationships is also generally related to rape supportive beliefs (Byers, 1988).

PERSONALITY CHARACTERISTICS

Although this category of dispositional factors has not been found to be highly predictive of date rape, the characteristics of aggression, hostility, and interpersonal control are critical factors. Aggression is related to both self-reported rape proclivity (Greendlinger & Byrne, 1987) and actual sexually aggressive behavior (Petty & Dawson, 1989). Higher aggression scores on various attitudinal, behavioral, and personality measures have been found in college men with histories of sexual aggression (Malamuth & Check, 1983). Similarly, positive relationships exist between hostility and both laboratory sexual arousal measures to rape scenes (Yates, Barbaree, & Marshall, 1984) and self-reported dating sexual aggression (Murphy, Coleman, & Haynes, 1986). Finally, the infliction of sexual aggression by male dating partners has been found to be positively related to interpersonal control (Stets & Pirog-Good, 1989).

PSYCHOPATHOLOGY

Hypothesizing that a behavior is the result of some underlying psychopathology, the psychopathology model has been a popular explanation for rape (Groth & Birnbaum, 1979). Although histories of antisocial behavior are common in DR perpetrators (Rapaport, 1984), clinically significant levels of psychopathology are generally not characteristic of self-reported DR perpetrators (Koss et al., 1985).

SEXUALITY

Components of sexuality related to the behavior of DR perpetrators include (a) sexual expectations, (b) nonaggressive sexual behavior, (c) sexual arousal, and (d) previous behavior. The sexual learning process results in very different sexual expectations for males and females. For example, almost 50% of males but only 25% of females believe that sexual intercourse is appropriate by the fifth date (Knox & Wilson, 1981). Differential sexual expectations appear to be important in date rape, with the initiation of sexual aggression related to the male definition of sexual relationships in an extremely determined motivational manner (Burkhart & Stanton, 1988).

Although not related to rape proclivity, nonaggressive sexual behavior has been found to be predictive of self-reported dating sexual aggression (Briere & Malamuth, 1983). For example, DR perpetrators tend to become sexually active at an early age and report more childhood voluntary and forced sexual experiences (Koss & Dinero, 1988); have greater sexual experience (Malamuth, 1986); and are more likely to use a mechanical device sexually, participate in group and anal sex, and stimulate genitals manually (McDermott, Sarvela, & Banracharya, 1988).

Studying college-aged DR perpetrators, Kanin (1984) concluded that these males have a comparatively strong desire for new sexual experiences, have considerably more sexual experience, are more successful sexually, and utilize more seductive or exploitative techniques in their sexual interactions than do nonaggressive males. Apt to have a history of group rape, these men were described as sexual predators whose self-worth is closely associated with sexual success. However, DR perpetrators report relatively greater sexual dissatisfaction than do less experienced, nonaggressive males.

Sexual arousal measures have also been found to be predictive of dating sexual aggression in males (Murphy et al., 1986). Finally, reports of past sexual aggression and coercion have been significantly correlated to date rape proclivity (Smeaton & Byrne, 1987) and are the most accurate predictors of future sexual aggression (Nagayama Hall, 1990).

SOCIAL PERCEPTION

Socialization teaches males to view the world in a pervasive sexualized manner (Goodchilds & Zellman, 1984) and, consequently, to interpret neutral cues as sexual (Abbey, 1982), overinterpret mildly sexual cues, and overestimate the sexual intent of females (Abbey et al., 1987). Deficit social cue-reading abilities can precipitate a series of misperceptions resulting in date rape (Abbey et al., 1987). Social perceptions have been found to be predictive of self-reported sexual aggression (McDonel & McFall, 1991; Murphy et al., 1986).

SUMMARY OF DISPOSITIONAL
FACTORS FINDINGS

As these findings reveal, DR perpetrators share a number of dispositional factors, including attitudes and values, personality characteristics, psychopathology, sexuality, and perception of others. One additional factor - the lack of any psychopathology as the underlying cause of dating sexual aggression - is also characteristic of these men. It is important to note that no single DR perpetrator is likely to have all of these dispositional factors. Furthermore, the strength of each characteristic will vary considerably across individuals.

RELEASERS:
EMPIRICAL FINDINGS

Called releasers, some factors are related to a specific behavior in that their presence or use seems to decrease normally existing inhibitions or encourage a propensity to engage in that behavior. Common releasers in date rape are alcohol/drugs and some types of pornography.

Alcohol reduces inhibitions against violence for both males and females (Barbaree et al., 1983), and many males take advantage of this impact to obtain sex from dates. For example, 18% of female and 39% of male high school students judged forced sex as acceptable if the female was drunk or stoned (Giarrusso et al., 1979), and 75% of males admitted having used alcohol/drugs in order to have sex with their dates (Mosher & Anderson, 1986). Alcohol is commonly used by DR perpetrators (Abbey, 1991; Koss & Dinero, 1988; Koss & Gaines, 1993; Richardson & Hammock, 1991). In fact, in their study of the sexual victimization of college women, Frintner and Rubinson (1993) found that 21.4% of women who reported experiencing sexual assault further reported that they "thought the man planned the incident and encouraged them to drink beyond their tolerance" (p. 279). Comparing sexually aggressive dates and recent nonaggressive dates, females reported similarity with respect to the use of alcohol or drugs (Muehlenhard & Linton, 1987). However, heavy usage by both persons was more common in the aggressive dates.

A releasing relationship between date rape and sexually violent and degrading pornography has been found (Demare, Briere, & Lips, 1988). However, nonviolent pornography has not been demonstrated to influence sexual aggression (Nutter & Kearns, 1993; Sapolsky, 1984).

PEERS: EMPIRICAL FINDINGS

A final significant factor underlying date rape is a peer subculture which espouses, supports, and/or shares such behavior (Garrett-Gooding & Senter, 1987). The peer subculture of college-aged DR perpetrators devalues male virginity and uses significant peer pressure to encourage members to be sexually active (Kanin, 1967, 1985; O'Sullivan, 1991; Sanday, 1990). These peers establish sex norms that demand an unreasonably high level of sexual behavior and legitimize the sexual utilization of women. For example, Frintner and Rubinson (1993) found an overrepresentation of group membership (fraternities and sports team members) in college-aged females' reports of characteristics of their alleged perpetrators. It is felt that being a member of a fraternity or a sports team increases the likelihood to traditional sex role stereotypes and a relative insensitivity to sensitive communication styles (Jackson, 1994). Date rape perpetrators are likely to have a history of collaborative sex, either group rape or sequential sexual sharing of a partner, and to have had intercourse with a peer identified as a sexually congenial female. Kanin (1985) stresses the hypererotic character of the peer group, which is perceived as approving of aggressive interactions with certain women who are seen as violating dating expectations (e.g., bar pick-ups, "loose" women, teasers, economic exploiters). The peers of DR perpetrators may seriously suggest the use of one of these "deviant" females for sexual success. Although not openly rewarding violence, these peers are seen as supporting the "sexual conquest." In a

12-year longitudinal study of males, a peer subculture was identified as a necessary but not sufficient condition for the occurrence of sexually aggressive behavior (Adler, 1985).

CLINICAL INTERVENTION WITH
DATE RAPE (DR) PERPETRATORS

The DR perpetrator findings previously reviewed underscore
the need for an assessment and treatment plan that encom-
passes multiple areas. In this section, specific treatment needs
are delineated, and appropriate assessment procedures are discussed. Finally, numerous treatment procedures are considered.

ASSESSMENT ISSUES

There are five major problem areas that may need attention in the assessment of DR perpetrators: (a) sexual arousal
patterns, (b) social skills, (c) sexual behavior, (d) cognitive/so-
cial functioning, and (e) anger control. Each of these possible
problem areas is considered individually.

Sexual Arousal Patterns. The assessment of an
individual's arousal pattern must include consideration of both
deviant and nondeviant arousal. Some DR perpetrators are
likely to have excessive arousal to deviant stimuli requiring the
application of aversive-suppressive techniques. Should an individual have deficit arousal to nondeviant sexual stimuli, interventions aimed at generating nondeviant arousal are needed.

A variety of methods can be used to assess an individual's
arousal pattern to deviant and nondeviant stimuli, including
penile tumescence measures, self-report measures, and clinical
interviews. Penile recordings offer an objective method of assessment but require laboratory equipment not possessed by
the majority of mental health professionals. For those interested in learning about this psychophysiological procedure, there
are many sources that delineate this assessment approach and
its use with sexual aggressives (Farrall & Card, 1988; Laws &

Osborn, 1983; McConaghy, 1993; Quinsey & Chaplin, 1988; Rosen & Beck, 1988). It must be stressed, however, that penile tumescence measures are not intended to serve as the basis for the making of diagnoses but rather to help identify deviant sexual arousal patterns that require treatment (Quinsey & Earls, 1990).

Some self-report measures aimed at identifying sexual interests, particularly deviant interests, are listed in Part I of Appendix 3-A (p. 80). A compendium of sexuality measures is also available (C. Davis, W. Yarber, & S. L. Davis, 1988). In light of reliability and validity problems, it is recommended that confirmatory measures be sought when self-report measures are used.

Clinical interviews can also be structured to assess sexual arousal patterns. McConaghy (1988) discusses the clinical interview as a technique for assessing sexual behavior, and Skinner and Becker (1985) offer general interviewing procedures in the assessment of sexual deviations. However, given the high level of denial, rationalization, and minimizing engaged in by DR perpetrators, interviews are the least valid measures, particularly of deviant arousal. Collateral data are very important and can frequently be used as a means of working through the patient's defensive manner.

Sexual Behavior. Clinical interviews, sexual inventories, and sex knowledge tests can be employed to assess sexual knowledge, sexual assault knowledge, and sexual expectations. The Rape Trauma Knowledge Test and the Rape Aversiveness Scale (Hamilton & Yee, 1990) measure sexual assault knowledge. Self-report measures and clinical interviews are appropriate to determine the presence of sexual dysfunctions. A problem-oriented interview format has been forwarded by Annon (1976) and general interviewing procedures in the assessment of sexual dysfunctions are available (Skinner & Becker, 1985).

Skills. An adequate assessment of a DR perpetrator must include consideration of the individual's social, assertiveness, and empathy skills. These skills can be evaluated through both clinical interviewing and self-report inventories. Part II of

Appendix 3-A (pp. 80-81) lists some appropriate paper-and-pencil instruments.

In addition, role-playing is a most appropriate assessment procedure for these skills. Several formats can be followed when conducting a role-play assessment of social, assertive, and empathy skills. Numerous devices have been developed, such as the Behavioral Assertiveness Test - Revised (Bellack, Hersen, & Turner, 1978) and a behavioral assessment device for social skills (Bellack, Hersen, & Lamparski, 1979). This assessment procedure has the advantages of fostering maximum patient involvement and allowing individualization (Becker & Heimberg, 1988). The ability to individualize the skills assessment is particularly important in the assessment of DR perpetrators.

Social Perception and Attitudes. A thorough evaluation of the treatment needs of DR perpetrators includes assessment of social information processing skills. Procedures for such an assessment component have been described elsewhere (Lipton, McDonel, & McFall, 1987). Some brief self-report instruments available for assessing various social attitudes are listed in Part III of Appendix 3-A (pp. 81-82). Although there is currently no standardized measure of distorted cognitions common among DR perpetrators, such beliefs can be drawn from attitude measurements.

Anger Control. Identification of the situations in which the DR perpetrator loses control of his aggression can be accomplished through an anger diary as well as through the recall of recent preassessment anger-eliciting situations. In addition to describing the specifics of the situations, a discussion of the antecedent and consequent events should be included. As part of the assessment procedures, it is important to determine if reported aggression is anger mediated or instrumental mediated because these two types of aggression require differential treatments.

Assessment Summary. A clinician conducting an assessment of a DR perpetrator should ensure that adequate attention is given to the five problem areas of sexual arousal pat-

terns, social skills, sexual behavior, cognitive and social functioning, and anger control. However, it is not likely that all DR
perpetrators require intervention in each of these areas. Subtypes of these men are likely to have differential treatment needs
(Skinner, Carroll, & Berry, in press). Regardless of the type of
DR perpetrator being seen, a complete assessment covering all
five areas should be the standard.

TREATMENT INTERVENTIONS

A clinician anticipating treating DR perpetrators should develop a general treatment program that includes procedures
for (a) modifying sexual arousal patterns, (b) increasing sexual
knowledge and addressing any existing sexual dysfunctions, (c)
enhancing social and/or assertive skills and improving sexual
communication, (d) modifying maladaptive cognitions and social perception, and (e) increasing anger control. Procedures
for addressing each of these treatment components are described
below.

Procedures to Modify Arousal Patterns. A variety of
behavioral interventions have been utilized to decrease excessive deviant arousal (e.g., assisted covert sensitization,
biofeedback-assisted suppression, chemical aversion, covert sensitization, electrical aversion, masturbatory satiation, olfactory
aversion, verbal satiation) and to increase deficit nondeviant
sexual arousal (e.g., exposure, fading, orgasmic reconditioning,
systematic desensitization). Most of these procedures meet the
minimal requirements of directness of effort, simplicity of approach, and procedure portability (Laws & Osborn, 1983). Because most of these procedures are standard behavioral or cognitive behavioral interventions, only selected interventions are
discussed below. Case summaries are presented to illustrate
these interventions.

Decreasing Deviant Arousal

Olfactory Aversion. This treatment consists of the repeated
pairing of the presentation of deviant sexual stimuli or fantasies with a very noxious but harmless odor, such as that pro-

duced by crushable spirit of ammonia capsules or valeric acid. Olfactory aversion is intended to be specific to deviant arousal.

Sam: Case Summary #1

Sam was in treatment to decrease his date rape fantasies. Seen twice a week, he was placed in a room and instructed to attend to the presentation of deviant stimuli. At some sessions, visual stimuli were used, while at other sessions, Sam was asked to verbalize his deviant fantasies. With the onset of the stimuli, Sam would crush the ammonia capsule and pass it back and forth at least 6 inches below his nostrils. After 12 sessions, Sam had lost his deviant arousal as determined by his verbal report and erection recordings. However, after the sixth session, he reported that he thought the treatment was negatively affecting his nondeviant arousal. Thus, following each subsequent session, Sam was instructed to masturbate to ejaculation using nondeviant fantasies and this step was effective in maintaining his nondeviant sexual arousal.

There are some cautions that must be taken with this treatment approach. For example, it must be explained to the patient that the fumes from the broken capsule can damage his nasal membranes if he places the capsule directly under his nostrils. In addition, spirit of ammonia, which is a poison, should not be used with patients who are suicide-prone (Laws & Osborn, 1983).

Satiation Procedures. Based on both behavioral and analytic analyses of the development of sexual arousal, masturbatory satiation is one of the more promising aversion techniques to correct sexual excesses. This treatment is intended to sever the deviant fantasy-pleasurable masturbatory orgasm relationship by the repeated pairing of deviant fantasies with the postorgasmic phase of masturbation (Abel, Becker, & Skinner, 1985; Quinsey & Earles, 1990). The deviant fantasies change from being arousing to becoming boring and then aversive. This treatment is specific to deviant arousal, leaving nondeviant sexual arousal intact.

Walter: Case Summary #2

Walter's penile recordings indicated that he experienced a significant level of sexual arousal to both consenting and date rape stimuli. Masturbatory satiation was utilized to decrease his deviant arousal. In the privacy of his home, Walter was instructed to masturbate to ejaculation as quickly as possible using nondeviant sexual fantasies. Following ejaculation, he was instructed to change his fantasies to his most erotic deviant fantasies and continue masturbating for a total of 1 hour masturbatory time. Walter had three masturbatory satiation sessions per week for 4 weeks when he reported that he had "wiped out" his supply of deviant fantasies. Assessment in the laboratory indicated that his deviant arousal had diminished significantly while his nondeviant arousal had remained at its pretreatment level.

If a patient reports that he is having trouble masturbating to ejaculation, he can be instructed to masturbate for his usual latency to ejaculation period plus 2 minutes and then switch the fantasy theme to deviant and continue masturbating for the prescribed time period, which should range from 30 minutes to 1 hour. It is also advisable to have the patient audiotape each treatment session so that the clinician can spot check the tape to ensure that the patient is implementing the procedures appropriately.

Jonathan: Case Summary #3

Jonathan had never engaged in rape behavior but sought treatment because he had recurring fantasies about raping his girlfriend and feared that he might lose control. During the interview, he denied masturbating, reporting that his religion forbade him to do so. Realizing that he would reject the use of masturbatory satiation, verbal satiation was suggested. He was instructed to verbalize his deviant fantasies for a 30-minute period three times. Within 5 weeks, he found his deviant fantasies to be boring and nonarousing. Penile recordings supported his verbal report.

If a sexual aggressor denies having deviant fantasies, a clinician can provide the individual with deviant phrases to repeat during the masturbatory sessions. The content of these phrases should be determined by the nature of his sexually deviant behavior.

Clinical Issues Related to Procedures for Modifying Sexual Arousal. A concern about the use of aversive procedures centers on the issue of control; that is, who imposes the negative consequence? In the procedures frequently utilized with DR perpetrators, such as those described previously, the application of the aversive component is always within the total control of the patient. For example, he decides to break the capsule, think about a deviant fantasy, or continue masturbating. This fact is particularly relevant when coercion to seek treatment is an issue.

A second issue focuses on the continued effectiveness of the treatment effect of these procedures. As effective as the aversion procedures may be, they are control procedures, and their impact can diminish over time. Patients should be made aware of this possibility and, rather than viewing treatment as a failure, be encouraged to use these portable procedures at their own initiation. Thus, it is imperative that the clinician teach the patient the techniques so that the aggressor can continue his treatment when needed. Additionally, the clinician should use follow-up "booster" sessions at needed intervals.

Increasing Nondeviant Arousal. With any individual who engages in date rape, it is imperative that an adequate level of nondeviant sexual arousal be present. It is clinically inappropriate to remove deviant arousal in the absence of nondeviant arousal. Although only a limited number of DR perpetrators will require treatment to increase nondeviant sexual arousal, assessment of this possible need should never be overlooked.

Exposure. Some men lack sufficient material to produce mutually consenting sexual fantasies and, consequently, pair deviant fantasies with masturbation and orgasm. The simple procedure of exposing an individual to stimuli depicting mutually consenting sexual interactions devoid of any deviant content can provide the patient with material from which he can then develop nondeviant sexual fantasies. If this procedure is to be used, it is imperative that the clinician carefully select the materials to be used and, initially, monitor the fantasies to ensure that themes of deviant (i.e., violent, nonconsenting) sex are excluded. With some men, it may be necessary to help create early fantasies. In such cases, homework assignments of writing nondeviant fantasies for review and further development during treatment sessions are suggested.

Orgasmic Reconditioning. Also known as masturbatory conditioning and masturbatory retraining, this counterconditioning procedure is intended to alter a person's masturbatory behavior by modifying the content of sexual fantasies. There are numerous variations of this procedure (Laws & O'Neil, 1981), with some involving such complexity that patients have difficulty complying with the instructions. Although perhaps paradoxical, the variation described below is easily implemented by patients and effective in increasing nondeviant sexual arousal.

Richard: Case Summary #4

With a long history of both date and stranger rapes, Richard had not experienced satisfactory consenting intercourse. His penile recordings indicated that he had very high deviant arousal and very low nondeviant arousal. After his deviant arousal had been treated successfully, orgasmic reconditioning was implemented to increase his nondeviant arousal. The procedure involved having him engage in three masturbatory sessions each week in the privacy of his home. During the first week, he was told to masturbate to ejaculation using deviant sexual fantasies. The next week, he was to rely on nondeviant fantasies during his masturbatory sessions. This weekly alternating of fantasy content continued throughout his 3 months of treatment. His progress was monitored weekly in the laboratory and when his nondeviant arousal was 63%, treatment was considered successful.

Although increasing nondeviant arousal is the goal of this treatment procedure, an occasional benefit is a decrease in deviant arousal.

Sexual Behavior. Sex is still a taboo topic in our society and, consequently, there is an abundance of sexual misinformation. College males, who represent a large percentage of DR perpetrators, believe more sexual myths than do females, and sexual experience has not been found to diminish the amount of misinformation accepted as "fact" (Mosher, 1979). Thus, standard sex education focusing on human sexuality, the anatomy and physiology of sex, reproduction, and sexual variations may be needed. In addition to increasing knowledge, sex education can modify attitudes toward date rape, with students becoming more rejecting of such assault (Fischer, 1986).

Some attention should be directed at sensitizing DR perpetrators to the frequent sexual expectation differences of males and females, as well as gender differences in the development and focus of sexuality. Specifically, this treatment component should include consideration of what males and females want sexually in a dating relationship and when in a relationship these behaviors are perceived as appropriate. Discussion of these differential sexual expectations is very much related to sexual communication and social perception, two other areas that frequently need addressing.

The sexuality treatment component should also include educational efforts to increase sexual assault knowledge. Increased knowledge about the impact of rape on the survivor is related to decreased rape proclivity (Hamilton & Yee, 1990), and personalization of the rape survivor has been an educational goal of some programs for sexual aggressives (Groth, 1983). The informational content of this treatment component can be drawn from the empirical literature on date rape survivors. In addition, videotapes of interviews with survivors are very effective.

Finally, sex dysfunction therapy may be needed by a small percent of DR perpetrators. Because this treatment component does not have to be tailored for DR perpetrators and an extensive body of literature on sex dysfunction therapy exists, this component will not be discussed here.

Skills. Both skills and sexual communication training are likely components in treatment programs for DR perpetrators. Many DR perpetrators can benefit from treatment addressing deficits in social and/or assertive skills. In fact, it has been suggested that social skills training may be one of the most crucial treatment programs for sexual aggressives (McFall, 1990). A good social skills training program should include the components of expressive elements, receptive elements (social perception), and interactive balance (Curran & Monti, 1982), and should be tailored for DR perpetrators. Behavioral rehearsal with response feedback is the most common procedure used for skills training, and modeling is considered essential in social skills training (Eisler et al., 1978). However, cognitive techniques (e.g., rational restructuring), can also be effective (Kaplan, 1982).

Just as people today are encouraged to discuss the use of safer sex procedures with a sexual partner *prior* to being sexual, it would help prevent date rape if dating partners openly discussed their behavioral and sexual boundaries before the potentially problematic situation arises. However, because most individuals are not initially comfortable in such sexual discussions, training in sexual assertive communication (Parrot, 1987) should be included as a treatment component in any program for DR perpetrators.

Cognitive and Social Functioning. Treatment techniques for problem areas in cognitive and social functioning are difficult to locate, leaving clinicians somewhat on their own. Nonetheless, treatment should include the modification of DR perpetrators' attitude structure supporting rape and aggression. Murphy (1990) notes that cognitive changes may be an unexpected consequence of treatments targeted at decreasing deviant arousal. However, serious consideration should be given to the inclusion of therapeutic procedures aimed specifically at cognitive and social functioning. In fact, it has been suggested that exclusive dependence on cognitive techniques in lieu of behavioral techniques may be sufficient in the treatment of sexually aggressive males (Quinsey & Earls, 1990).

A cognitive restructuring component aimed at identifying and modifying the cognitions underlying the DR perpetrator's behavior is critical in a good treatment program. This component allows the opportunity for some "reality testing" in that an aggressor, with the help of the therapist or peers, becomes aware of his misperceptions and rationalizations about his behavior, irrational beliefs and cognitive distortions, rape myth acceptance, and attitudes and beliefs. A Socratic approach to cognitive restructuring therapy has been recommended as being preferable to a direct confrontational approach (Murphy, 1990).

Jim: Case Summary #5

Jim sought treatment after being arrested for attempted rape of a woman he had been dating for about 3 months. From the beginning of treatment, Jim adamantly denied that he had attempted a rape, insisting instead that his girlfriend was just trying to get even with him for some earlier slight. In his sessions with the therapist, he resisted all attempts to reformulate this perception. Eventually, he joined a therapy group of DR perpetrators. When Jim first suggested that he did not belong there because he was "different," the group members began challenging his perceptions about his behavior. Each of his explanations and rationalizations was confronted by group members, and he found himself offering increasingly irrational explanations. Within four sessions, even Jim admitted that he had trouble believing what he was saying.

Reverse role-playing is another variation of this procedure that is very effective with DR perpetrators. The perpetrator can assume the role of the DR survivor, a family member of the survivor, or a prosecuting attorney, while another group member or the therapist plays the role of the perpetrator, echoing his irrational statements, excuses, and beliefs.

Group therapy can be an ideal vehicle for cognitive restructuring. In addition to the power of a group, fellow DR perpetrators are particularly skilled at recognizing the distorted cognitions of others, and their challenges are very potent. Additionally, the process of assisting others in modifying their beliefs can help an individual recognize and re-evaluate his own distortions.

Treatment efforts directed at increasing the empathy of DR perpetrators may be most effectively accomplished through group therapy (Murphy, 1990). In addition, the involvement of DR survivors' counselors is most helpful. Rather than including a survivor-perpetrator confrontation, empathy treatment can incorporate the reading of survivors' impact statements or personal accounts of their assaults (Herman, 1990).

Anger Control. Most commonly, problem-solving skills are taught to help a DR perpetrator increase his control over his anger. In the case of anger-mediated aggression, assertion training may have some effectiveness. When a therapist determines that the patient's anger and aggression are instrumental-mediated, stress inoculation (Novaco, 1975, 1976) is usually the preferred approach.

RELAPSE PREVENTION

The final component of any treatment package for a DR perpetrator should sensitize him to the possibility of relapse and help him prepare to cope with risk situations. However, this component of the overall treatment package should not be implemented until the individual has evidenced considerable change as a result of treatment (Hall, 1989). Relapse prevention is intended to enhance the patient's decision-making skills and behavior to maintain treatment progress after the termination of treatment. Because this prevention program must be individualized for each DR perpetrator, both assessment and treatment procedures must be included in the relapse prevention process. The initial phase entails the identification of high-risk situations, assessment of the man's coping skills, and the identification of apparent determinants and antecedents of his deviant behavior. The treatment component involves assisting the DR perpetrator in identifying precursor events to avoid lapses and in helping him develop specific coping and problem-solving skills to use when a lapse cannot be avoided (Pithers et al., 1988). An excellent description of relapse prevention programs for use with sexual aggressives can be found in Pithers et al. (1983).

Treatment Summary. The necessary components for a comprehensive treatment program for DR perpetrators have been discussed previously. Clinicians should address each component separately and be prepared to individualize treatment as necessary. Furthermore, to ensure the success of any intervention, pre- and posttreatment measures should be collected for each treatment component. Relapse prevention training should be included in the treatment program. Finally, it is most important that the therapist realize that DR perpetrators can be treated successfully.

ETHICAL ISSUES
IN WORKING WITH
DATE RAPE PERPETRATORS

When dealing with individuals whose problem behavior has both serious consequences for a survivor of the behavior and legal consequences for the perpetrator, it is imperative that a therapist be sensitive to ethical issues, particularly the issues of informed consent, confidentiality, and the duty to take reasonable steps to protect others. Each of these issues is discussed below.

INFORMED CONSENT

A clinician treating a patient without having obtained informed consent is technically committing battery and at risk of prosecution (Bohmer, 1983). The basic elements of informed consent include competency, knowledge, and voluntariness.

Competency. The competency issue is relatively straightforward if the patient is of legal age and has the cognitive abilities to comprehend the information provided. However, when the patient is an adolescent or mentally retarded, special problems are posed. Weiner (1985) recommends that informed consent be obtained from both the adolescent and one of his parents, particularly if invasive or aversive procedures are to be employed. The presence of mental retardation does not necessarily rule out a DR perpetrator's ability to give informed consent. Rather, determinations must be made on a case-by-case basis. If it is determined the individual is not legally competent to give consent, it should be sought from a legal guardian.

Knowledge. There is some controversy as to how much information must be provided to enable a person to make a knowledgeable decision. The minimum elements that should be included in any informed consent form include the following: (a) the purpose of assessment or treatment (e.g., to decrease deviant arousal, modify cognitive distortions); (b) the specifics of the proposed assessment or treatment, including its nature and duration; (c) possible risks specific to the assessment or treatment procedures; (d) the likelihood of success; (e) alternative assessment or treatment options; (f) possible consequences of foregoing assessment or treatment altogether; (g) possible risks stemming from participation in assessment or treatment but not specific to procedures selected (e.g., identity as sexual aggressor may become known); (h) services provided should the patient experience negative side effects resulting from assessment or treatment; and (i) any limitations on confidentiality (e.g., duty to take reasonable steps to protect others).

It is particularly important to discuss confidentiality limitations because the DR perpetrator is seeking treatment for behavior that is illegal and could cause serious legal consequences for him. Informed consent should also be obtained before an assessment is done, as legally potentially damaging information is obtained during that phase. The mere provision of information is not sufficient. The therapist must ensure that the DR perpetrator understands the material for the consent to be informed.

Voluntariness. This issue is always complicated when the DR perpetrator is involved in the legal system because an incarcerated individual or one under legal coercion to seek treatment may not be capable of making a voluntary decision. It is likely that most DR perpetrators will be seen on an outpatient basis but some may be under legal coercion to participate in treatment in lieu of incarceration. Weiner (1985) points out that even coerced individuals are able to make a choice between treatment or imprisonment. This choice can be complicated when the treatment procedures are intrusive, as with Depo Provera (a pharmacological treatment designed to inhibit pituitary gonadotropin secretion), or experimental, and more care may need to be taken to assess the presence and extent of possible coercion.

Informed Consent Procedures. Informed consent should always be written and free from jargon and legalese. It is best if the presentation of the information is witnessed, and the patient should be given a copy of the informed consent form. New informed consent should be obtained each time a new treatment procedure is implemented, and periodic review of it during treatment is advised. At the completion of a treatment procedure, it is helpful if the relevant consent form is reviewed to determine if the patient believes that all needed information to make an informed decision was provided. This last step does not benefit the patient specifically but can be educational for the therapist and can assist in improving the informed consent procedure.

CONFIDENTIALITY

Confidentiality is an important issue for any patient in therapy and one that all therapists deal with daily. However, the issue of security of patient data records is particularly sensitive when a patient is seeking treatment for a behavior which can have legal consequences. Some specific procedures have been recommended for therapists who work with sexual aggressors (Abel et al., 1985). For example, a DR perpetrator should be told that a breach of confidentiality is not possible if the therapist does not have details about a crime. He should be instructed to discuss his assaults in general terms and with no identifying information about the assault or the survivor (e.g., names, dates, times, locations). Should the patient allow such information to slip, the therapist should not include it in the patient's records. This is particularly likely in the treatment of DR perpetrators since many of these assaults occur in the context of ongoing relationships. In addition, it is recommended that a clinician treating a DR perpetrator keep two separate files: one containing necessary identifying information needed for business purposes (e.g., name, address, telephone number, place of employment) and a second file for all clinical information. No identifying information, including the patient's name, should be in this clinical file. Code numbers can be used for these files. As with all patient files, the DR perpetrator's files should be kept in locked cabinets. The identifying and clinical files should be kept in separate cabinets.

An additional issue results from requests from outside sources, including third-party payers, for patient information. All too frequently, patients sign release of information forms without appreciating the consequences such releases may hold. A possible protection for these situations is to provide any report on the patient's assessment or treatment progress directly to the patient and then allow him, after having the opportunity to read the report, to decide if it is to be sent to the requester (Abel et al., 1985). In fact, the patient can be given the responsibility for mailing the report so that he maintains control.

A final suggestion centers on patient participation in group therapy. The maintenance of confidentiality is always difficult and generally out of the therapist's control when the treatment format is group therapy. To decrease the likelihood of a breach of confidentiality, patients should be reminded not to reveal any specific details about their aggressive behaviors during the treatment sessions. A patient may choose to use a false name in the group to protect his identity. In addition, the importance of maintaining confidentiality should be stressed to group members periodically during group meetings.

When measures such as these are taken to protect patient records and confidentiality, an added benefit can be the fostering of valid reports about urges and deviant behavior during the treatment process.

DUTY TO TAKE REASONABLE
STEPS TO WARN/PROTECT

Mental health professionals working with potentially dangerous or violent patients must always contend with their legal obligation to warn/protect endangered third parties. There continues to be legal debate surrounding the exact obligation of the therapist, but generally a therapist who is aware that a patient plans to harm an identifiable third person who is not likely to be aware of this possible harm must take some action to protect the third person. Thus, if a therapist is aware that a sexual aggressor is intending to assault a specific individual who is unaware of the impending harm, the therapist has the legal responsibility to take some action to protect the intended party. All of this information should be a standard part of the informed consent procedures so that the patient is very much aware of this limitation on confidentiality.

The duty to take reasonable steps to protect generally does not pose a major problem for a therapist working with DR perpetrators. Most of these assaults are not planned in advance but instead are impulsive and, consequently, a therapist is not likely to have an awareness of impending harm. There are occasions when a DR perpetrator may have plans to rape a specific individual and discusses this information during a therapy session. At such a time, a therapist may choose to stop the patient as soon as the therapist is aware of the nature of the disclosure and remind him of the limits on confidentiality and the therapist's legal obligations. If, after such a warning, the patient continues revealing the plans and the therapist fulfills her or his legal and ethical responsibility, the therapist may find that the subsequent action taken is less disruptive to the therapeutic relationship. In addition, the therapist should inform the patient of any action that is to be taken and, if possible, incorporate the patient in that action.

SUMMARY

Although considerable research has been focused on the serious problem of sexual aggression in dating relationships, research on the DR perpetrator is still very much in its infancy. The research of the last 10 years has focused upon dispositional factors and proclivity toward date rape and serves as a foundation for the identification of assessment and treatment needs of DR perpetrators. An adequate assessment program for this group of aggressives must address the problem areas of sexual arousal patterns, social skills, sexual behavior, cognitive/social functioning, and anger control. Procedures for addressing these treatment needs were considered, as was the issue of relapse prevention in the treatment of DR perpetrators. Finally, the discussion of the ethical issues of informed consent, confidentiality, and duty to warn/protect was tailored for the clinical intervention with DR perpetrators.

APPENDIX 3-A:
ASSESSMENT MEASURES

PART I:
Self-Report Measures to
Assess Sexual Arousal Patterns

Sexual Behavior Inventory	Bentler (1968)
Sexual Opinion Survey	Fisher, Byrne, and White (1983)
Sexual Experiences Survey	Koss and Oros (1982)
Attraction to Sexual Aggression Scale	Malamuth (1989a, 1989b)
Endorsement of Force Scale	Rapaport and Burkhart (1984)
Coercive Sexuality Scale	Rapaport and Burkhart (1984)
Coercive Sexual Fantasies Scale	Greendlinger and Byrne (1987)
Submissive Sexual Fantasies Scales	Greendlinger and Byrne (1987)

PART II:
Skills Self-Report Instruments

SOCIAL SKILLS

Heterosexual Interaction Survey	Twentyman and McFall (1975)
Situation Questionnaire	Rehm and Marston (1968)
Social Activity Questionnaire	Arkowitz et al. (1975)
Social Avoidance and Distress Scale	Watson and Friend (1969)
Test of Reading of Affective Cues	Hall (1990)

ASSERTIVENESS SKILLS

Adult Self-Expression Scale	Gay, Hollandsworth, and Galassi (1975)
Assertion Questionnaire	Callner and Ross (1976)
Assertion Self-Statement Test	Schwartz and Gottman (1976)
Assertiveness Inventory	Gambrill and Richey (1975)
College Self-Expression Scale	Galassi et al. (1974)
Conflict Resolution Inventory	McFall and Lillesand (1971)
Interpersonal Situation Inventory	Goldsmith and McFall (1975)
Rathus Assertiveness Schedule	Rathus (1973)
Wolpe-Lazarus Assertiveness Schedule	Wolpe and Lazarus (1966)

PART III:
Attitudinal and
Sex Role Orientation Measures

ATTITUDES TOWARD SEXUALITY

Adversarial Sexual Beliefs Scale	Burt (1980)
Sexuality Irrationality Questionnaire	Jordan and McCormick (1988)

ATTITUDES TOWARD WOMEN

Attitudes Toward Women Scale	Spence, Helmreich, and Stapp (1973)
Hostility Toward Women	Check and Malamuth (1983b)
Sexist Attitudes Toward Women Scale	Benson and Vincent (1980)

ATTITUDES TOWARD SEXUAL
ASSAULT AND VIOLENCE

Acceptance of Interpersonal Violence Scale	Burt (1980)
Attitudes Toward Rape Victims	Ward (1988)
Rape Empathy Scale	Borden, Karr, and Caldwell-Colbert (1988)
Rape Myth Acceptance Scale	Burt (1980)
Rape Stereotype Scale	Marolla and Scully (1979)
Rape Vignettes	Williams and Holmes (1981)
Sexual Beliefs Scale	Muehlenhard and MacNaughton (1988)
Sexual and Dating Attitude Survey	Dull and Giacopassi (1987)

SEX ROLE ORIENTATION

Bem Sex Role Inventory	Bem (1974)
Extended Personal Attributes	Spence, Helmreich, and Holahan (1979)
Sex Role Stereotyping Scale	Burt (1980)

REFERENCES

Abbey, A. (1982). Sex differences in attributions for friendly behavior: Do males misperceive females' friendliness? *Journal of Personality and Social Psychology, 42*, 830-838.

Abbey, A. (1991). Acquaintance rape and alcohol consumption on college campuses: How are they linked? *Journal of the American College Health Association, 39*, 165-169.

Abbey, A., Cozzarelli, C., McLaughlin, K., & Harnish, R. J. (1987). The effects of clothing and dyad sex composition on perceptions of sexual intent: Do women and men evaluate these cues differently? *Journal of Applied Social Psychology, 17*, 108-126.

Abel, G. G., Becker, J. V., & Skinner, L. J. (1985). Behavioral approaches to treatment of the violent sex offender. In L. H. Roth (Ed.), *Clinical Treatment of the Violent Person* (pp. 100-123). Rockville, MD: National Institute of Mental Health.

Adler, C. (1985). An exploration of self-reported sexually aggressive behavior. *Crime & Delinquency, 31*, 306-331.

Annon, J. S. (1976). *Behavioral Treatment of Sexual Problems: Brief Therapy*. Hagerstown, MD: Harper & Row.

Arkowitz, H., Lichtenstein, E., McGovern, K., & Hines, P. (1975). The behavioral assessment of social competence in males. *Behavioral Therapy, 6*, 3-13.

Barbaree, H. E., Marshall, W. L., Yates, E., & Lightfoot, L. O. (1983). Alcohol intoxication and deviant arousal in male social drinkers. *Behavior Research and Therapy, 21*, 365-374.

Becker, R. E., & Heimberg, R. G. (1988). Assessment of social skills. In A. S. Bellack & M. Hersen (Eds.), *Behavioral Assessment: A Practical Handbook* (3rd ed., pp. 365-395). New York: Pergamon.

Bellack, A. S., Hersen, M., & Lamparski, D. (1979). Roleplay tests for assessing social skill: Are they valid? Are they useful? *Journal of Consulting and Clinical Psychology, 47*, 335-342.

Bellack, A. S., Hersen, M., & Turner, S. M. (1978). Roleplay tests for assessing social skill: Are they valid? *Behavior Therapy, 9*, 448-461.

Bem, S. L. (1974). The measurement of psychological androgyny. *Journal of Consulting and Clinical Psychology*, *43*, 155-162.

Benson, P. L., & Vincent, S. (1980). Development and validation of the Sexist Attitudes Toward Women Scale (SATWS). *Psychology of Women Quarterly*, *5*, 276-291.

Bentler, P. M. (1968). Heterosexual behavior assessment-I. Males. *Behaviour Research and Therapy*, *6*, 21-25.

Bernard, J. L., Bernard, S. L., & Bernard, M. L. (1985). Courtship violence and sex-typing. *Family Relations Journal of Applied Family and Child Studies*, *34*, 573-576.

Bohmer, C. (1983). Legal and ethical issues in mandatory treatment: The patient's rights versus society's rights. In J. G. Greer & I. R. Stuart (Eds.), *The Sexual Aggressor: Current Perspectives on Treatment* (pp. 3-21). New York: Van Nostrand Reinhold.

Borden, L. A., Karr, S. K., & Caldwell-Colbert, A. T. (1988). Effects of a university rape prevention program on attitudes and empathy toward rape. *Journal of College Student Development*, *29*, 132-136.

Briere, J., & Malamuth, N. M. (1983). Self-reported likelihood of sexually aggressive behavior: Attitudinal versus sexual explanations. *Journal of Research in Personality*, *17*, 315-323.

Burke, P. J., Stets, J. E., & Pirog-Good, M. A. (1988). Gender identity, self-esteem, and physical and sexual abuse in dating relationships. *Social Psychology Quarterly*, *51*, 272-285.

Burkhart, B. R., & Stanton, A. L. (1988). Acquaintance rape. In G. Russell (Ed.), *Violence in Intimate Relations* (pp. 43-65). New York: PMA Publishing Corp.

Burt, M. R. (1980). Cultural myths and support for rape. *Journal of Personality and Social Psychology*, *38*, 217-230.

Burt, M. R., & Albin, R. S. (1981). Rape myths, rape definitions, and probability of conviction. *Journal of Applied Social Psychology*, *11*, 212-230.

Byers, S. E. (1988). Effects of sexual arousal on men's and women's behavior in sexual disagreement situations. *The Journal of Sex Research*, *25*, 235-254.

Callner, D. A., & Ross, S. M. (1976). The reliability of three measures of assertion in a drug addition population. *Behavior Therapy, 7,* 659-667.

Check, J. V. P., & Malamuth, N. M. (1983, June). *The Hostility Toward Women Scale.* Paper presented at the Western Meeting of the International Society for Research on Aggression, Victoria, Canada.

Curran, J. P., & Monti, P. M. (Eds.). (1982). *Social Skills Training: A Practical Handbook for Assessment and Treatment.* New York: Guilford.

Davis, C., Yarber, W., & Davis, S. L. (Eds.). (1988). *Sexuality Related Measures: A Compendium.* Lake Mills, IA: Graphic Publishing Company.

Demare, D., Briere, J., & Lips, H. M. (1988). Violent pornography and self-reported likelihood of sexual aggression. *Journal of Research in Personality, 22,* 140-153.

Dull, R. T., & Giacopassi, D. J. (1987). Demographic correlates of sexual and dating attitudes: A study of date rape. *Criminal Justice and Behavior, 14,* 175-193.

Eisler, R. M., Blanchard, E. B., Fitts, H., & Williams, J. G. (1978). Social skill training with and without modeling for schizophrenic and non-psychotic hospitalized psychiatric patients. *Behavior Modification, 2,* 147-172.

Farrall, W. R., & Card, R. D. (1988). Advancements in physiological evaluation of assessment and treatment of the sexual aggressor. In R. A. Prentky & V. L. Qunisey (Eds.), *Human Sexual Aggression: Current Perspectives* (Vol. 528, pp. 261-273). New York: The New York Academy of Sciences.

Fischer, G. J. (1986). College student attitudes toward forcible date rape: Changes after taking a human sexuality course. *Journal of Sex Education and Therapy, 12,* 42-46.

Fischer, G. J. (1992). Sex attitudes and prior victimization as predictors of college student sex offenses. *Annals of Sex Research, 5,* 53-60.

Fisher, W. A., Byrne, D., & White, L. A. (1983). Emotional barriers to contraception. In D. Byrne & W. A. Fisher (Eds.), *Adolescents, Sex, and Contraception* (pp. 207-239). Hillsdale, NJ: Lawrence Erlbaum.

Frintner, M. P., & Rubinson, L. (1993). Acquaintance rape: The influence of alcohol, fraternity membership, and sports team membership. *Journal of Sex Education and Therapy, 19,* 272-284.

Galassi, J. P., DeLo, J. S., Galassi, M. D., & Bastien, S. (1974). The College Self-Expression Scale: A measure of assertiveness. *Behavior Therapy, 5,* 165-171.

Gambrill, E. D., & Richey, C. A. (1975). An assertion inventory for use in assessment and research. *Behavior Therapy, 6,* 550-561.

Garrett-Gooding, J., & Senter, R., Jr. (1987). Attitudes and acts of sexual aggression on a university campus. *Sociological Inquiry, 57,* 348-371.

Gay, M. L., Hollandsworth, J. G., & Galassi, J. P. (1975). An assertiveness inventory for adults. *Journal of Counseling Psychology, 22,* 340-344.

Giarrusso, R., Johnson, P., Goodchilds, J. D., & Zellman, G. L. (1979, April). Adolescents' cues and signals: Sex and assault. In P. Johnson (Chair), *Acquaintance Rape and Adolescent Sexuality.* Symposium conducted at the meeting of the Western Psychological Association, San Diego, CA.

Goldsmith, J. B., & McFall, R. M. (1975). Development and evaluation of an interpersonal-skill training program for psychiatric inpatients. *Journal of Abnormal Psychology, 84,* 51-58.

Goodchilds, J. D., & Zellman, G. L. (1984). Sexual signaling and sexual aggression in adolescent relationships. In N. M. Malamuth & E. Donnerstein (Eds.), *Pornography and Sexual Aggression* (pp. 233-243). Orlando, FL: Academic Press.

Greendlinger, V., & Byrne, D. (1987). Coercive sexual fantasies of college men as predictors of self-reported likelihood to rape and overt sexual aggression. *Journal of Sex Research, 23*(1), 1-11.

Groth, A. N. (1983). Treatment of the sexual offender in a correctional institution. In J. G. Greer & I. R. Stuart (Eds.), *The Sexual Aggressor: Current Perspectives on Treatment* (pp. 160-176). New York: Van Nostrand Reinhold.

Groth, A. N., & Birnbaum, H. J. (1979). *Men Who Rape: The Psychology of the Offender.* New York: Plenum.

Hall, R. L. (1989). Relapse rehearsal. In D. R. Laws (Ed.), *Relapse Prevention With Sex Offenders* (pp. 197-206). New York: Guilford.

Hamilton, M., & Yee, J. (1990). Rape knowledge and propensity to rape. *Journal of Research in Personality, 24,* 111-122.

Herman, J. L. (1990). Sex offenders: A feminist perspective. In W. L. Marshall, D. R. Law, & H. E. Barbaree (Eds.), *Handbook of Sexual Assault* (pp. 177-193). New York: Plenum.

Holcomb, D. R., Holcomb, L. C., Sondag, K. A., & Williams, N. (1991). Attitudes about date rape: Gender differences among college students. *College Student Journal, 25,* 434-439.

Jackson, T. (1994). Sexual responsibility: Assault prevention and safe dating. In *NCAA Life Skills Programs.* Overland Park, KS: NCAA.

Jenkins, M. J., & Dambrot, F. H. (1987). The attribution of date rape: Observers' attitudes and sexual experiences and the dating situation. *Journal of Applied Social Psychology, 17,* 875-895.

Jordan, T. J., & McCormick, N. B. (1988). Sexual Irrationality Questionnaire (SIQ). In C. Davis, W. Yarber, & S. L. Davis (Eds.), *Sexuality Related Measures: A Compendium* (pp. 46-49). Lake Mills, IA: Graphic Publishing Company.

Kanin, E. J. (1967). Reference groups and sex conduct norm violations. *Sociological Quarterly, 8,* 495-504.

Kanin, E. J. (1984). Date rape: Unofficial criminals and victims. *Victimology: An International Journal, 1,* 95-108.

Kanin, E. J. (1985). Date rapists: Differential sexual socialization and relative deprivation. *Archives of Sexual Behavior, 14,* 219-231.

Kaplan, D. A. (1982). Behavioral, cognitive, and behavioral cognitive approaches to group assertion training therapy. *Cognitive Therapy and Research, 6,* 301-314.

Knox, D., & Wilson, K. (1981). Dating behaviors of university students. *Family Relations, 30,* 255-258.

Koss, M. P., & Dinero, T. E. (1988). Predictors of sexual aggression among a national sample of male college students. In R. A. Prentky & V. L. Qunisey (Eds.), *Human Sexual Aggression: Current Perspectives* (Vol. 528, pp. 133-146). New York: The New York Academy of Sciences.

Koss, M. P., & Gaines, J. A. (1993). The prediction of sexual aggression by alcohol use, athletic participation, and fraternity affiliation. *Journal of Interpersonal Violence, 8,* 94-108.

Koss, M. P., Goodman, L. A., Browne, A., Fitzgerald, L. F., Keita, G. P., & Russo, N. F. (1994). *No Safe Haven: Male Violence Against Women at Home, at Work, and in the Community.* Washington, DC: American Psychological Association.

Koss, M. P., Leonard, K., Beezley, D., & Oros, C. J. (1985). Nonstranger sexual aggression: A discriminant analysis of the psychological characteristics of undetected offenders. *Sex Roles, 12,* 981-992.

Koss, M. P., & Oros, C. J. (1982). Sexual Experiences Survey: A research instrument investigating sexual aggression and victimization. *Journal of Consulting and Clinical Psychology, 50,* 455-457.

Laws, D. R., & O'Neil, J. A. (1981). Variations on masturbatory conditioning. *Behavioural Psychotherapy, 9,* 111-136.

Laws, D. R., & Osborn, C. A. (1983). How to build and operate a behavioral laboratory to evaluate and treat sexual deviance. In J. G. Greer & I. R. Stuart (Eds.), *The Sexual Aggressor: Current Perspectives on Treatment* (pp. 293-335). New York: Van Nostrand Reinhold.

Lipton, D. N., McDonel, E. C., & McFall, R. M. (1987). Heterosocial perception in rapists. *Journal of Consulting and Clinical Psychology, 55,* 17-21.

Malamuth, N. M. (1986). Predictors of naturalistic sexual aggression. *Journal of Personality and Social Psychology, 50,* 953-962.

Malamuth, N. M. (1989a). The Attraction to Sexual Aggression Scale: Part one. *Journal of Sex Research, 26,* 26-49.

Malamuth, N. M. (1989b). The Attraction to Sexual Aggression Scale: Part two. *Journal of Sex Research, 26,* 324-354.

Malamuth, N. M., & Check, J. V. P. (1983). Sexual arousal to rape depictions: Individual differences. *Journal of Abnormal Psychology, 92,* 55-67.

Marolla, J., & Scully, D. (1979). Rape and psychiatric vocabularies of motive. In E. Gomberg & V. Franks (Eds.), *Gender and Disordered Behavior: Sex Differences in Psychopathology* (pp. 301-318). Larchmont, NY: Brunner-Mazel.

McConaghy, N. (1988). Sexual dysfunction and deviation. In A. S. Bellack & M. Hersen (Eds.), *Behavioral Assessment: A Practical Handbook* (3rd ed., pp. 490-541). New York: Pergamon.

McConaghy, N. (1993). *Sexual Behavior: Problems and Management.* New York: Plenum.

McDermott, R. J., Sarvela, P. D., & Banracharya, S. M. (1988). Nonconsensual sex among university students: A multivariate analysis. *Health Education Research, 3,* 233-241.

McDonel, E. C., & McFall, R. M. (1991). Construct validity of two heterosocial perception skill measures for assessing rape proclivity. *Violence and Victims, 6,* 17-30.

McFall, R. M. (1990). The enhancement of social skills. In W. L. Marshall, D. R. Laws, & H. E. Barbaree (Eds.), *Handbook of Sexual Assault* (pp. 311-330). New York: Plenum.

McFall, R. M., & Lillesand, D. B. (1971). Behavior rehearsal with modeling and coaching in assertion training. *Journal of Abnormal Psychology, 77,* 313-323.

Mosher, D. L. (1979). Sex guilt and sex myths in college men and women. *Journal of Sex Research, 15,* 224-234.

Mosher, D. L., & Anderson, R. D. (1986). Macho personality, sexual aggression, and reactions to guided imagery of realistic rape. *Journal of Research in Personality, 20,* 186-196.

Muehlenhard, C. L. (1988). Misinterpreted dating behaviors and the risk of date rape. *Journal of Social and Clinical Psychology, 6,* 20-37.

Muehlenhard, C. L., & Linton, M. A. (1987). Date rape and sexual aggression in dating situations: Incidence and risk factors. *Journal of Counseling Psychology, 34,* 186-196.

Muehlenhard, C. L., & MacNaughton, J. S. (1988). Women's beliefs about women who "lead men on." *Journal of Social and Clinical Psychology, 7,* 65-79.

Murphy, W. D. (1990). Assessment and modifications of cognitive distortions in sex offenders. In W. L. Marshall, D. R. Laws, & H. E. Barbaree (Eds.), *Handbook of Sexual Assault* (pp. 331-342). New York: Plenum.

Murphy, W. D., Coleman, E. M., & Haynes, M. R. (1986). Factors related to coercive sexual behavior in a nonclinical sample of males. *Violence and Victims, 1,* 255-278.

Nagayama Hall, G. C. (1990). Prediction of sexual aggression. *Clinical Psychology Review, 10,* 229-245.

Novaco, R. W. (1975). *Anger Control: The Development and Evaluation of an Experimental Treatment.* Lexington, MA: Heath.

Novaco, R. W. (1976). The functions and regulation of the arousal of anger. *American Journal of Psychiatry, 133,* 1124-1128.

Nutter, D. E., & Kearns, M. E. (1993). Patterns of exposure to sexually explicit material among sex offenders, child molesters, and controls. *Journal of Sex & Marital Therapy, 19,* 77-85.

O'Sullivan, C. S. (1991). Acquaintance gang rape on campus. In A. Parrott & L. Bechhofer (Eds.), *Acquaintance Rape: The Hidden Crime* (pp. 140-157). New York: Wiley.

Parrot, A. (1987). *Acquaintance Rape and Sexual Assault Prevention Training Manual* (2nd ed.). Ithaca, NY: Cornell University Press.

Petty, G. M., & Dawson, B. (1989). Sexual aggression in normal men: Incidence, beliefs, and personality characteristics. *Personality and Individual Differences, 10,* 355-362.

Pithers, W. D., Kashima, K. M., Cumming, G. F., Beal, L. S., & Buell, M. M. (1988). Relapse prevention of sexual aggression. In R. A. Prentky & V. L. Quinsey (Eds.), *Human Sexual Aggression: Current Perspectives* (Vol. 528, pp. 244-260). New York: The New York Academy of Sciences.

Pithers, W. D., Marques, J. K., Gibat, C. C., & Marlatt, G. A. (1983). Relapse prevention with sexual aggressives: A self-control model of treatment and maintenance of change. In J. G. Greer & I. R. Stuart (Eds.), *The Sexual Aggressor: Current Perspectives on Treatment* (pp. 214-239). New York: Van Nostrand Reinhold.

Quinsey, V. L., & Chaplin, T. C. (1988). Preventing faking in phallometric assessments of sexual preference. In R. A. Prentky & V. L. Quinsey (Eds.), *Human Sexual Aggression: Current Perspectives* (Vol. 528. pp. 49-58). New York: The New York Academy of Sciences.

Quinsey, V. L., & Earls, C. M. (1990). The modification of sexual preferences. In W. L. Marshall, D. R. Laws, & H. E.

Barbaree (Eds.), *Handbook of Sexual Assault* (pp. 279-295). New York: Plenum.

Rapaport, K. (1984). *Sexually Aggressive Males: Characterological Features and Sexual Responsiveness to Rape Predictions*. Unpublished doctoral dissertation, Auburn University, Auburn, AL.

Rapaport, K., & Burkhart, B. (1984). Personality and attitudinal characteristics of sexually coercive college males. *Journal of Abnormal Psychology, 93*, 186-196.

Rathus, S. A. (1973). A 30-item schedule for assessing assertive behavior. *Behavior Therapy, 4*, 398-406.

Rehm, L. P., & Marston, A. R. (1968). Reduction of social anxiety through modification and self-reinforcement: An instigation therapy technique. *Journal of Consulting and Clinical Psychology, 32*, 565-574.

Richardson, D. R., & Hammock, G. S. (1991). Alcohol and acquaintance rape. In A. Parrott & L. Bechhofer (Eds.), *Acquaintance Rape: The Hidden Crime* (pp. 83-95). New York: Wiley.

Rosen, R. C., & Beck, J. G. (1988). *Patterns of Sexual Arousal: Psychophysiological Processes and Clinical Applications*. New York: Guilford.

Sanday, P. R. (1990). *Fraternity Gang Rape: Sex, Brotherhood, and Privilege on Campus*. New York: New York University Press.

Sapolsky, B. S. (1984). Arousal, affect, and the aggression-moderating effect of erotica. In N. M. Malamuth & E. Donnerstein (Eds.), *Pornography and Sexual Aggression* (pp. 85-113). Orlando, FL: Academic.

Schwartz, R., & Gottman, J. M. (1976). Toward a task analysis of assertive behavior. *Journal of Consulting and Clinical Psychology, 44*, 910-920.

Skinner, L. J., & Becker, J. V. (1985). Sexual dysfunctions and deviations. In M. Hersen & S. M. Turner (Eds.), *Diagnostic Interviewing* (pp. 205-242). New York: Plenum.

Skinner, L. J., Carroll, K. A., & Berry, K. K. (in press). A typology for sexually aggressive males in dating relationships. *Journal of Offender Rehabilitation*.

Smeaton, R. G., & Byrne, D. (1987). The effects of R-rated violence and erotica, individual differences and victim characteristics on acquaintance rape proclivity. *Journal of Research in Personality, 21*, 171-184.

Spence, J. T., Helmreich, R. L., & Holahan, C. K. (1979). Negative and positive components of psychological masculinity and femininity and their relationships to self-reports of neurotic and acting out behaviors. *Journal of Personality and Social Psychology, 37*, 1673-1682.

Spence, J. T., Helmreich, R. L., & Stapp, J. (1973). A short version of the Attitudes Toward Women Scale. *Bulletin of the Psychonomic Society, 2*, 219-220.

Stets, J. E., & Pirog-Good, M. A. (1989). Patterns of physical and sexual abuse for men and women in dating relationships: A descriptive analysis. *Journal of Family Violence, 4*, 63-76.

Twentyman, C. T., & McFall, R. M. (1975). Behavioral training of social skills in shy males. *Journal of Consulting and Clinical Psychology, 43*, 384-395.

Ward, C. (1988). The Attitudes Toward Rape Victims Scale. *Psychology of Women Quarterly, 12*, 127-146.

Watson, D., & Friend, R. (1969). Measurement of social-evaluative anxiety. *Journal of Consulting and Clinical Psychology, 33*, 448-467.

Weiner, B. A. (1985). Legal issues raised in treating sex offenders. *Behavioral Sciences and the Law, 3*, 325-340.

Williams, J., & Holmes, K. A. (1981). *The Second Assault: Rape and Public Attitudes*. Westport, CT: Greenwood.

Wolpe, J., & Lazarus, A. A. (1966). *Behavior Therapy Techniques: A Guide to the Treatment of Neuroses*. Oxford: Pergamon.

Yates, E., Barbaree, H. E., & Marshall, W. L. (1984). Anger and deviant sexual arousal. *Behavior Therapy, 15*, 287-294.

4

The Rape Trauma Syndrome: Symptoms, Stages, and Hidden Victims

Patricia A. Petretic-Jackson
and
Susan Tobin

This chapter will describe the nature and course of symptomatic responses manifested by victims of acquaintance rape. We begin the chapter with several vignettes which illustrate the complex and variable nature of the crime of acquaintance rape and its aftermath.

Vignette 1

Kathy was a divorced 32-year old who had returned to school to complete her undergraduate degree in nursing. Late one evening she was interrupted from her studies by loud knocking on her door. Keeping the chain on her door latched, she looked out to see a man she had been acquainted with casually. He appeared highly distraught. Sobbing, he apologized for bothering her at such an hour but said he desperately needed to talk to someone. He told her that he had just found out an hour previously that his mother was diagnosed with terminal cancer. He felt that although he did not know Kathy well, given her academic major in nursing, she could probably help him to cope with this family crisis.

Kathy initially was hesitant to let him enter her apartment. Yet, at the same time, she was feeling guilty for her "paranoia" in not letting him in, and she berated herself silently for her lack of compassion. She told him that she felt uncomfortable with the situation and wasn't sure she could be helpful to him since they really didn't know each other all that well. She then suggested he might be better off contacting any of several mutual acquaintances whom she felt knew him better. He replied that he had already called or stopped by the homes of three of these individuals and none were available. He then begged her to let him in because he desperately needed to talk to someone.

Kathy decided to let him in, thinking she shouldn't "be so cautious to think that anyone she didn't know well should automatically be considered dangerous." She rationalized her decision by the fact that she had seen him at a half dozen or so parties in the past year, talking to him briefly on several occasions. She recalled that he had not behaved inappropriately toward her in any way. He had not made any sexual overture or even asked her out, and he had never before made any attempt to contact her outside of these casual group get-togethers. Kathy then opened the door. He entered the apartment, thanking her profusely. After the door was closed his manner changed abruptly. He shoved her up against the wall, told her to keep quiet or he would really hurt her, and raped her in her living room.

To Kathy it had all seemed so unreal, "like a bad dream." She sought medical treatment in the week following her rape because of fears of contracting a sexually transmitted disease. She also confided in a female friend who was supportive, but Kathy refused her friend's suggestion that she seek counseling. She said she felt "stupid" for being "taken in" the way she had, that "she should have known better." She did not tell anyone in her family about the assault since she believed they would think "less of her" for it. After all, she had acted carelessly in allowing her rapist into her home late at night.

Nine months later she commented that "It's terrible to live every day afraid to trust people." Increasingly becoming more socially isolated and depressed, she refused to date and had not attended any parties out of fear she would see her assailant. In a low voice, she said, "I'm not sure what I would do. . . . I try to blank it out most of the time, but sometimes on campus I find myself looking around, and I realize I'm afraid I'll come face to face with him. . . . At night I still have bad dreams. . . . Sometimes I think about moving, starting fresh in a new place, but I love this place and I don't want to let him win. . . . Moving means him winning . . . still controlling me and what I do. . . . Sometimes it takes so much energy just to get up and go to class or just to talk to people and try to act normal, whatever that is."

Vignette 2

Brenda was a 22-year-old student in her last year of college. Her boyfriend of 2 years was attending graduate school in another state. They had been having problems in their relationship in the last several months, primarily due to his failure to make a firm commitment to the relationship. As Brenda became increasingly dissatisfied with this aspect of the relationship, she began spending more and more time talking to a male student who was taking a class with her. Over the past 2 months in the semester, they had talked several times a week either before or after class. She felt her self-esteem was getting a much needed boost from his concern and attention, given her deteriorating relationship with her boyfriend. In the last several weeks her classmate had begun to stop by almost every day to visit her while she was working at the university library. Although she was not seriously interested in beginning a relationship with him, she enjoyed his company and looked forward to their daily talks.

One day, while shopping off campus on a street near her apartment, Brenda ran into her classmate. He introduced her to a male friend he was with and they started to talk. During the course of the conversation he asked her where she lived, which was nearby, and asked if he and his friend might come over to have a cup of coffee and continue their talk. She invited them to her apartment, and after they had been there an hour or so, she was startled when he suggested that they go into her bedroom and have sex. She began to feel a growing sense of panic, suddenly aware of how uncomfortable the situation had become. Her motives really weren't sexual. At least she hadn't thought they were. She viewed flirting as an "enjoyable and harmless diversion" which validated her attractiveness to men. It also allowed her a "safe" way of "getting back at" her boyfriend for his lack of commitment to her. She had not intended her invitation for coffee to have sexual connotations since she had not wanted this relationship to become sexual in nature. At the same time, she was worried that she "must have led him on by asking him to come to her apartment." Perhaps her behavior with him could have been construed as "teasing" since she had been laughing and flirting. She tried to stall for time, joking that he "couldn't be serious." Her classmate said that he "could tell by the way she acted that she really wanted sex." After all, he remarked, she had acted interested in him and did, after all, invite him to her apartment. Why else would she invite him there?

Brenda's sense of panic increased. She suggested that they were having a "misunderstanding," reminding him of her relationship with her boyfriend. She couldn't be sexually involved with anyone else. Her classmate continued to verbally pressure her for sex and was unwilling to comply with her increasingly anxious requests, punctuated by nervous laughter, to leave her apartment. It began to dawn on Brenda that if she did not cooperate she could be hurt or even killed. After all there were two of them. She realized, with a start, that she had no idea of the kind of person this man really might be. She didn't know his friend at all, and no one knew they were there in her apartment. She decided that she would be better off just to comply with his wishes and "get it over with." The strongest motivator in this decision was her thought that he might harm her, perhaps using a knife from her own kitchen where they had been having coffee. It was reinforced by the fact that, as he talked to her about having sex with him, he began to play with a knife that was laying on her kitchen counter. While he did not actually threaten her with it, she was intimidated by this behavior and was still concerned that he might use it against her if she did not comply with his wishes.

Brenda went into the bedroom with him. After he had intercourse with her, her classmate casually mentioned that his friend had just been released from the state penitentiary and that perhaps she might want to provide him with sex as well. At this point Brenda was so confused and upset that she couldn't decide if he was telling her the truth about his friend. If he were, maybe this other man was dangerous. She could still be hurt, even killed. At that point, she began to cry and scream and throw things at him, hoping that a neighbor might hear her screams. She thought that even if they killed her to keep her quiet, maybe it would be better to die than to have to be forced to have sex with both of them, particularly a man she had just met an hour before. Her classmate first appeared surprised by this reaction and tried to calm her down. When that failed, calling her "a crazy bitch" and "a tease," the classmate dressed and the two men left.

After she heard the door close behind them, Brenda walked out of the bedroom and into the hall to lock the door to the apartment. She began to shake, and sat down on the floor by the door. She felt "dirty" and went into the bathroom to take a shower. She scrubbed herself until her skin was raw and bleeding in spots. She just couldn't get "clean." An hour later her classmate returned to her apartment. She let him in to her apartment although she was afraid he might force her to have sex again. She wasn't sure why she opened the door, but thought she should "play along" to keep him from hurting her physically. He might do that if he believed her to be a threat to him. He asked her if she was "all right." He said after thinking about things he just wanted to be sure "she was okay." She tried to be cheerful and told him what had happened between them was "not a problem, but should not happen again because she could not do that to her boyfriend." He then commented that his friend was concerned that if she was upset about the sex she might try to complain to someone and get his friend and him in trouble. She quickly promised to not tell anyone if he wouldn't expect it to happen again. He agreed and left, saying "We'll just forget this ever happened, okay?"

Brenda sat alone in her apartment for the next 4 days, skipping her classes and work. She was concerned about pregnancy but was afraid she would "just lose it if they ask me any questions about what happened" if she sought medical services. She was too embarrassed to tell anyone, particularly her boyfriend, whom she was sure would think that she was responsible for what had happened. A male friend, concerned when she did not answer the phone, came to her apartment on the fifth day. When she wouldn't tell him what had happened to her, he surmised some type of major trauma and drove her to the office of a crisis counselor. He was concerned because she looked so terrible and kept saying she just wanted to be left alone and wished she were dead. When asked by the crisis counselor what had happened, she responded, "I think I was raped. I don't know. I just wish I were dead."

Over the course of a year her symptoms ran the gamut. Her moods alternated between periods of depression accompanied by suicidal ideation and angry outbursts, often directed at male friends and her boyfriend. Deciding he would never forgive her if he knew what had happened ("I know he would blame me for what happened") she eventually provoked a fight and broke off the relationship. Initially socially isolated and highly anxious, she stopped wearing makeup and wore baggy, shapeless clothes. This was followed by a period wherein she dressed in short, tight clothing, wore much more make-up than was typical and flirted with men at any opportunity. During this period she said, "I'm a tramp. Why not dress the part and let everyone know?" Yet, during this year, she did not date, saying the thought of a man touching her made her physically ill. For a period of several months she reported a substantial increase in her alcohol consumption. She reported a variety of somatic complaints and missed a number of days of school.

Vignette 3

Meredith was an 18-year-old freshman at a state university. She went with a group of her friends to a local bar following a football game. After a few drinks she began talking to one of the members of the football team, and they danced and talked for the next several hours. Although Meredith wasn't much of a drinker, the bar was hot and the football player kept buying her drinks. After about three drinks she began to feel lightheaded and stopped drinking. She noticed that he had had about four or five beers, but "wasn't acting all that drunk." She was secretly thrilled that he seemed interested in her, and thought she would be the envy of all her friends if she began dating him.

When the bar closed he offered to take her home but said he needed to stop by a friend's house on the way to pick up a letter which contained a check. When they arrived at the apartment complex, he suggested she come up with him and not sit alone in the car. She hesitated, but he teasingly asked if she was afraid he might take advantage of her. He laughed and reminded her that he only needed to stop by the apartment briefly. Not wanting to look unsophisticated or "like a baby," she agreed to go to the apartment with him. No one was home, but he used a key he said his friend had lent him.

After they entered the apartment, he looked around the living room, complaining that the letter was not there and he would have to spend some time checking around for it. He got a beer from the refrigerator for himself and offered her one. When she refused, he asked her "what her problem was." He asked her to help him look around, and made a pretext of looking in the bedrooms while asking her to check the living room and kitchen again. He suggested she sit on the couch and check through a pile of mail again. As she began sorting he came over and sat by her. He leaned over and kissed her. She returned the kiss, but as he became more aggressive sexually she attempted to politely push him away. She suggested they might "slow down." He looked confused and said, "I thought you liked me. What's the problem?" Trying to sound confident and assertive, she suggested they should probably leave. He began to laugh and told her "to relax, not be a baby, he wouldn't hurt her." He began kissing her. Not responding, she began to cry and tried to push him away. She kept asking him to stop, repeatedly saying "No," and tried to break away as he persisted. He moved back and she thought for a moment he was going to stop. Instead, he grabbed her wrists tightly, and pushed her down on the couch. He then laid on top of her, pinning her to the couch. Despite her protests, he forced her skirt up and penetrated her.

After he ejaculated he asked her if she had "enjoyed it." He said that he knew she was a nice girl and that nice girls couldn't say yes to sex even when they really wanted to. He also told her that she should not worry. He still respected her and would call her. He then drove her back to her dormitory, talking about a number of things along the way. He was seemingly oblivious to the fact that she was crying quietly. At the dorm, he leaned over and kissed her, told her what a great time he had with her, and reminded her that he'd call her in the coming week.

Meredith couldn't understand where the evening had gone wrong. She was embarrassed and confused. She had been a virgin and hadn't imagined her first sexual experience would happen this way. She hadn't been ready, had wanted a relationship first. She had actually fantasized earlier in the evening about what it would be like to date him and, just maybe, have a sexual relationship with him - in time. He said he would call, so obviously he had liked her. Then why had he forced her to have sex when she said "No"? Was this what dating was like in college? Did you have to have sex with a guy even if you didn't want to? Was he really going to call her? Should she go out with him if he did call? He didn't seem to think anything wrong had happened. Why did she feel so guilty, so dirty if nothing was wrong?

She was bleeding vaginally, but felt she could not face the staff at the student health center. She was too embarrassed to say anything to her roommate initially. When she tentatively told her about the incident a few days later, her roommate couldn't see why Meredith was so upset. "Why the big deal over this? So he was an animal. He's a catch. A lot of girls on campus would be glad to trade places with you." Meredith found herself spending a lot of time in the next several weeks going over and over the events of that evening. How exactly did it all happen? What did she do wrong? It just didn't make sense.

* * *

The reality of sexual violence is that as children, as adolescents, and as adults, women are most likely to be victimized by their protectors, families and intimate partners. . . . By count and by context, victimization is a woman's lot in life. To the degree that women participate in culturally prescribed contexts, according to culturally prescribed gender roles and with those culturally prescribed as their most appropriate male partners, they are, to that degree, likely to be victimized. (Mandoki & Burkhart, 1991, p. 177)

Each of the women described in the vignettes was raped by a man known to her - an acquaintance, not a stranger. In the rape literature the distinction has been made between sexual assault perpetrated by a stranger and that perpetrated by an acquaintance. Although the term acquaintance may sometimes be used in a narrow way, referring to a person "known but not a close friend" (Bechhofer & Parrot, 1991, p. 12), Bechhofer and Parrot note that the more common usage within the acquaintance rape literature has broader definitional scope. In this context an *acquaintance* is defined as *anyone not a stranger who is known to a person.* Acquaintances are further delineated into four types: (a) *nonromantic acquaintances* (e.g., friend, co-worker, or neighbor); (b) *casual dates*; (c) *steady dates* (e.g., boyfriend or lover); and (d) *spouses or other family members* (Koss et al., 1988). For the purpose of this chapter, this broad definition of acquaintance will be used, with a focus on the symptomatic impact of sexual assault when perpetrated by a nonromantic acquaintance, casual date, intimate partner, or family member. *Acquaintance rape* will be defined as *nonconsensual sex between two individuals who are known to each other.* The focus of the chapter will be restricted to exploration of the impact of acquaintance rape on adolescent or adult females.*

A woman who is sexually victimized by a man with whom she is acquainted does not "fit" the culturally stereotypic picture of the "typical/stranger rape victim." The "typical" rape victim is often perceived as a woman who has been unsuccessful in her attempts to ward off forced intercourse by a physically violent and mentally disturbed stranger. However, for the majority of women who are raped, their assailant will be a man known to them, an acquaintance and not a stranger (Koss, Gidycz, & Wisniewski, 1987; Russell, 1984). Within this group, a small number will seek help immediately following their assault. These women will be referred to as *acknowledged acquaintance rape* victims. As part of that group of women who have sought formal assistance in the immediate postassault period, the nature and course of their behavioral, physiological, and cognitive symptomatic response to victimization have been well documented in the clinical and research literature. However, the overwhelming majority of women assaulted by ac-

---

*While recognizing the legitimate status of both male and child assault victims and the commonalities of their assault response, the reader is referred to other sources for a more in-depth discussion of the concerns of these groups (D. Everstine & L. Everstine, 1989; Lew, 1988; Sgroi, 1982; Struckman-Johnson, 1991).

quaintances will choose not to seek any form of legal, mental health, or health-related services in this early postassault period (Koss, 1988a). These women also commonly fail to confide in a significant other or even define their experience as rape. In some instances an unacknowledged victim of acquaintance rape may view herself as a victim, but not as a "legitimate crime victim" (Estrich, 1987). Koss (1983) has used the terms *unacknowledged* or *hidden* victim of acquaintance rape to characterize this population of women who remain unidentified following their rape.

In this chapter we will describe the range of symptoms that may be experienced by both groups of women who have been assaulted by acquaintances. Clinicians will encounter women from both groups among their clients. Although the cluster of core symptoms is similar to that exhibited by victims of stranger rape, both acknowledged and unacknowledged acquaintance rape victims will be at greater risk for long-term behavioral, emotional, and cognitive symptoms and impairment due to the unique, malevolent social-psychological context of sexual victimization by an acquaintance (Burt & Katz, 1987).

Rape in any context is a very real trauma. Rape violates not only the body but the spirit as well, bringing in its wake a sense that any control over one's physical safety is now gone. In the case of rape by a stranger, a woman may be able to maintain a sense of a "zone of protection" (Warshaw, 1988), drawing on the support provided by family and friends who validate her experience by their sympathetic reaction to her victimization. For the victim of acquaintance rape this is often not the case. The trauma of her rape is exacerbated by the impact of the violation of trust inherent in a rape committed by an acquaintance. But in addition to this violation of trust, the support provided by friends and family is often lacking. As Burkhart (1991) has commented, "excepting the absolute magnitude of the prevalence data for acquaintance rape . . . perhaps the most striking aspect . . . is how hidden it has been from awareness" (p. 288). Like incest, acquaintance rape often becomes a "dirty little secret," known only to the woman and her rapist. Many individuals the victim encounters daily make a distinction between "real" rapes and "date" rapes. Implicit in this language is the notion that stranger rape is *not* the same as being raped by an acquaintance.

The reality of such victim-blaming attributions in society is validated by the literature on attribution of victimization blame and is further reflected in "the lack of medical, social, psychological and legal support for victims" (Calhoun & Townsley, 1991, p. 67). Negated are the facts of the assault which may legally define it as rape, and put in their place is a social re-definition of the event as "something other than rape," something that is "no big deal." As Burkhart and Stanton (1988) have indicated

> Relationship status is a very powerful component of the social definition of rape (Burt, 1980; S. H. Klemmack & D. L. Klemmack, 1976; Koss, 1985; Skelton & Burkhart, 1980) with the degree of acquaintance being negatively correlated with an attribution of rape by victims, offenders, and other citizens. (p. 44)

The primary distinction that will be made by the present authors between acquaintance and stranger rape and other forms of traumatic victimization is a recognition of the unique challenges to the personal belief system of the woman (Gidycz & Koss, 1991a) that may be operating in the case of acquaintance rape, beliefs which compound the traumatic effects of the assault.

Women who acknowledge their status as acquaintance rape victims (e.g., acknowledged victims) will "fit" the prototypic rape Posttraumatic Stress Disorder (PTSD) symptoms pattern that is commonly identified with stranger rape. However, certain symptoms may prove to be more salient in this group when they are compared to victims of stranger assault. Acknowledged acquaintance rape victims typically seek treatment in the immediate postassault period or several months following the assault when core postassault symptoms (e.g., depression, anxiety, sexual, and relationship problems) have not abated. When women in the unacknowledged group have contact with a clinician, one of several symptom patterns may be present. Within this group, delayed treatment seeking is the norm, and the woman may or may not spontaneously label herself as a rape victim, respond affirmatively to clinician inquiries concerning a history of sexual assault, or identify her prior assault as a causal factor contributing to her current distress.

The salience of cognitive symptoms must be thoroughly investigated by the clinician when treating victims of acquaintance rape. The clinican should be aware of two common cognitive response styles which reflect the classic double bind inherent with this form of sexual victimization. Koss and Burkhart (1989) describe a type of cognitive-emotional paralysis which commonly occurs in many women as a result of the conflict between the traumatic subjective experience of the assault and the response of a nonaffirming, often-blaming, external social environment. Koss and Burkhart (1989) comment

> Led to believe she is responsible for any sexual outcome and faced with an unsupportive environment (including an assailant who may even ask her to go out with him again), the woman experiences herself as having only the choice of responsibility and self-blame, or denial. It may not be until years later through a chance remark or exposure to similar circumstances that she will recognize her own victimization and her accommodation to it. Without the opportunity to develop a positive or, at least, strengthening reinterpretation of her experience, the rape victim may assimilate degradation and helplessness into her beliefs and behavior. To the extent that a victim sees herself as damaged and unworthy, she may become compromised in her ability to see herself as powerful and able, or even willing to affirm her dignity. (p. 35)

Thus, we see that cognitive appraisals and coping styles play a critical mediating role in the long-term behavioral/emotional symptomatic response of the victim of acquaintance rape. However, given the steadily increasing number of acquaintance rape victims who seek treatment in the immediate postassault period, we will first discuss immediate posttrauma symptomatic responses to acquaintance rape. Characteristic of many acknowl-edged victims of acquaintance rape, this constellation of symp-toms may also be observed in the delayed treatment seeker as well, often in response to symbolic cueing to the unresolved trauma.

SYMPTOMS OF ACKNOWLEDGED ACQUAINTANCE RAPE VICTIMS: THE RAPE TRAUMA SYNDROME

Currently there is a substantial research and clinical litera-ture which documents the consequences of rape. However, until the last several years the descriptions of postassault symp-tomatology of rape victims limited the documentation of rape sequelae to that group of women who were acknowledged or identified rape victims. That is, much was known about the symptom picture of women who reported their sexual assaults to agencies or who responded to research advertisements solic-iting women who had experienced rape. Several reviews are available which comprehensively describe the postassault symptomatology of this group of women. For further details, the reader is referred to Ellis (1983), Holmes and St. Lawrence (1983), and Resick (1993).

It has been argued that descriptions of rape symptomatology published prior to 1985 fail to provide a good "fit" with the symptom picture of acquaintance rape victims. Instead, it has been suggested that these early studies, which chronicled the postassault responses in acknowledged rape victims, more ac-curately described postassault responses of victims of stranger rape. In fact, did these studies, examining as they did the postassault symptoms in samples of acknowledged rape victims, provide accurate descriptions of assault sequelae only for women victimized by strangers? Were the findings not at all applicable to women assaulted by acquaintances? A closer examination of these studies, along with the women described in them, is war-ranted.

As a group, women raped by strangers tend to report their rapes more often than victims who have been assaulted by men known to them (Williams, 1984). Examining a sample of 246 women who contacted a rape crisis center, Williams found that victims of stranger rape were more likely to report their assault to the police because they perceived themselves to be true crime victims. *Women raped by men they knew*, in social settings or at home, *were far less likely to report because they questioned their role and responsibility in the attack.* Because assaults by acquaintances usually involved less violence, women often lacked the physical evidence needed to convince both themselves and others that they were indeed true victims. Thus, many more victims of stranger rape were represented in groups of acknowledged rape victims.

Additionally, the *specific impact of being raped by an acquaintance* had not been studied prior to the early 1980s. Even though acquaintance rape victims were represented in groups of acknowledged victims, the impact of a victim's degree of relationship to the assailant on her symptomatic response to rape had not been examined extensively. In 1988, when Koss first reported that substantial numbers of women in a national college sample had been victims of rape - the vast majority perpetrated by acquaintances - and that 95% of these women had failed to seek treatment or assistance of any kind, it raised a host of issues. Among them was the issue of whether the symptomatic response of these hidden (nonidentified) victims of acquaintance rape would be similar to or different from that of women who had sought services and whose response to rape had been chronicled in the earlier clinical studies of acknowledged rape victims.

Upon closer examination, it appears that these early clinical studies of acknowledged rape victims frequently included a substantial number of women who had been acquainted with their assailants prior to their assault. For example, Kilpatrick and his colleagues (Kilpatrick, Best, et al., 1985; Kilpatrick, Best, Saunders, Amick-McMullan, et al., 1988; Kilpatrick, Best, Saunders, & Veronen, 1988; Kilpatrick, Resick, & Veronen, 1984; Kilpatrick & Veronen, 1984; Kilpatrick, Veronen, & Best, 1985) analyzed the aftermath of rape by comparing a sample of victimized women with a nonvictimized control group, using as subjects those women who entered their model treatment/research program. Kilpatrick documented the assailant-victim relationship in describing the demographic characteristics of his victim group. One-half of the sample of victims had been raped by complete strangers, 28% by acquaintances, 9% by friends/dates, 3% by family members, and 10% by others. All these women were acknowledged rape victims and had sought treatment.

It appears, then, that a subset of women raped by men known to them do acknowledge their assault and seek treatment in the immediate postassault period. It is also apparent that this group of women experiences a significant level of postassault trauma. The subset of treatment-seeking women victimized by acquaintances commonly experience severe rape sequelae consistent with the symptom picture of Rape Trauma Syndrome (RTS) or Posttraumatic Stress Disorder (PTSD) (*DSM-IV;* American Psychiatric Association, 1994). However, cognitive symptoms, particularly attributions of self-blame, appear more salient in this group when compared to victims of stranger assault despite their common status as acknowledged victims.

However, the fact that acquaintance rape victims comprise a substantial subset of acknowledged victims who seek medical or mental health assistance does not necessarily imply that symptom patterns are identical to those of victims of stranger rape who seek such assistance. Does, in fact, the symptomatology for acknowledged rape victims assaulted by acquaintances differ from the symptomatology of acknowledged victims assaulted by strangers? Unfortunately, this question was not initially addressed in the research conducted with acknowledged victims in the 1970s. Rather than focus on differences in symptomatology that might exist within a heterogeneous group of acknowledged victims as a function of the victim-offender relationship, researchers instead compared victims to nonvictims. This focus can best be understood in a historical context, which reflects the developmental status of rape research in the 1970s and early 1980s. At issue during this period was the necessity of validating the existence of trauma associated with rape.

VALIDATING TRAUMA
ASSOCIATED WITH RAPE IN
ACKNOWLEDGED VICTIM GROUPS:
THE RAPE TRAUMA SYNDROME (RTS)

It had not been until the 1970s that societal attitudes regarding rape were challenged in the writings of feminists. Concomitantly the first publications in the psychiatric literature departed from a victim-provocation perspective. Sutherland and Scherl documented the three-phase reaction syndrome to rape in 1970. This syndrome included symptoms of fear, anxiety, and depression. In 1974 the somatic, cognitive, psychological, and behavioral symptoms identified with Rape Trauma Syndrome (RTS) were documented by Burgess and Holmstrom (1974). Burgess and Holmstrom differentiated victim responses to rape into two phases, acute and long-term. The acute phase was characterized by general stress response symptoms, while the long-term reorganization process was characterized by rape-related symptoms (e.g., anxiety/fear, depression, and sexual dysfunction, etc.).

Burgess and Holmstrom described Rape Trauma Syndrome as a response pattern characterized by the following essential symptoms:

1. a sense of helplessness
2. intensified conflicts about dependence and independence
3. self-criticism and guilt
4. impaired interpersonal relationships
5. intrusive imagery
6. psychic numbing expressed by a range of emotions
7. constrained activities

They also identified a host of associated symptoms which might be present. These included

1. self-blame
2. concentration difficulties
3. avoidance/fears/phobias
4. sleep disturbances
5. hyperalertness

Burgess and Holmstrom subsequently related the stress patterns of the Rape Trauma Syndrome to *DSM* criteria of Posttraumatic Stress Disorder (PTSD; Burgess & Holmstrom, 1985). Today, RTS is commonly conceptualized as an example of PTSD (Allen, 1994; Becker & Kaplan, 1991; Foa, Rothbaum & Steketee, 1993; Frieze, 1987; Goodman, Koss, & Russo, 1993; Kilpatrick, Veronen, & Best, 1985; Rothbaum et al., 1990). Although many of the same symptoms identified by Burgess and Holmstrom overlap with the essential and associated features of PTSD described in *DSM-IV*, the primacy of specific symptoms varies somewhat, as can be noted when comparing the symptom list of Burgess and Holmstrom with the diagnostic criteria for Posttraumatic Stress Disorder provided in *DSM-IV*. *DSM-IV* criteria are listed in Table 4-1 (pp. 110-111), with symptoms particularly salient for victims of acquaintance rape highlighted in **bold print**.

Among the PTSD diagnostic criteria changes made within *DSM-IV* is how criteria A, the stressor, is now defined. The definition of "outside usual experience" used in *DSM-III-R* was altered and expanded to allow for the impact of personal perceptions of distress to be considered in situations in which an individual experiences symptoms of PTSD as delineated in criteria B, C, and D. This change recognizes the importance of an individual's cognitive conceptualization of perceived trauma or danger. This change also makes PTSD a viable diagnostic option to consider in instances when acquaintance rape victims experience the rape as highly traumatic, as evidenced by symptoms of PTSD in Criteria B, C, and D. However, the symptom duration requirement for a diagnosis of PTSD (i.e., symptoms must be present for more than 1 month) make this diagnosis inappropriate for women seen in the immediate postassault period. A new diagnostic option available for women who are symptomatic during this time period is (308.3) Acute Stress Disorder. This diagnosis is appropriate for victims experiencing classic PTSD symptoms (at least one symptom from each of the three PTSD symptom clusters) and at least three dissociative symptoms, whose symptoms last a minimum of 2 days and a maximum of 4 weeks. Symptom onset must be within 4 weeks of the assault. For individuals initially given the diagnosis of

TABLE 4-1:
DSM-IV DIAGNOSTIC CRITERIA FOR 309.81 POSTTRAUMATIC STRESS DISORDER - SALIENCE FOR ACQUAINTANCE RAPE VICTIMS*

A. The person has been exposed to a traumatic event in which both of the following were present:

    (1) the person experienced, witnessed, or was confronted with an event or events that involved actual or threatened death or serious injury, or a threat to the physical integrity of self or others

    (2) the person's response involved intense fear, helplessness, or horror

B. The traumatic event is persistently **reexperienced** in one (or more) of the following ways:

    (1) **recurrent and intrusive distressing recollections of the event, including images, thoughts, or perceptions**

    (2) **recurrent distressing dreams of the event**

    (3) **acting or feeling as if the traumatic event were recurring (includes a sense of reliving the experience, illusions, hallucinations, and dissociative flashback episodes,** including those that occur on awakening or when intoxicated)

    (4) **intense psychological distress at exposure to internal or external cues that symbolize or resemble an aspect of the traumatic event**

    (5) physiological reactivity on exposure to internal or external cues that symbolize or resemble an aspect of the traumatic event

C. Persistent **avoidance of stimuli associated with the trauma** and **numbing of general responsiveness (not present before the trauma)**, as indicated by three (or more) of the following:

---

*Note: From *Diagnostic and Statistical Manual of Mental Disorders* (DSM-IV, 4th ed., pp. 427-429, by American Psychiatric Association, 1994, Washington, DC: American Psychiatric Association. Copyright © 1994 by American Psychiatric Association. Reprinted with permission.

(1) efforts to **avoid thoughts, feelings, or conversations associated with the trauma**

(2) efforts to **avoid activities, places, or people** that arouse **recollections of the trauma**

(3) inability to recall an important aspect of the trauma

(4) markedly **diminished interest or participation in significant activities**

(5) **feeling of detachment or estrangement from others**

(6) restricted range of affect (e.g., unable to have loving feelings)

(7) sense of a foreshortened future (e.g., does not expect to have a career, marriage, children, or a normal life span)

D. Persistent symptoms of **increased arousal** (not present before the trauma), as indicated by two (or more) of the following:

(1) **difficulty falling or staying asleep**

(2) irritability or outbursts of **anger**

(3) difficulty **concentrating**

(4) hypervigilance

(5) exaggerated startle response

Acute Stress Disorder whose symptoms persist longer than 1 month, the diagnosis is changed from Acute Stress Disorder to PTSD.

DSM-IV retains the basic tripartite division of essential symptoms into intrusive (Criterion B), avoidant and numbing (Criterion C), and hyperarousal (Criterion D) categories used in the *DSM-III-R*. However, the discussion of associated symptoms is vastly improved in the *DSM-IV*, and the relationship between interpersonal traumas and associated symptoms is clarified. Associated features of PTSD identified within *DSM-IV* include "impaired affect modulation; self-destructive and impulsive behavior; dissociative symptoms; somatic complaints; feelings of ineffectiveness, shame, despair or hopelessness; feeling permanently damaged; loss of previously sustained beliefs; hostility; social withdrawal; feeling constantly threatened; impaired relationships with others; or a change from the individual's previous personality characteristics" (p. 425). Such associated features are more commonly seen with interpersonal stressors such as sexual and physical assault, and so are commonly observed in victims of acquaintance rape.

In a prospective study, Rothbaum et al. (1990) reported that 94% of rape victims meet PTSD criteria in the immediate postassault period while 47% met criteria 3 months later. In a recent longitudinal survey of a national probability sample of over 4,000 women (Kilpatrick, Edmunds, & Seymour, 1992), in which one in eight women reported being raped at least once, 31% of all rape victims developed PTSD at some time and 11% had PTSD at the time of the survey. Kilpatrick et al. (1992) estimated that 3.8 million adult American women have experienced rape-induced PTSD, while 1.3 million currently experience rape-induced PTSD.

However, recent conceptualizations of PTSD (Silver & Sprock, 1991) suggest that trauma victims are not a homogeneous group. Rape victims typically experience a unique subset of salient symptoms, while sharing common core symptoms with other trauma groups. The most salient PTSD symptoms exhibited by rape victims do not necessarily reflect *DSM-IV* essential symptoms (Silver & Sprock, 1991). Instead, it appears that the most salient symptoms more closely correspond to those originally identified by Burgess and Holmstrom (1974) in their conceptualization of RTS. These symptoms include both essential and associated features within the *DSM-IV* diagnostic criteria.

As previously discussed, early clinical and research studies failed to specify whether the symptom constellation associated with RTS and PTSD accurately described the experience of the subset of women raped by acquaintances. Would the symptom picture of women who are victims of acquaintance rape be different from that of women who are victims of stranger rape in terms of severity, duration, or pattern of symptoms experienced? It was not until the early 1980s that within-group differences of acknowledged rape victims as a function of the victim-assailant relationship were addressed.

COMPARING SYMPTOMS OF ACKNOWLEDGED VICTIMS OF ACQUAINTANCE AND STRANGER RAPE

Several studies in the early 1980s examined the effects of rape on postassault psychological adjustment as a function of the victim-assailant relationship in clinical samples of acknowledged rape victims (Atkeson et al., 1982; Becker et al., 1982; Ellis, Atkeson, & Calhoun, 1981; Frank, Turner, & Stewart, 1980; Kilpatrick, Veronen, & Best, 1985). In virtually all of these studies, researchers failed to establish that post-rape levels of fear, depression, or social maladjustment were predicted by the victim-offender relationship. In only one study (McCahill, Meyer, & Fischman, 1979) were any differences found. McCahill et al. (1979) rated the severity of post-rape trauma in a group of victims interviewed four times during the first year following the assault. When the offender was a casual acquaintance or relative stranger, victims were rated as *more* severely maladjusted than when the offender was a friend, family member, or total stranger.

In all of the studies identified herein, assessment of symptomatology was limited to the year subsequent to the assault. Research addressing the issues of long-term patterns of response to rape, coping strategies, or the relationship between coping efforts and the recovery process has only begun within the last several years (Burt & Katz, 1988; Frieze, 1987). When issues in long-term recovery and coping strategies are examined, an interesting pattern has emerged. Findings from recent long-term follow-up studies conducted with acknowledged rape victims now suggest that the majority of acknowledged rape victims do not experience a rapid recovery. This clinical documentation of long-term problems in response to rape trauma contradicts the premise of rape as a time-limited, acute trauma followed by a period of reorganization and recovery as described in initial crisis model conceptualizations. Instead, there is now a growing body of evidence that a substantial number of acknowledged rape victims experience continued interpersonal dysfunction, fears, depression, suspiciousness, confusion, and sexual problems several years postassault (Becker et al., 1982; Burgess & Holmstrom, 1979; Kilpatrick et al., 1984; Nadelson et al., 1982). Consequently, it is not surprising to find that as many as 30% to 48% of rape victims sampled more than 1 year postassault report that they eventually sought psychotherapy, sometimes years following the assault (Ellis, Atkeson, & Calhoun, 1982; Koss, 1985).

In one study, Kilpatrick and his colleagues (Kilpatrick, Best, et al., 1985) surveyed 43 adult victims and 96 female nonvictims drawn from a random community sample of 391 women used in a lifetime prevalence study of criminal victimization experiences. The two groups of women were administered the Mental Health Problem Interview, a structured interview which assessed major depressive disorder, agoraphobia, social phobia, simple phobia, panic disorder, obsessive-compulsive disorder, posttraumatic stress disorder, and disorders of sexual desire and/or sexual functioning. Kilpatrick et al. found that victims reported depression, social phobia, obsessions, and sexual dysfunction. Compared to nonvictims, victims were 11 times more likely to be clinically depressed, 6 times more likely to be anxious in social situations, 2½ times more likely to experience sexual dysfunction, and 3 times more likely to have an obsessive-compulsive disorder, despite the fact that, on the average, it had been nearly 15 years since the assault. Date rapes were most likely to produce a subjective cognitive appraisal of life threat or injury, while husband and stranger assaults were less likely to have done so. Assailant identity did not predict differences in the prevalence of current mental health problems in the victim sample.

In summary, a number of research studies indicate that, among women who seek treatment following assault, the identity of their assailant is not a salient variable that predicts differential symptom pattern. It appears that being raped by an acquaintance affects the victim in much the same way as being raped by a stranger - if the assault has motivated the victim to seek immediate assistance or if victim cognitively labels the assault as rape. Symptomatically, acknowledged acquaintance rape victims show a higher rate of significant primary symptoms of PTSD, with elevations of clinical depression, sexual dysfunction, and anxiety. Co-occurrence of Mood and Anxiety Disorders is also common. Although studies specifically addressing cognitive symptomatology have been limited, both clinical and research findings identify obsessions, ruminations, and attributions of self-blame as common problems within the cognitive domain (Katz & Burt, 1988; Mandoki & Burkhart, 1991).

Early clinical case descriptions of women who sought treatment following rape by acquaintances validated the symptom pattern identified in research studies of acknowledged rape victims. This correspondence between clinical and research data should not be surprising, given that these women had, by seeking mental health services, acknowledged their victimization as such and reported substantial postassault trauma. It then follows that the earliest conceptualizations of sequelae to acquaintance rape, based on such clinical reports, highlighted the similarities of acquaintance rape to stranger rape.

However, although it can be concluded that the identity of the rapist is not a predictor of the presence or severity of affective, behavioral, or cognitive symptoms among acknowledged rape victims, one could still question if status as an acknowledged versus an unacknowledged acquaintance rape victim might affect symptom pattern or course. That is, would the pattern of symptomatology documented in the studies of acknowledged victims be representative of the symptom pattern of acquaintance rape victims who fail to seek therapy, identify their assault as "rape," or view themselves as a legitimate crime victim?

THE UNACKNOWLEDGED VICTIM
OF ACQUAINTANCE RAPE:
THE HIDDEN RAPE VICTIM

There is some disagreement among clinical researchers whether a clearly identifiable differential response pattern exists in unacknowledged acquaintance rape victims which would discriminate them from acknowledged acquaintance rape victims. Findings from several studies suggest that unacknowledged rape victims cannot be discriminated symptomatically from victims of stranger or acquaintance rape who have acknowledged their assaults. However, researchers investigating sequelae of assault in the population of unacknowledged acquaintance rape victims suggest that subtle differences may exist between these women and their counterparts who have sought treatment.

Findings from the Kilpatrick, Best, et al. (1985) community study summarized previously suggest that postassault symptomatology is similar between acknowledged and unacknowledged victims of rape. Kilpatrick et al. found that acknowledgement of rape had little relationship to mental health consequences when victims were compared to nonvictims. Separating acknowledged and unacknowledged victims, Kilpatrick found, with both groups more likely than nonvictims to have a major depressive episode, current social phobia, and sexual problems. Also, when the groups of acknowledged and unacknowledged victims were compared, no differences were found in characteristics of the offense. Violence during rape was associated with victim acknowledgement of the incident as rape, and acknowledged victims were significantly more likely to have developed PTSD.

COMPARING HIDDEN VICTIMS OF STRANGER AND ACQUAINTANCE RAPE IN A COLLEGE POPULATION

Currently there exists a nonclinical data base which focuses on the symptomatic response to unacknowledged rape in a college population, a group demographically at considerable risk for this problem. Based on recent incidence and prevalence studies, it is also apparent that such "hidden" rape victims are far more prevalent than victims of rape by strangers. Of the 3,187 women who participated in a national survey of college students at 32 institutions (Koss, 1988a), 15.4% reported experiencing an act that met the legal definition of rape at some time since the age of 14. In classifying these assaults, Koss found that the typical acquaintance rape victim profile for her sample did not match the profile of rapes reported by traditional crime statistics/surveys. In the Koss study, only 16% of the females who were sampled reported rape perpetrated by strangers. The vast majority of assaults reported were perpetrated by an individual (95%), usually close acquaintances or dates (84%). Only 5% of these rapes had been reported to police and only 5% of victims had sought crisis services. Of assaults which met legal criteria for rape, 27% were acknowledged by the victim as such.

Based on the numbers of "hidden rape" victims, this group of women whose symptomatic response to rape had not been previously documented, Koss (1988a) called for further study of

> the traumatic cognitive and symptomatic impact of rape on victims who do not report, confide in significant others, seek services, or even identify themselves as victims. It is possible that the *quality of many women's lives is reduced* by the effects of encapsulated, hidden sexual victimization and the victim's subsequent *accommodation to the experience through beliefs and behavior* [italics added]. (p. 22)

Research examining the pattern of symptomatic response to acquaintance rape in this previously unidentified sample of nontreatment-seeking women attending college has only recently begun. In addition to the analysis of the national college sample data by Koss and her colleagues (Gidycz & Koss, 1991a, 1991b; Koss et al., 1988), Burkhart and his colleagues at Auburn University (Mandoki, 1989; Sommerfeldt, Burkhart, & Mandoki, 1989) have conducted a series of investigations with this population.

From the college national sample of 3,187 women, Koss et al. (1988) identified a total of 489 rape victims. They made two comparisons in this group of victims who had largely underreported their assaults. First, they compared victims of stranger ($n = 52$) versus acquaintance ($n = 416$) rape. They then compared four different groups, classifying groups by type of acquaintance: nonromantic acquaintances, such as friends, coworkers, or neighbors ($n = 122$); casual dates ($n = 103$); steady dates, including boyfriends or lovers ($n = 147$); and spouses/other family members ($n = 44$).

Four symptoms were assessed: depression (using the Beck Depression Inventory), anxiety (using the Trait Anxiety Scale), relationship satisfaction (e.g., able to trust others, to make friends, get close to others, and to maintain relationships), and sexual satisfaction (obtaining satisfaction ratings of different sexual activities, such as kissing and hugging, petting and stroking, and sexual intercourse, using items developed by the researchers).

Compared to stranger rape victims, victims of acquaintance rape believed the man was less responsible for what happened and rated the offender as less aggressive and themselves as less "scared." Anger ratings and depression were not rated differently, nor were there differences in ratings of responsibility. Groups were similar in the numbers who considered suicide postassault; 27.8% considered it to the point of thinking about methods.

Examining coping strategies postassault, victims of acquaintance rape were less likely to discuss the experience with someone, seek crisis services, and report their assault to the police. In retrospect, victims of acquaintance rape also believed they should have had counseling following their assault. In this sample only 1.7% of acquaintance rape victims sought crisis services, while a similar percentage informed the police. Women who were raped by acquaintances (23.1%) were less likely to identify the assault as rape than were women raped by strangers (55%). Comparatively, 62% raped by acquaintances "did not view their assaults as any type of crime" compared to 29% of women who were raped by strangers (Koss et al., 1988, p. 13).

Within the acquaintance rape victim group, the four subgroups differed significantly in perceptions of the rape, rating of offender aggression, feelings of anger and depression at time of assault, and degree of responsibility for assault. All felt equally "scared" and showed similar ratings of resistiveness. Women raped by casual dates, steady dates, or nonromantic acquaintances viewed themselves as more responsible than those raped by family members. Many women did not view their experience as any kind of crime (52.1% in the nonromantic acquaintance versus 73% and 71.2%, respectively, in the casual date and steady date perpetrator groups).

Symptomatically, groups did not differ on depression, anxiety, or sexual satisfaction ratings. Findings were consistent with those of studies of stranger rape (Ellis et al., 1981; Frank et al., 1980, Kilpatrick, Best, et al., 1985; Ruch & Chandler, 1983). However, all groups of victims had scores on standardized psychological scales that were elevated. Beck Depression Inventory scores were one standard deviation above the nonvictim group, consistent with a clinical label of mild depression. State anxiety scores were almost a standard deviation above the mean of nonvictimized women, at an elevation "characteristic of college students with emotional problems" (Koss et al., 1988, p. 22). Both relationship and sexual difficulties were present. Women reported a reduction in the frequency of sexual contact and less satisfaction with a number of sexual activities. Koss concluded, "The responses to psychological symptom scales among all groups of victims indicated a lingering, potentially clinically significant impact of rape which did not vary in severity according to the victim-offender relationship" (p. 22).

Confirmation of these findings has occurred in samples using both quantitative and qualitative methods. For example, Gidycz and Koss (1989) assessed levels of depression and anxiety in high school-aged adolescent victims of assault using the Beck Depression Inventory and Trait Anxiety Scale and found similar elevations for this age group. They also found the frequency of suicidal ideation, plans, and attempts similar to those found in the college-aged group. In a community sample, Burnam et al. (1988) found an increased risk of phobic, obsessive-compulsive, and panic disorders and a severity of depression that was consistent with a diagnosis of Major Depression. In the popular press report of Koss's survey for *Ms.* magazine, Warshaw (1988) interviewed acquaintance rape victims. Victims reported relationship difficulties. They also incurred genital and other forms of physical injuries from the man's actions or their resistance to the assault. They were fearful of increased risk of pregnancy, sexually transmitted diseases (STDs), and AIDS. With pregnancy, there was the issue of abortion. When this option was selected there were associated symptoms of suicidal ideation, guilt, depression, and anniversary reactions. Common cognitive errors reported included beliefs of oneself as worthless, helpless, and alone. These women also reported a loss of trust and had a heightened sense of their own vulnerability and risk of serious harm in a world in which safety was now proven to be an illusion.

In another study of college females, Rogers (1984) identified symptoms of anxiety, guilt about sexual behavior, and poor social and family adjustment in a sample of undergraduate women who experienced sexual victimization. Symptomatic responses did not diminish over time. In a study of coping and attitudes by Mandoki (1989), women sampled from the acquaintance/date rape group were also asked to provide written descriptions of their assaults (Sommerfeldt et al., 1989). The most common symptomatic response was an increase in cautiousness and mistrust of others, particularly men. Other symptomatic responses reported included feelings of anger, fear, depression, shame, and decreased self-esteem. Approximately half reported some type of self-blame.

These studies of postassault symptomatology of unacknowledged acquaintance rape victims suggest that behavioral and affective responses may indeed be similar to responses of stranger rape and acknowledged rape victims. However, Sales, Baum, and Shore (1984) have suggested that a victim's symptomatic response to rape may be independent from her cognitive responses. Along similar lines, Koss et al. (1988) have suggested that the nature of the victim-offender relationship may predict changes in life circumstances and other coping responses/postassault actions. What then is known about coping and other cognitive strategies in the postassault period and their relationship to behavioral and emotional symptoms?

COGNITIVE PROCESSES:
ATTITUDES AND COPING IN
VICTIMS OF ACQUAINTANCE RAPE

Until quite recently the research in rape-induced trauma used a behavioral or conditioning framework to account for core symptom development. Such models were used to explain anxiety and sexual dysfunctions, typically in the acute postassault period. However, an emphasis on cognitive and attitudinal processes has become a recent focus of current symptomatology research with both acknowledged and unacknowledged victims. Researchers in this area have theorized that "the key in understanding . . . chronic patterns may have more to do with the kinds and consequences of the victim's perceptions and cognitive appraisals of her experience than with simple or complex conditioning effects" (Koss, 1990, p. 376). The recognition of the role played by cognitive factors in symptom manifestation and course has been reflected in recent recommendations that cognitive assessment be incorporated into evaluations of rape trauma in the immediate postassault period (Ruch et al., 1991).

Empirical research on cognitive coping strategies in rape victims has been minimal (Santello & Leitenberg, 1993). In one study, Burt and Katz (1988) "systematically document[ed] the real patterns that are observed in women as they cope with rape over time and specifically as their recovery progresses" (p. 345). They used Lazarus and Folkman's (1984) domains of coping strategies to sample rape victims solicited from crisis centers and through newspaper advertisements. Lazarus and Folkman (1984) divided coping strategies into two broad domains: problem-focused and emotion-focused. Problem-focused coping (e.g., helping with management/solving the problem) strategies are directed at the environment and inward. For sexual assault, they include tasks to get through. The woman may have used such strategies during the rape itself. Problem-focused coping views recovery as a performance to be achieved. However, Burt and Katz (1988) note that some things, like rape, cannot be mastered; they must be lived with and endured. In contrast, emotion-focused coping strategies (e.g., accept or manage prior events and chronic, unalterable situations) should be recognized as important coping mechanisms as well. Emotion-focused coping strategies may involve reconceptualizing the situation, selective attention, narrowing/minimizing strategies, avoidance, venting anger and other emotions, and seeking emotional support. Emotion-focused coping conceptualizes recovery as something to be endured.

Burt and Katz predicted that higher levels of stress indicators and negative symptomatology (e.g., fear, anxiety, and depression) would be associated with more active coping. Negative coping techniques would include self-destructive behaviors, avoidance, and restrictive strategies. Burt and Katz found that all coping behaviors (including expressive ones) were elevated when high fear, anxiety, and depression were present. Use of coping strategies was associated with levels of generalized guilt and self-blame. This effect was the strongest for self-destructive behaviors and next strongest for avoidance strategies. Expressive strategies were the only coping behaviors which were not associated with current generalized guilt and self-blame (Burt & Katz, 1988).

Burt and Katz also identified rape victims in terms of primary coping styles although they also noted that some individuals could not be categorized into a pure type. Their coping types included

1. *Avoiders:* Use of sleep, distracting activities, forgetting, ignoring, alcohol/drugs to "make it go away"
2. *Back to Business:* Use of role responsibilities
3. *Sturdy Battlers:* Determined to face feelings and work through to achieve resolution
4. *Ingestion:* Use of foods, cigarettes, alcohol, drugs, or rape center telephone reassurance to allay anxiety or other feelings
5. **Hapless:** Philosophy of rape as one more, albeit severe, blow to "sea of troubles"

Mandoki (Mandoki, 1989; Mandoki & Burkhart, 1989) also examined the effects of attributions and coping strategies on postassault adjustment. A sample of 813 female undergraduates completed anonymous questionnaires in which they reported victimization history, attributions, coping strategies employed, and psychological effects of assault experience. Acquaintance/date rape victims were compared to noncoital sexual aggression victims and nonvictims. Nonvictims were asked to rate the distress of their most negative academic failure as a comparison. Based on Symptom Checklist 90-Revised (SCL-90-R) scores, victims reported significantly higher levels of distress. Time since assault was not predictive of level of distress. Blame attributions were most useful in predicting postassault adjustment. Characterological self-blame was associated with initial and current distress levels. As was found in the Katz and Burt study, self-blame was also related to greater use of all forms of coping strategies. Blaming society or one's own behavior did not have a strong relationship to adjustment. It then appears that cognitions of (behavioral) self-blame, while thought to play a positive role by facilitating mastery in some trauma patients, have a negative effect on coping in rape victims (see also Davidson & Foa, 1991). Self-blame is thought to affect one's sense of mastery negatively, producing guilt and self-recrimination in acquaintance rape victims.

Women from the acquaintance/date rape group in the Mandoki (1989) study were also asked to provide written descriptions of their assaults. These responses were reported in a paper by Sommerfeldt et al. (1989). Descriptions were categorized to evaluate attributions of causality as well as effects of victimization. In the acquaintance rape group, 40% of the women acknowledged self-blame. Other cognitive symptoms reported by these women included increased mistrust, feelings of shame, and lowered self-esteem.

Koss and her colleagues (Gidycz & Koss, 1991b; Koss, 1990; Koss & Burkhart, 1989) have provided a conceptual analysis of rape victimization which focuses on the role of cognitive appraisal in mediating the long-term effects of rape. Lacking a strong empirical data base in the area of rape on which to base their conceptualization, Koss and her colleagues derive their cognitive model from one developed within the natural trauma (e.g., disasters, terminal illness) victimization literature. Borrowing from the work of Janoff-Bulman (1985) and Taylor (1983), among others, Koss has observed that victims of rape hold cognitive assumptions regarding the world which are shared by victims of many different forms of trauma. For example, the victimization experience appears to alter three basic beliefs: (a) personal invulnerability ("It can't happen to me"), (b) the world is meaningful and has a just order ("I am safe in my world"), and (c) a positive view of self ("Only bad girls have bad things happen to them"). The process of victimization triggers negative self-images (e.g., "I am weak . . . needy . . . frightened . . . out of control"). Generally, victimization leads to a sense of loss of equilibrium (Bard & Sangrey, 1979), that things are "out of kilter."

However, Koss and her colleagues also believe that the trauma of acquaintance rape imposes unique rape-related cognitions due to two factors: (a) the intensely interpersonal nature of rape, and (b) the negative social context in which acquaintance rape is viewed. For example, it will be critical for the victim to deal with the sense of meaning of interpersonal relationships and her identity in them (e.g., "Can I trust others?" "Can I trust myself to be able to judge my safety with others?" "What will others think of me now?" "Who would want to have a relationship with me now?"). According to Koss, the conflict between the reality of the trauma of rape and the societal response of minimization and attribution of victim blame produces a type of "cognitive-emotional paralysis" (Koss, 1990, p. 376) in which there is denial that the experience "really" happened (Taylor, Wood, & Lichtman, 1983).

Women make cognitive adjustments in response to others' judgments about the abuse. Faced with conflicts between their subjective experiences and the response of their social environment, victims may engage in reconstructions of the rape to help them cope (Koss, 1988b). For example, victims may engage in (a) denial (e.g., "It didn't happen"), (b) alteration of affective response (e.g., "It happened, but didn't really mean anything. It was not that important."), or (c) modification of the meaning of the rape (e.g., "It happened, but I provoked it so it can't be rape.") (Rieker & Carmen, 1986, p. 363).

Resolution of the trauma must involve dealing with cognitive, behavioral, and affective symptom domains. The need to develop a positive reinterpretation of the assault is critical to inhibit victim accommodation to the assault and foster resolution and personal growth. Comment Koss and Burkhart (1989)

> Without the opportunity to develop a positive, or at least, strengthening reinterpretation of her experience, the rape victim may assimilate degradation and helplessness into her beliefs and behavior. To the extent that a victim sees herself as damaged and unworthy, she may be-

come compromised in her ability to see herself as powerful and able, or even willing to affirm her dignity. Symptomatically, such beliefs could lead to a clinical picture that varies from a constricted, fear-dominated, withdrawn person to a person who acts out her sense of unworthiness and powerlessness by repeated involvement in abusive relationships. (p. 35)

Koss and Burkhart also believe that adolescents, given their level of cognitive development, may be "more vulnerable to guilt, self-blame, and a sense of helplessness and unworthiness" (p. 35). Obviously, identification of cognitions and coping styles is a critical task for the clinician treating such women. Multiple levels of intervention may be necessary to address the different levels of cognitive and emotional processes affected by acquaintance rape (Koss, 1990). Clinician strategies which support and promote affirming self-cognitions and successful cognitive reappraisal of the assault which affirms that the victim was truly victimized (Koss & Burkhart, 1989) are discussed in the chapter by Burkhart and Fromuth in this volume.

SUMMARY AND CONCLUSIONS

Based on the findings from the preceding empirical and clinical studies, a number of cognitive, behavioral, and emotional sequelae to acquaintance rape have been identified. A listing of these symptoms is provided in table form in an appendix at the end of this chapter (see pp. 127-133). A final caveat is offered. The clinician must remember that the pattern, duration, and intensity of a victim's response to acquaintance rape can undoubtedly be moderated by a complex number of factors: crime characteristics, idiosyncratic coping style, concurrent life stress, premorbid history, preexisting personality variables, age at the time of the assault, and the response of her social support network (particularly the quality of the support), as well as other factors (Resick, 1987). How such factors interact, why some victims and not others exhibit chronic effects, and the identity of critical mediating variables which can predict outcome remain unknown.

Again, although core behavioral and affective symptoms of victims of acquaintance rape are highly similar to those exhibited by acknowledged stranger rape victims, symptoms that are more cognitively based, such as self-blame and decreased self-esteem and isolation, appear to be more intense in the acquaintance rape victim group. Women who fail to acknowledge their assault as rape experience a considerable degree of emotional distress despite their failure to acknowledge their abuse as such or to seek treatment. Their level of distress is of a magnitude comparable to that of peers identified as having other forms of emotional distress. Their relabeling and minimization of their assault experience may result in a symptom picture which meets RTS or PTSD symptom criteria. Distress is further compounded by the inability of these unacknowledged acquaintance rape victims to recognize the source of what appears to them to be global distress. Given the conspiracy of silence involved in "hidden" rape, it is imperative that the clinician assess for the possibility of assault when female clients present for treatment with target symptoms of anxiety, depression, or the constellation of symptoms characteristic of PTSD or RTS, particularly when the client is unable to identify an immediately recognizable precipitant. The clinician must also be sensitive when inquiring about sexual assault and rape history, using language appropriate to the client. A client's initial denial of a history of rape per se does not necessarily imply that her past unwanted or forced sexual experiences did not meet the legal criteria for rape. Koss cautions that clinicians must meet the challenge of women who "may reveal in their current behavior the entanglement of survival strategies, stamped in coping behaviors, and accommodation to the reactions of others" (Koss, 1990, p. 379). Only with recognition of the symptoms of acquaintance rape can the clinician begin to appropriately meet the treatment needs of this group of women.

APPENDIX 4-A:
SYMPTOMATIC RESPONSES
TO ACQUAINTANCE RAPE -
SUGGESTIONS FOR ASSESSMENT

Assessment of acquaintance rape victims will generally include information about two domains: the stressor/assault and postassault symptoms. However, since the scope of this chapter focuses on the symptomatic response to acquaintance rape, the reader is referred to Kilparick, Veronen, et al. (1987), Resnick and Newton (1992), and Saunders et al. (1989) for information about interview questions related to the assessment of the nature and type of assault.

Chapters by Jackson, Quevillon, and Petretic-Jackson (1985) and Resnick and Newton (1992) provide more detailed discussion of the areas of specific symptomatic functioning which should be assessed in interviews, along with a listing of specific interview questions in outline form. Areas included in interviews reflect the three broad clusters of symptoms discussed below: behavioral and affective symptoms, cognitive processes, and relational skills.

CLUSTER 1:
BEHAVIORAL AND
AFFECTIVE SYMPTOMS

As indicated previously, a number of specific behavioral and affective symptoms in response to acquaintance rape have been documented. Standardized measures which provide an assessment of general distress, as well as specific symptomatic distress, include the Symptom Checklist 90-Revised (SCL-90-R; Derogatis, 1977) and the Trauma Symptom Inventory (TSI; Briere, 1991). Specific behavioral and affective symptoms, along with suggested methods/measures for assessment, are listed below:

1. *DEPRESSION*

- May be related to increased suicidal ideation, formulated plans, and attempts.
- Assess by interview and standardized measures, such as the Beck Depression Inventory (Beck et al., 1961); Scale 2 of Minnesota Multiphasic Personality Inventory-2 (MMPI-2; Butcher et al., 1989); and the Center for Epidemiology Study Depression Scale (CES-D Depression Scale; Radloff, 1977).

2. *ANXIETY*

- Social anxiety may be related to increased isolation.
- Assess by interview and the Beck Anxiety Inventory (Beck & Steer, 1990, 1993).

3. *PHOBIC ANXIETY/FEARS*

- May be cue-specific to events and/or characteristics of offender; may also generalize to a fear of men in general.
- Assess by interview; Modified Fear Survey (MFS; Veronen & Kilpatrick, 1980).

4. *ANGER/HOSTILITY*

- May be both self- and other-directed.
- Assess by the State-Trait Anger Scale (Spielberger, 1988); Novaco's Anger Index (Novaco, 1975); or the Buss-Durkee Hostility Inventory (Buss & Durkee, 1957). Several self-report measures will differentiate between forms of aggression and assertion (e.g., Mauger, Adkinson, & Simpson, 1979). The Assertiveness and Aggressiveness Inventory (Bakker, Bakker-Rabdau, & Breit, 1978), which has been used in domestic violence research, may be useful in assessing anger expressed in a victim's relationship with her partner.

5. *REPETITION COMPULSION*

- May involve risk-taking behaviors, which are incorrectly interpreted as "acting out"; means of regaining a sense of control in environment. An example would be a woman continuing to walk alone in the area where the rape occurred.
- Assess by interview.

6. *REDUCED LEVELS OF POSITIVE AFFECT/ANHEDONIA*

- May involve reports of decreased levels of joy, contentment, vigor, and affection; view of world with "gray-colored glasses."
- Assess by interview and Beck Hopelessness Scale (Beck & Steer, 1988).

7. *ALCOHOL AND OTHER DRUG ABUSE*

- May be used as a "self-medication" strategy to deal with cognitive intrusions, flashbacks, and so forth. Oftentimes prescription drug abuse/misuse may be present.
- Assess by interview to determine behavioral patterns. Consider using a brief (10 item) version of the Michigan Alcohol Screening Test (Pokorny, Miller, & Kaplan, 1972), or use the original Michigan Alcoholism Screening Test (MAST; Selzer, 1971). An alternative is to score the MacAndrews scale if using the MMPI-2 in assessment. While drug and alcohol scales on the Millon Clinical Multiaxial Inventory (MCMI; Millon, 1983) may be employed, generally the MCMI is not recommended for use with victims experiencing acute trauma. Many PTSD victims obtain false positive diagnoses of Borderline Personality Disorder if administered the MCMI while in acute distress (e.g., immediately following traumatic incidents; in concurrent domestic violence situations). The MCMI is best used if the client has been in a safe environment for at least 6 months to 1 year following any acute trauma.

8.   *PTSD-RELATED SYMPTOMS*

- Examples include psychic numbing, constrained range of activities, sleep disturbances, reexperiencing of trauma, avoidance of stimuli associated with trauma or numbing of general responsiveness, hyperalertness, conflicts about dependence and independence.
- Assess in interview using *DSM-IV* symptoms for guidelines. Be sure to assess subjective perception of threat and client's judgment of the impact of the rape. Refer to Saunders et al. (1989) and Resnick and Newton (1992) for additional information regarding interviewing suggestions. For paper-and-pencil measures assessing PTSD symptoms consider using the Crime-Related PTSD Subscale of the SCL-90-R (Saunders, Mandoki, & Kilpatrick, 1990); the Impact of Event Scale (IES; Horowitz, Wilner, & Alvarez, 1979); the PTSD scales associated with the MMPI-2); or the Rape Aftermath Symptom Test (RAST; Kilpatrick, 1988).

CLUSTER 2:
COGNITIVE PROCESSES

A number of cognitive symptoms are documented as highly salient among acquaintance rape victims. Unfortunately, the absence of empirically validated, standardized measures of assessment of the cognitive area of functioning hampers clinicians in planning treatment aimed at changing distorted cognitions related to the self, situation, and future (Koss, 1990). However, Resick and Schnicke (1992) have developed a scale, the Personal Beliefs and Reactions Scale (PBRS), to assess self-blame, beliefs about rape and judgments about safety, trust, power/competence, esteem, and intimacy. This measure may be used to provide a comprehensive evaluation of postassault cognitive appraisals and attributions. Cognitive symptoms documented in acquaintance rape victims include

1. Denial of Victimization
2. Minimization
3. Self-Deprecation
4. Vulnerability
5. Self-Blame/Guilt and Self-Recrimination
6. Shame
7. Suppression
8. Sense of Helplessness/Insecurity
9. Confusion
10. Sense of Worthlessness
11. Reduced Sense of Self-Esteem; Negative Self-Images
12. Concerns about Interpersonal Relationships and One's Identity in Them
13. Sense of Loss of Equilibrium; Environment and Victim Within It Are "Out of Kilter"
14. No Sense of Meaning or Order to the World
15. Suicidal Ideation

The clinician has several options. One is to use one of several coping inventories which presently exist as research tools. However, these measures are not designed for primary use as clinical measures. As such they will provide useful, albeit qualitative, information. However, it could be valuable for a clinician to use these measures and develop a set of "local norms." One such measure is the Ways of Coping Scale-Revised (Vitaliano et al., 1985). Additionally, several researchers working with other traumatized populations have derived instruments which may prove useful to the clinician in assessing PTSD-related cognitions, such as the Impact of Events Scale (Horowitz et al., 1979). Another consideration is the use of a psychometrically sound measure of self-esteem that is sensitive to aspects of esteem altered by victimization. One promising measure is the Multidimensional Self-Esteem Inventory (MSEI; O'Brien & Epstein, 1988). A second strategy is to adapt general cognitive-behavioral assessment strategies designed for use with other populations (e.g., depressed clients) for use with rape victims. For example, clients can be asked to keep a diary/log of dysfunctional thoughts.

CLUSTER 3:
RELATIONAL SKILLS AND
INTERPERSONAL FUNCTIONING

1. *INTERPERSONAL DIFFICULTIES*

   - May involve physical and emotional "distancing" of self from others in relationships. Either a pattern of separation or arguments; "testing of relationships" may occur.
   - Assess by interview and by use of the Inventory of Interpersonal Problems (Horowitz et al., 1988). This measure is designed to describe types of interpersonal problems and the associated level of distress. Specific factors measured include assertiveness, sociability, submissiveness, intimacy, responsibility, and controlling behavior. To assess the variable of social adjustment also consider administration of the Social Adjustment Scale (SAS; Weissman & Paykel, 1974). The SAS yields an overall social adjustment score as well as scale scores for work, social and leisure, extended family, parental, family unit, and economic functioning.

2. *PERCEPTIONS OF PERSONAL*
   LIKABILITY AND LOVABILITY

   - May reflect intimacy and trust issues in both primary intimate relationships and friendships. Perception of "damaged goods," that no one would want them after their assault.
   - A standardized measure of self-esteem, the Multidimensional Self-Esteem Inventory (MSEI; O'Brien & Epstein, 1988) includes two subscales - Likability and Lovability - that relate to an individual's perception of his or her social value. These subscales have been found to discriminate adults who have experienced a history of childhood abuse from those who have not been abused. Abused individuals obtain significantly lower scores on both scales compared to nonabused adults.

3. *SEXUAL PROBLEMS*

- May involve decreased activity and/or satisfaction.
- Assess by interview and the Sexual Arousal Inventory (E. F. Hoon, P. W. Hoon, & Wincze, 1976) or the Index of Sexual Satisfaction (Hudson, 1982).

REFERENCES

Allen, S. N. (1994). Psychological assessment of post-traumatic
    stress disorder: Psychometrics, current trends and future
    directions. *Psychiatric Clinics of North America, 17,* 327-
    349.
American Psychiatric Association. (1994). *Diagnostic and Sta-
    tistical Manual of Mental Disorders* (DSM-IV, 4th ed.) Wash-
    ington, DC: Author.
Atkeson, B., Calhoun, K. S., Resick, P. A., & Ellis, E. (1982).
    Victims of rape: Repeated assessment of depressive symp-
    toms. *Journal of Consulting and Clinical Psychology, 50,*
    96-102.
Bakker, C. B., Bakker-Rabdau, M. K., & Breit, S. (1978). The
    measurement of assertiveness and aggressiveness. *Journal
    of Personality Assessment, 42,* 277-284.
Bard, M., & Sangrey, D. (1979). *The Crime Victim's Book.* New
    York: Basic Books.
Bechhofer, L., & Parrot, A. (1991). What is acquaintance rape?
    In A. Parrot & L. Bechhofer (Eds.), *Acquaintance Rape: The
    Hidden Crime* (pp. 9-25). New York: Wiley.
Beck, A. T., & Steer, R. A. (1988). *Beck Hopelessness Scale.*
    San Antonio, TX: Psychological Corporation.
Beck, A. T., & Steer, R. A. (1990). *Beck Anxiety Inventory.*
    San Antonio, TX: Psychological Corporation.
Beck, A. T., Ward, C. H., Mendelson, M., Mock, J., & Erbaugh,
    J. (1961). An inventory for measuring depression. *Archives
    of General Psychiatry, 4,* 53-63.
Becker, J. V., & Kaplan, M. S. (1991). Rape victim: Issues, theo-
    ries, and treatment. *Annual Review of Sex Research, 2,* 267-
    292.
Becker, J. V., Skinner, L. J., Abel, G. G., & Treacy, E. C. (1982).
    Incidence and types of sexual dysfunctions in rape and in-
    cest victims. *Journal of Sex and Marital Therapy, 8,* 65-74.
Briere, J. (1991). *The Trauma Symptom Inventory.* Unpub-
    lished psychological test, University of Southern California
    School of Medicine, Los Angeles, CA.
Burgess, A. W., & Holmstrom, L. L. (1974). Rape trauma syn-
    drome. *American Journal of Psychiatry, 131,* 981-985.

Burgess, A. W., & Holmstrom, L. L. (1979). Rape: Sexual disruption and recovery. *American Journal of Orthopsychiatry*, *49*, 648-657.

Burgess, A. W., & Holmstrom, L. L. (1985). Rape trauma syndrome and posttraumatic stress response. In A. Burgess (Ed.), *Rape and Sexual Assault* (pp. 46-60). New York: Garland.

Burkhart, B. R. (1991). Conceptual and practical analysis of therapy for acquaintance rape victims. In A. Parrot & L. Bechhofer (Eds.), *Acquaintance Rape: The Hidden Crime* (pp. 287-303). New York: Wiley.

Burkhart, B. R., & Stanton, A. (1988). Sexual aggression in acquaintance relationships. In G. Russell (Ed.), *Violence in Intimate Relationships* (pp. 43-65). Englewood Cliffs, NJ: Spectrum.

Burnam, M. A., Stein, J. A., Golding, J. M., Siegel, J. M., Sorenson, S. B., Forsythe, A. B., & Telles, C. A. (1988). Sexual assault and mental disorders in a community population. *Journal of Consulting and Clinical Psychology*, *56*, 843-850.

Burt, M. R., & Katz, B. L. (1988). Coping strategies and recovery from rape. In R. A. Prentky & V. L. Quinsey (Eds.), *Human Sexual Aggression: Current Perspectives* (Vol. 528, pp. 345-358). New York: Annals of the New York Academy of Sciences.

Burt, M. R. (1980). Cultural myths and support for rape. *Journal of Personality and Social Psychology*, *38*, 217-230.

Burt, M. R., & Katz, B. L. (1987). Dimensions of recovery from rape: Focus on growth outcomes. *Journal of Interpersonal Violence*, *2*, 57-82.

Buss, A. H., & Durkee, A. (1957). An inventory for assessing different kinds of hostility. *Journal of Clinical and Consulting Psychology*, *21*, 343-349.

Butcher, J. N., Dahlstrom, W. G., Graham, J. R., Tellegen, A., & Kaemner, B. (1989). *Minnesota Multiphasic Personality Inventory (MMPI-2) Manual for Administration and Scoring*. Minneapolis, MN: University of Minnesota Press.

Calhoun, K. S., & Townsley, R. (1991). Attributions of responsibility for acquaintance rape. In A. Parrot & L. Bechhofer

(Eds.), *Acquaintance Rape: The Hidden Crime* (pp. 57-69). New York: Wiley.

Davidson, J. R., & Foa, E. B. (1991). Diagnostic issues in post-traumatic stress disorder: Considerations for the DSM-IV. *Journal of Abnormal Psychology, 100*, 346-355.

Derogatis, L. R. (1977). *SCL-90-R: Administration, Scoring, and Procedure Manual-I for the R (Revised) Version.* Baltimore: Johns Hopkins School of Medicine.

Ellis, E. M. (1983). A review of empirical rape research: Victim reactions and response to treatment. *Clinical Psychology Review, 3*, 473-490.

Ellis, E. M., Atkeson, B. M., & Calhoun, K. S. (1981). An assessment of long-term reaction to rape. *Journal of Abnormal Psychology, 90*, 263-266.

Ellis, E. M., Atkeson, B. M., & Calhoun, K. S. (1982). Examination of differences between multiple and single incident victims of sexual assault. *Journal of Abnormal Psychology, 91*, 221-224.

Estrich, S. (1987). *Real Rape.* Cambridge, MA: Harvard University Press.

Everstine, D., & Everstine, L. (1989). *Sexual Trauma in Children and Adolescents: Dynamics and Treatment.* New York: Brunner/Mazel.

Foa, E. B., Rothbaum, B. O., & Steketee, G. S. (1993). Treatment of rape victims. *Journal of Interpersonal Violence, 8*, 256-276.

Frank, E., Turner, S. M., & Stewart, B. D. (1980). Initial response to rape: The impact of factors within the rape situation. *Journal of Behavioral Assessment, 2*, 39-53.

Frieze, I. H. (1987). The female victim: Rape, wife battering and incest. In G. VandenBos & B. Bryant (Eds.), *Cataclysms, Crises and Catastrophes: Psychology in Action.* Washington, DC: American Psychological Association.

Gidycz, C. A., & Koss, M. P. (1989). The impact of adolescent sexual victimization: Standardized measures of anxiety, depression, and behavioral deviancy. *Violence and Victims, 4*, 139-149.

Gidycz, C. A., & Koss, M. P. (1991a). The effects of acquaintance rape on the female victim. In A. Parrot & L. Bechhofer

(Eds.), *Acquaintance Rape: The Hidden Crime* (pp. 270-283). New York: Wiley.

Gidycz, C. A., & Koss, M. P. (1991b). Predictors of long-term sexual assault trauma among a national sample of victimized college women. *Violence & Victims, 6,* 175-190.

Goodman, L. A., Koss, M. P., & Russo, N. F. (1993). Violence against women: Physical and mental health effects. Part I: Research findings. *Applied and Preventive Psychology, 2,* 79-89.

Holmes, M. R., & St. Lawrence, J. S. (1983). Treatment of rape induced trauma: Proposed behavioral conceptualization and review of the literature. *Clinical Psychology Review, 3,* 417-433.

Hoon, E. F., Hoon, P. W., & Wincze, J. P. (1976). An inventory for the measurement of female sexual arousability: The SAI. *Archives of Sexual Behavior, 5,* 291-300.

Horowitz, L. M., Rosenberg, S. E., Baer, B. S., Ureno, G., & Villasenor, V. S. (1988). Inventory of Interpersonal Problems: Psychometric properties and clinical applications. *Journal of Consulting and Clinical Psychology, 56,* 885-892.

Horowitz, L. M., Wilner, N., & Alvarez, W. (1979). Impact of Event Scale: A measure of subjective stress. *Psychosomatic Medicine, 41,* 209-218.

Hudson, W. W. (1982). *The Clinical Measurement Package: A Field Manual.* Homewood, IL: Dorsey.

Jackson, T., Quevillon, R., & Petretic-Jackson, P. (1985). Assessment and treatment of sexual assault victims. In P. A. Keller & L. G. Ritt (Eds.), *Innovations in Clinical Practice: A Source Book* (Vol. 4, pp. 51-78). Sarasota, FL: Professional Resource Exchange.

Janoff-Bulman, R. (1985). The aftermath of victimization: Rebuilding shattered assumptions. In C. R. Figley (Ed.), *Trauma and Its Wake: The Study and Treatment of Post-Traumatic Stress Disorder* (pp. 15-35). New York: Brunner/Mazel.

Katz, B. L., & Burt, M. R. (1988). Self-blame in recovery from rape: Help or hindrance? In Ann Burgess (Ed.), *Rape and Sexual Assault II* (pp. 151-168). New York: Garland.

Kilpatrick, D. G. (1985). The Sexual Assault Research Project: Assessing the aftermath of rape. *Response, 8*, 20-24.

Kilpatrick, D. G. (1988). Rape Aftermath Symptom Test. In M. Hersen & A. S. Bellack (Eds.), *Dictionary of Behavioral Assessment Techniques* (pp. 366-367). Elmsford, NY: Pergamon.

Kilpatrick, D. G., Best, C. L., Ruff, G. A., Veronen, L. J., & Ruff, M. H. (1985, November). *Predicting Mental Health Consequences of Sexual Assault: A Random Community Survey.* Paper presented at the Annual Meeting of the Association for Advancement of Behavior Therapy, Houston, TX.

Kilpatrick, D. G., Best, C. L., Saunders, B. E., Amick-McMullan, A. E., Lipovsky, J. A., & Haskett, M. (1988). *Does Victim's Acknowledgement Influence Risk of Mental Health Disorders?* Paper presented at the annual meeting of the American Psychological Association, Atlanta, GA.

Kilpatrick, D. G., Best, C. L., Saunders, B. E., & Veronen, L. J. (1988). Rape in marriage and in dating relationships: How bad is it for mental health? In R. A. Prentky & V. L. Quinsey (Eds.), *Human Sexual Aggression: Current Perspectives* (Vol. 528, pp. 335-344). New York: Annals of the New York Academy of Sciences.

Kilpatrick, D. G., Edmunds, C. N., & Seymour, A. K. (1992). *Rape in America: A Report to the Nation.* Arlington, VA: National Victim Center.

Kilpatrick, D. G., Resick, P. A., Veronen, L. J. (1984). Effects of a rape experience: A longitudinal study. *Journal of Social Issues, 37*, 105-121.

Kilpatrick, D. G., & Veronen, L. J. (1984). *Assessing Victims of Rape: Methodological Issues* (Final Report, Grant No. R01 MH38052). Rockville, MD: National Institute of Mental Health.

Kilpatrick, D. G., Veronen, L. J., & Best, C. L. (1985). Factors predicting psychological distress among rape victims. In C. R. Figley (Ed.), *Trauma and Its Wake: The Study and Treatment of Post-Traumatic Stress Disorder* (pp. 113-141). New York: Brunner/Mazel.

Kilpatrick, D. G., Veronen, L. J., Best, C. L., Amick-McMullan, A., & Paduhovich, J. (1987). *The Psychological Impact of*

Crime: A Study of Randomly Surveyed Crime Victims (Final Report, Grant No. 84-IJ-CX-0039). Washington, DC: National Institute of Justice.

Klemmack, S. H., & Klemmack, D. L. (1976). The social definition of rape. In M. J. Walker & S. L. Brodsky (Eds.), *Sexual Assault* (pp. 135-147). Lexington, MA: D. C. Heath & Co.

Koss, M. P. (1983). The scope of rape: Implications for clinical treatment of victims. *The Clinical Psychologist, 36*, 88-91.

Koss, M. P. (1985). The hidden rape victim: Personality, attitudinal and situational characteristics. *Psychology of Women Quarterly, 9*, 193-212.

Koss, M. P. (1988a). Hidden rape: Incidence, prevalence, and descriptive characteristics of sexual aggression in a national sample of college students. In A. W. Burgess (Ed.), *Sexual Assault* (Vol. II, pp. 3-25). New York: Garland.

Koss, M. P. (1988b). *The Women's Mental Health Research Agenda: Violence Against Women*. Rockville, MD: National Institute of Mental Health, Office of Women's Programs.

Koss, M. P. (1990). The women's mental health research agenda: Violence against women. *American Psychologist, 45*, 374-380.

Koss, M. P., & Burkhart, B. R. (1989). A conceptual analysis of rape victimization: Long-term effects and implications for treatment. *Psychology of Women Quarterly, 13*, 27-40.

Koss, M. P., Dinero, T. E., Seibel, C. A., & Cox, S. (1988). Stranger and acquaintance rape: Are there differences in the victim's experience? *Psychology of Women's Quarterly, 12*(1), 1-24.

Koss, M. P., Gidycz, C., & Wisniewski, N. (1987). The scope of rape: Incidence and prevalence of sexual aggression and victimization in a national sample of higher education students. *Journal of Consulting and Clinical Psychology, 55*, 162-170.

Lazarus, R. S., & Folkman, S. (1984). *Stress, Appraisal, and Coping*. New York: Springer.

Lew, M. (1988). *Victims No Longer: Men Recovering from Incest and Other Sexual Child Abuse*. New York: Nevraumont Publishing.

Mandoki, C. A. (1989). *Coping with Sexual Victimization: An Analysis of the Relationship Between Appraisals, Coping*

Strategies, and Adjustment. Unpublished doctoral dissertation, Auburn University, Auburn, AL.

Mandoki, C. A., & Burkhart, B. R. (1989, August). *Coping and Adjustment to Rape.* Paper presented at the annual convention of the American Psychological Association, New Orleans, LA.

Mandoki, C. A., & Burkhart, B. R. (1991). Women as victims: Antecedents and consequences of acquaintance rape. In A. Parrot & L. Bechhofer (Eds.), *Acquaintance Rape: The Hidden Crime* (pp. 176-191). New York: Wiley.

Mauger, P. A., Adkinson, D. R., & Simpson, D. G. (1979). *The Interpersonal Behavior Survey Manual.* Los Angeles: Western Psychological Services.

McCahill, T. W., Meyer, L. C., & Fischman, A. M. (1979). *The Aftermath of Rape.* Lexington, MA: D. C. Heath.

Millon, T. (1983). *Millon Clinical Multiaxial Inventory.* Minneapolis, MN: National Computer Systems.

Nadelson, C., Notman, M., Jackson, H., & Gornick, J. (1982). A follow-up study of rape victims. *American Journal of Psychiatry, 139*, 1266-1270.

Novaco, R. W. (1975). *Anger Control: The Development and Evaluation of an Experimental Treatment.* Lexington, MA: Lexington Books.

O'Brien, E. J., & Epstein, S. (1988). *Multidimensional Self-Esteem Inventory (MSEI): Professional Manual.* Odessa, FL: Psychological Assessment Resources.

Pokorny, A. D., Miller, B. A., & Kaplan, H. B. (1972). The brief MAST: A shortened version of the Michigan Alcoholism Screening Test. *American Journal of Psychiatry, 129*, 342-345.

Radloff, L. S. (1977). The CES-D Scale: A self-report depression scale for research in the general population. *Applied Psychological Measurements, 1*, 385-401.

Reiker, P. P., & Carmen, E. H. (1986). The victim-to-patient process: The disconfirmation and transformation of abuse. *American Journal of Orthopsychiatry, 56*, 360-370.

Resick, P. A. (1987, September). *The Impact of Rape on Psychological Functioning.* Paper presented at the conference "State of the Art in Sexual Assault," Charleston, SC.

Resick, P. A. (1993). The psychological impact of rape. *Journal of Interpersonal Violence, 8*, 223-255.

Resick, P. A., & Schnicke, M. K. (1992). Cognitive processing therapy for sexual assault victims. In E. B. Foa (Chair), *Treatment of PTSD: An Update.* Symposium presented at the annual meeting of the International Society for Traumatic Studies, Los Angeles, CA.

Resnick, H. S., & Newton, T. (1992). Assessment and treatment of post-traumatic stress disorder in adult survivors of sexual assault. In D. W. Foy (Ed.), *Treating PTSD: Cognitive-Behavioral Strategies* (pp. 99-126). New York: Guilford.

Rogers, L. C. (1984). *Sexual Victimization: Social and Psychological Effects in College Women.* Unpublished doctoral dissertation, Auburn University, Auburn, AL.

Rothbaum, B. O., Foa, E. B., Murdock, T., Riggs, D., & Walsh, W. (1990). *Post-Traumatic Stress Disorder in Rape Victims.* Unpublished manuscript.

Ruch, L. O., & Chandler, S. M. (1983). Sexual assault trauma during the active phase: An exploratory model and multivariate analysis. *Journal of Health and Social Behavior, 24*, 174-185.

Ruch, L. O., Gartrell, J. W., Ramelli, A., & Coyne, B. J. (1991). The Clinical Trauma Assessment: Evaluating sexual assault victims in the emergency room. *Psychological Assessment, 3*, 405-411.

Russell, D. E. (1984). *Sexual Exploitation.* Beverly Hills, CA: Sage.

Sales, E., Baum, M., & Shore, B. (1984). Victim readjustment following assault. *Journal of Social Issues, 37*, 5-27.

Santello, M. D., & Leitenberg, H. (1993). Sexual aggression by an acquaintance: Methods of coping and later psychological adjustment. *Violence & Victims, 8*, 91-104.

Saunders, B. E., Kilpatrick, D. G., Resnick, H. S., & Tidwell, R. P. (1989). Brief screening for lifetime history of criminal victimization at mental health intake: A preliminary study. *Journal of Interpersonal Violence, 4*, 267-277.

Saunders, B. E., Mandoki, K. A., & Kilpatrick, D. G. (1990). Development of a crime-related post-traumatic stress disorder scale within the Symptom Checklist-90-Revised, *Journal of Traumatic Stress, 3*, 439-448.

Selzer, M. L. (1971). The Michigan Alcoholism Screening Test: The quest for a new diagnostic instrument. *American Journal of Psychiatry, 127*, 1653-1658.

Sgroi, S. (1982). *Handbook of Clinical Intervention in Child Sexual Abuse*. Lexington, MA: Lexington Books.

Silver, C. J., & Sprock, J. (1991, May). *Classification of Psychological Sequelae Associated with Rape and War Trauma: Are There Two Distinct PTSD Subtypes?* Paper presented at the Midwestern Psychological Association Meeting, Chicago, IL.

Skelton, C. A., & Burkhart, B. R. (1980). Sexual assault: Determinants of victim disclosure. *Criminal Justice and Behavior, 7*, 229-236.

Sommerfeldt, T. G., Burkhart, B. R., & Mandoki, C. A. (1989, August). *In Her Own Words: Victims' Descriptions of Hidden Rape Effects*. Paper presented at the annual convention of the American Psychological Association, New Orleans, LA.

Spielberger, C. D. (1988). *State-Trait Anger Expression Inventory*. Odessa, FL: Psychological Assessment Resources.

Struckman-Johnson, C. (1991). Male victims of acquaintance rape. In A. Parrot & L. Bechhofer (Eds.), *Acquaintance Rape: The Hidden Crime* (pp. 192-213). New York: Wiley.

Sutherland, S., & Scherl, D. (1970). Patterns of response among victims of rape. *American Journal of Orthopsychiatry, 40*, 503-511.

Taylor, S. (1983). Adjustment to threatening events: A theory of cognitive adaptation. *American Psychologist, 38*, 1161-1173.

Taylor, S., Wood, J., & Lichtman, R. (1983). It could be worse: Selective evaluation as a response to victimization. *Journal of Social Issues, 39*, 19-40.

Veronen, L. J., & Kilpatrick, D. G. (1980). Self-reported fears of rape victims: A preliminary investigation. *Behavior Modification, 4*, 383-396.

Vitaliano, P. P., Russo, J., Carr, J. E., Maiuro, R. D., & Becker, J. (1985). The Ways of Coping Checklist: Revision and psychometric properties. *Multivariate Behavioral Research, 20,* 3-26.

Warshaw, R. (1988). *I Never Called It Rape: The Ms. Report on Recognizing, Fighting and Surviving Date and Acquaintance Rape.* New York: Harper and Row.

Weissman, M. M., & Paykel, C. S. (1974). *The Depressed Woman: A Study of Social Relationships.* Chicago: University of Chicago Press.

Williams, L. S. (1984). The classic rape: When do victims report? *Social Problems, 31,* 459-467.

5

The Victim: Issues in Identification and Treatment

Barry R. Burkhart
and
Mary Ellen Fromuth

We begin this chapter by presenting two clinical vignettes which, in their poignancy, have the power to establish what is felt to be the foundation for therapeutic work with acquaintance rape survivors:

Vignette 1

A participant in a research project investigating courtship sexual violence was asked to describe her rape. She was assaulted at a fraternity party by her date whom she had helped to his room after he feigned illness. It was clearly a premeditated assault and the emotional damage to her was still present and evident 2 years after the assault. Tearfully, she described her terror as she struggled with him, weeping and pleading with him to stop. However, when asked, as part of the research protocol, how her assailant had responded to her re-

sistance, her demeanor abruptly changed, with head held down
and in a halting, shame-filled voice she replied . . . "Even as I
say this now it sounds crazy to me, after what he did . . . but I
didn't scream, not because I didn't think about it. I remember thinking I should scream. I even sort of tried to scream as
I tried to fight him off, but I didn't. I don't know why . . . but
I remember thinking I shouldn't scream because it might
embarrass him. Isn't that crazy? What must be wrong with
me?"

Vignette 2

A young woman in therapy for a debilitating posttraumatic
stress disorder with dissociative features consequent to being
raped and to being sexually abused as a child described recurring nightmares in which she is in danger, but when she tries
to scream, cannot. After much work in therapy focused on
her assault and its impact on her, she began to recover memories of her assault. With much anguish she recalls how, during the assault, she had screamed and screamed. Because of
the isolation of the place, she knew her cries were futile; however, it was her attempt to resist that was significant to her
sense of being able to do something. With horror and shame,
however, she finally recalls, that after the assault, her assailant, with leering conviction, told her that he "would have never
guessed she was a screamer," that she was "such a nice little
girl, he didn't expect that she would get off like that." Absolutely stricken, she went home, bathed herself over and over,
trying to wash away the horror of her memory. She described
hearing her screams echoing in her head for months after the
assault; no longer simply futile, they had become representative of her shame and guilt - a stigmata which became a powerful impetus for a crushing depression a year after the assault.

The most frequent and potentially harmful response to the
acquaintance rape victim is to not be heard, just as these two
women were not heard: not to be heard when they plead with
the assailant, not to be heard when they call for support, or
more poignantly, not to be heard even in their internal dia-
logue when they stand alone as witness to their victimization.

Victims of acquaintance rape are not heard because of the powerful and pervasive denial of the reality of acquaintance rape. This process of denial defines the experience of the acquaintance rape victim so completely that the assault, in Koss's (1985) descriptive term, is hidden - hidden from perpetrators who assert not just their innocence, but also their entitlement to a legitimate and praiseworthy (i.e., manly) goal. It is also hidden from society at large, which defines the term acquaintance rape as an oxymoron. Finally, it is even hidden from those who are designated as society's caregivers (police, physicians, counselors, and so forth) who often draw a clear distinction between "real" rapes and "date" rapes. This distinction is meant to imply that there is a fundamental difference between acquaintance/ date rape and stranger rape, a difference that reflects a fundamental distinction of reality; that is, one is real and one is not (Burkhart, 1991).

The fundamental and central precepts of treatment are to hear the true voices of victims and to confront the denial of their victimization. In doing so, a therapist can affirm for and with the victim/survivor "the most fundamental need of any human being: the need to have reality as a referent, to have what is experienced affirmed as real" (Burkhart, 1991, p. 289). Thus, therapy is driven by this organizing precept - the focal point of recovery from assaultive trauma must be the reality of the victim's experience. To this end, therapist and client must be able to stand as collaborative witnesses to the memories, affects, and effects consequent to the harm done by sexual victimization. This therapeutic stance is the necessary crucible wherein victim will be transformed into survivor. However, if this task is failed by an accommodation to a denial of the reality of the experience of victimization, then the victim is only recycled into new forms of victimization: shame-filled self-deprecation; vulnerable, frightened withdrawal; or repetition-compulsion-driven acting out.

The first and continued task, therefore, of the therapist is to be aware of the pathogenic impact of denial on the coping of victims and the iatrogenic effects of any amplification of this process via acceptance or encouragement of self-blame, minimization, suppression, or outright denial of the reality of the victimization. Simply put, recovery is the process of assimilation or acceptance of the trauma rather than accommodation to the trauma. Clearly, assimilation, integration, and growth beyond a trauma can only occur as denial of the trauma is confronted.

In this chapter, we will seek to indicate how this central task and its specific corollaries are to be accomplished in successful treatment. We will begin by examining briefly the direct implications of our conceptual analysis for the development of a treatment model. Next, the processes of assessment and intervention which follow from this analysis will be described. Finally, throughout this chapter, we will try to help the therapist hear the voices, however expressed, of those who are so often not heard, the victims of acquaintance rape.

It is necessary to first state a conceptual assumption upon which much of the rest of this chapter is predicated. Because of the dearth of work focused on acquaintance rape, not much direction is to be found in the scholarly or empirical literature directly relevant to the acquaintance rape victim. However, several excellent descriptions of treatment protocols for stranger assault victims are available (Foa et al., 1991; Jackson, Quevillon, & Petretic-Jackson, 1985; Kilpatrick & Veronen, 1982; Koss & Harvey, 1987; Resick & Schnicke, 1992; Rose, 1991), and therapists should be familiar with the processes, techniques, issues, and caveats reviewed and presented in these works. The present chapter, while drawing on these works, will be oriented toward the unique and specific issues of the acquaintance rape context. For a number of reasons detailed in previous work (Burkhart, 1991; Burkhart & Fromuth, 1991), we believe that the issues relevant to treatment of child sexual abuse survivors (Courtois, 1988; Courtois & Sprei, 1988; Summit, 1983) provide useful parallels to treatment of acquaintance rape victims. Thus, drawing upon this rich literature (Briere, 1989; Courtois, 1988) allows for the initial conceptual development of a treatment model for acquaintance rape victims. Additionally, we have found that clinicians with experience in the treatment of adult survivors of child sexual abuse find much that is familiar in the treatment of acquaintance rape survivors. For clinicians with limited contact with child sexual abuse survivors, we recommend that some attempt be made to familiarize themselves with the principles of and issues involved in the treatment of the child sexual abuse survivor. The isomorphism between the therapy of acquaintance rape and that of child sexual abuse survivors is so striking that the development of therapeutic competence is markedly enhanced by such exposure. Becoming familiar with the work of Summit (1983), Briere (1989), and Courtois (1988; Courtois & Sprei, 1988) can enhance and accelerate the development of professional competence with victims of acquaintance rape. To augment this conceptual generalization, we draw heavily upon our clinical experience with victims of acquaintance rape. In the final analysis, their voices are what call us to this task and inform us of our progress toward developing helpful therapeutic intervention.

Treatment of rape victims is difficult. It is difficult for victims and, without theoretical and practical guidance, it is difficult for therapists. In a previous work (Burkhart, 1991), we identified 10 facets of the therapeutic process and described the critical issues associated with resolving the emotional damage of an acquaintance rape within each of these. In the present chapter, we have drawn from this previous work, but have incorporated several additional themes and emphases. In particular, we have expanded our discussions of the conceptual and practical errors which we see as compromising successful treatment. Acquaintance rape presents in a context which, because of persistent and pervasive social myths, can be easily misunderstood. Thus, even with the best of intentions, the background context can make it easy for a therapist to violate the cardinal canon of healing: "First of all, do no harm."

THEORETICAL CONSIDERATIONS

The conceptual foundations for the treatment model to be outlined in this chapter have been described in several previous works (Burkhart, 1991; Burkhart & Stanton, 1988; Fromuth & Burkhart, 1992; Koss & Burkhart, 1989; Mandoki & Burkhart, 1991). For a more in-depth presentation of this conceptual analysis, interested readers are referred to these writings. As a precursor to the technical description of the treatment model, however, several essential theoretical themes and empirical findings must be presented herein. In part, this is necessary because most of the previous work dealing with the treatment of rape victims has been developed for populations of stranger rape victims (Ellis, 1983; Holmes & St. Lawrence, 1983). Thus, therapists treating acquaintance rape victims will find little direction from this literature which is specifically relevant to the treatment of acquaintance rape victims. Furthermore, several issues which are distinctly salient to the acquaintance rape context and, in our view, are critical to the success of treatment with victims of acquaintance rape have not been the focus of much work in the treatment of stranger rape (Koss & Burkhart, 1989). For example, most treatment work and research with rape victims has been conducted with victims seeking treatment immediately post-rape; however, only 5% of rape victims in a college student sample sought immediate post-rape treatment (Koss, 1985). Moreover, many victims who immediately enter treatment fail to complete a standard course of therapy (Frank & Stewart, 1983). Finally, Kilpatrick, Veronen, and Resick (1979) found that less than half of victims offered treatment during the 3-month post-rape period accepted therapy. As expressed by Resick (1983), the most typical response in describing the response of rape victims is "the hope that if they don't talk about the assault and try not to think about it, they will forget it and recover" (p. 131).

This hope, however, is not likely to be realized. Long-term follow-up studies with rape victims consistently indicate that recovery from rape is not rapid nor inevitable. Burgess and Holmstrom (1976) asked rape victims 4 to 6 years after their sexual assault if they felt "'normal,' that is, the way you felt prior to the rape." Twenty-six percent of the victims did not feel recovered, and another 37% felt that their recovery had taken years to accomplish.

Thus, for a number of reasons, the typical therapy presentation by an acquaintance rape victim is that of a delayed treatment seeker. This delayed presentation has a number of implications for therapeutic involvement. For example, in comparing immediate and delayed treatment seekers among a sample of rape victims, Stewart et al. (1987) found that delayed treatment seekers were more likely to have been raped in an acquaintance context and, in fact, were characterized by a different clinical presentation, including higher levels of affective distress. Stewart et al. (1987) also identified what we believe to be a critical issue: Delayed treatment seekers have more conflict and guilt about their assault and, in particular, have higher levels of self-blame and self-denigration as part of their symptom picture.

Moreover, in studies directly comparing victims of acquaintance versus stranger rape, despite the commonly held assumption that "date" rapes are less harmful than stranger rapes, no significant differences in impact of these assaults have been found (Koss et al., 1988). As stated by Kilpatrick et al. (1988), following their analysis of the possible differential effects of stranger versus acquaintance rape, there was

> No evidence to support the assumption that rape by a husband or boyfriend had less severe long-term psychological consequences than rape by a stranger. Multivariate analysis revealed that women assaulted by spouses or dates were just as likely as those assaulted by strangers to be depressed, fearful, obsessive compulsive, and sexually dysfunctional years after the assault. Common assumptions about women assaulted by strangers having a more difficult time adjusting to the event than women raped by husbands and boyfriends appear to be incorrect.

> The best conclusion at this time is that the impact of rape is severe whether the assailant is a stranger, husband, or boyfriend. There are no differences in either the immediate or long-term effect of rape based upon the role of the perpetrator. (p. 343)

Despite these data, the assumption of the relative benignness of an acquaintance rape is widely held. Thus, in addition to the direct effects of their victimization, there is a second-order effect with a powerfully malevolent impact. That is, for victims of acquaintance rape, there is no opportunity for an affirmation of the injury which they have suffered. This failure to be affirmed, to have their victimization and its effects validated, creates an entirely different demand on the coping skills of acquaintance rape victims. They must cope with the impact of an event which, they are told in effect, did not *really* happen, or if it did, it did not matter. Burkhart (1991) has described the consequences of this peculiar context as being that

> Victims do not define their rape as real (Koss, 1985); they do not report it to the authorities, nor do they seek treatment from socially sanctioned healers (Koss et al., 1988). In effect, every opportunity for external support and affirmation is denied and they must cope on their own. Thus, victims of acquaintance rape have to cope with the victimization itself and with the pervasive, malignant denial of the victimization. (pp. 290-291)

When victims deny their own experiences and have no off-setting affirmation, then a very specific kind of coping develops with a symptom picture colored by denial, self-doubt, or self-blame.

Rather than being able to actively confront their trauma, victims of an acquaintance rape experience "a sort of cognitive-emotional paralysis wherein their only recourse is to simply deny the experience ever happened" (Koss & Burkhart, 1989, p. 32). This particular symptom picture is powerfully illustrated in research by Mandoki and Burkhart (1989). In this study of 813 college-aged women, 19% ($N = 155$) reported having experienced forced intercourse, and the large majority of these experiences involved an acquaintance or dating partner. Rape victims were found to have significantly higher levels of psychological distress compared to nonvictims even though for 80% of these victims their assault had occurred more than 1 year before the study. Moreover, the level of psychological distress was significantly correlated with the degree of self-blame endorsed by the victim. Furthermore, the higher the level of self-blame, the less positive change in distress from immediate postassault ratings to current ratings.

In a follow-up study with part of this sample, Sommerfeldt, Burkhart, and Mandoki (1989) conducted a content analysis of written responses of 189 rape and attempted rape victims to four open-ended questions requesting the women to describe their perception of the cause of their victimization and the emotional and psychological consequences of being victimized. Almost half of these victims (46%) engaged in some form of self-blame for their victimization, describing themselves as being responsible, in some fashion, for being raped. However, such self-blame provided no defense against the toxic effects of being raped. In fact, self-blame appeared to amplify the psychological damage produced by the sexual assault and served to prevent any resolution of the trauma. Powerful illustration of these effects could be found in the actual words of these victims as they described the consequences of their assault:

> Losing my virginity in that way gave me a feeling of guilt I never felt before. The feeling was so intense that suicide came into my mind very often.

Moreover, it is possible to hear in the words of women how the psychological damage was amplified by the self-blame:

> Makes me feel used even though I did not put my foot down and make the situation stop. Makes me feel sometimes that the only way for me to receive love is to lay down.
>
> This experience lowered my self-esteem. I turned to drugs just after it happened. I would not talk to any males on a personal, one-on-one level. I felt used, worthless, and abused. I had a bad attitude, didn't want anyone (including my friends and family) to care about me. *They were too good for me.* I was filled with hate and anger.

And finally, these few words capture the essence of the traumatic effects: "I cried, felt violated, alone, and unclean."

How then, can therapists confront and bring resolution to these processes of self-blame and denial? Moreover, how will therapists even know about the victim's experiences given the power and pervasiveness of these defenses in the post-rape coping process? Clearly, the task of assessment is rendered more difficult and, thus, requires a special kind of attention which goes beyond the ordinary intake assessment. For example, Jacobson, Koehler, and Jones-Brown (1987) found that ordinary assessment procedures often fail to detect histories of sexual assault among psychotherapy patients. Thus, clearly one of the important tasks of the therapist is to enable a client to reveal her trauma and to be sensitive to the symptom configurations characteristic of the acquaintance rape victim. In the next section of this chapter, the issues involved in the sensitive assessment process necessary for acquaintance rape victims will be delineated. Again, as stated earlier, the classic warning must be heeded: "Above all else, do no harm."

IDENTIFICATION

Of course, the first way that a clinician can do harm is by a misdiagnosis or a missed diagnosis. Such clinical errors are likely because, although some women who have been raped may seek treatment immediately, most victimized women will not seek therapy until much later, often years later (Koss, 1990; Koss & Burkhart, 1989; Koss et al., 1994; Stewart et al., 1987). For these women, the history of rape and its etiological significance may not be immediately known to the therapist or even to the woman herself. For example, the research on child sexual abuse suggests that unless specifically asked, women may not reveal their victimization (Briere & Runtz, 1987). Further, there are a number of reasons, even if asked, a woman may not initially reveal her victimization. Here, it is instructive to review the parallel literature in child sexual abuse. As Courtois (1988) noted with incest, factors associated with victimization, such as shame, guilt, stigma, secrecy, and mistrust, may make it difficult for a woman to disclose the abuse. In the study by Sommerfeldt et al. (1989) of acquaintance rape victims, self-blame and guilt were the most usual emotional consequences to the victimization. Additionally, as Courtois (1988) further

noted, the abuse may be denied as a protective device involving
repression of painful memories or a dissociative response such
that the survivor herself may not remember the abuse. Though
full-scale dissociative responses have not been common responses to acquaintance rape, denial of the reality of the victimization is a very common coping response. Additionally,
specifically pertinent to acquaintance rape is the denial due to
the lack of perception that a rape occurred. Because of acceptance of the cultural view of rape as involving a stranger, many
women who had experiences fitting the legal definition of rape,
but involving acquaintances, do not define themselves as having been raped (Koss et al., 1988). For example, a patient in
treatment for marital difficulties described being gang raped as
an adolescent. She, however, did not consider herself raped
because she had been friends with the boys and had eagerly
gone with them. She perceived herself as getting what she de-
served and, thus, as being the truly guilty party. It is very
common for this denial of victimization to be a central motif of
the victim's coping and, thus, for a victimized patient to not
reveal her victimization or even connect it to her problems.

Thus, as has been advocated in the child sexual abuse field
and in the rape treatment literature, there is a critical need to
routinely and comprehensively inquire in the intake and early
stages of treatment about any type of sexual assault. Even if
the patient initially denies the victimization, the inquiry will
convey to the patient that such information is important and
relevant to treatment and that the therapist is willing to discuss these topics (Courtois, 1988). It is not unusual for a patient who initially denied the abuse to state later in treatment,
"Remember when you asked about. . . ?"

Critical, also, is how the therapist raises inquiry about the
rape experience. Simply asking during the intake about a history of "rape" is not sufficient and will fail to identify many
who have a history of acquaintance rape. The sensitive inter-
viewer would do better to inquire about any unwanted or un-
pleasant sexual experience and then explore from there.

Simply asking the "right" question, however, is not enough.
As has been noted in the field of child sexual abuse, and recently by Burkhart (1991) in the field of acquaintance rape, the

attitude and stance of the therapist toward victimization may determine whether the victimization is disclosed and may affect the patient's willingness to discuss the experience. As Sgroi (1978) aptly stated with regard to child sexual abuse, "Recognition of sexual molestation in a child is entirely dependent on the individual's inherent willingness to entertain the possibility that the condition may exist" (p. xvi). Similarly, in order to help an acquaintance rape victim, we must first be willing to admit that it occurs and acknowledge that it has profound psychological impact on victims. In all aspects, the therapeutic atmosphere must be conducive to disclosure. Courtois (1988), in discussing incest, for example, notes the need to be "approachable, understanding, and responsive to the survivor" (p. 141).

Recent research in child sexual abuse focusing on survivors' perception of therapy has highlighted the importance of the therapists' response to disclosure (Armsworth, 1989; Frenken & Van Stolk, 1990; Josephson & Fong-Beyette, 1987). Armsworth (1989) describes four basic responses that survivors found helpful: validation, advocacy, empathetic understanding, and absence of contempt or derision in response to the client. According to the survivors, negative or harmful responses included exploitation and victimization of the client, lack of validation, blaming responses, and negative or absent responses from the therapist. Other negative therapist behavior according to survivors include discomfort on the part of the therapist, excessive interest in sexual details, and anger at the client or the offender (Josephson & Fong-Beyette, 1987).

Unfortunately, as described in Frenken and Van Stolk (1990), these responses are not infrequent among professionals when dealing with child sexual abuse. Further, as described in the Josephson and Fong-Beyette (1987) study, negative responses from the therapist may engender negative survivor responses including not trusting the therapist, not discussing the experience again, or simply stopping treatment. Similar dynamics and issues exist for acquaintance rape. With self-blame and guilt being prominent responses to acquaintance rape, the importance of validation and a nonjudgmental, supportive stance on the part of the therapist cannot be overstated.

Finally, there is a need to be aware of symptoms which suggest that a woman has been sexually victimized even if the woman is currently denying the victimization. In the study by Sommerfeldt et al. (1989), acquaintance rape victims were asked to describe the emotional, psychological, and physical effects consequential to the sexual assault which they had experienced. Using these written descriptions, Sommerfeldt et al. identified several specific domains of effects representing the victims' sense of the sequelae of an acquaintance rape.

The most common effect, identified by half of all victims, was damage to their capacity to trust, particularly their ability to trust men. However, in many subjects this inability to trust generalized into many spheres of functioning. Thus, clinicians should expect that difficulties with trust would play a role in the symptom picture of acquaintance rape victims. In fact, often the precipitant for a delayed treatment seeker to finally seek treatment initially involves another breach of trust or an awareness of the limiting effects of trust issues in current relationships.

The second most common symptom response was shame or guilt. Subjects frequently described themselves as dirty or sinful and carrying an intense burden of shame. Of particular note is that these feelings were described by many victims as being unremitting; their sense of shame never left them. This particular dynamic of shame appears to have a powerful role in impeding a full recovery and calls for close inspection by therapists. As might be expected, a sizable number of subjects reported a sense of worthlessness, diminished self-esteem, or specific depressive symptoms, including crying, social withdrawal, and suicidal ideation. Additionally, approximately 15% of the sample reported specific sexual maladjustment.

Anger was reported by 22% of the sample. Though usually focused on their assailant, many victims reported their anger had generalized to other men or men in general. A significant number reported that the target of their anger was themselves.

Interestingly, 17% of subjects denied that the experience had any impact on them. Whether this response represented a style of callous self-regard, dissociative defenses, or a powerful accommodation to the role of victim cannot be determined from these data. However, in our clinical experience, this sort of denial often appears to be a cover for shame syndromes.

ASSESSMENT

To assess the impact of acquaintance rape, the therapist needs not only to elicit the details and patient's response to the event, but her perception of the assault. As with child sexual abuse (Courtois, 1988; McCann et al., 1988), women may have idiosyncratic responses and meaning that they attach to acquaintance rape.

In order to understand the context of the assault, it is also important to take a complete family and social history. Of particular importance will be a history of previous assaults and victimizations. McCann et al. (1988), in discussing child sexual abuse, notes that, depending in part on her history and existing schemata, a victim may have different responses to child sexual abuse. Clearly, a similar situation exists for acquaintance rape. For example, a woman who was emotionally and sexually abused as a child may view the acquaintance rape as confirmation of her badness and powerlessness and her view of the world as an unfair and unsafe place. The same experience may lead to a different response in a woman who did not experience childhood victimization. It is also clear that the early history and overall adjustment will mediate the effects of the victimization. Moreover, there are some data which suggest that early sexual trauma increases vulnerability to subsequent victimization (Koss & Dinero, 1989).

Part of the initial assessment will involve exploring specific areas of concern and difficulty for the victim. Finkelhor and Browne (1985) conceptualized the traumagenic dynamics of child sexual abuse as falling into four domains: betrayal, powerlessness, traumatic sexualization, and stigmatization. Similar processes are involved in acquaintance rape. As E. L. Rowan and J. B. Rowan (1984) note, "intimacy and trust issues are paramount in acquaintance rape" (p. 237). Not only is an acquaintance rape victim betrayed and victimized by someone she knows, but she may also feel betrayed by her own judgment. She may now doubt herself as a good judge of character and as a capable person. Finkelhor and Browne (1985) describe traumatic sexualization as a "process in which a child's sexuality (including both sexual feelings and sexual attitudes) is shaped in a developmentally inappropriate and interpersonally dysfunctional fashion as a result of sexual abuse" (p. 530). Similarly, not only does acquaintance rape typically occur at a young age (Ageton, 1983), but the rape may be the victim's first experience with sex (Mandoki & Burkhart, 1989). E. L. Rowan and J. B. Rowan (1984), in discussing rape and the college student, describe the developmental tasks that the late adolescent must accomplish in moving into adulthood, with two of these tasks being development of mature sexuality and the establishment of intimate relationships. Rape at such an early age has marked potential for interfering with the normal accomplishments of these tasks (Burkhart & Sherry, 1993). Thus, future sexual interactions and relationships are colored by this experience. For example, a patient who had been raped by her boyfriend described how it took 2 years before she would even double date and how 5 years later, she continues to remain extremely cautious in selecting dates.

The feelings of stigmatization and powerlessness consequent to rape have been frequently described. These issues, however, may have additional significance for the victim of acquaintance rape. The powerlessness of the acquaintance rape victim may be exacerbated by not being able to trust herself as a good judge of character. Because these rapes are less likely to be reported, they do not experience the potential empowerment of being involved with the legal system or experiencing support from a rape crisis center. Not viewing herself as a rape victim, she may not even experience the empowerment of being able to attribute her current difficulties to an identifiable source.

TREATMENT THEMES

As should be very clear, the philosophical stance which must be adopted by a therapist is one framed by the conceptual and empirical work reviewed to this point; that is, victims of acquaintance rape *are* victims and they are not responsible for the harm to which they have been exposed. Therapists have to be able to support the victim's understanding of this fact. Before one can go beyond the abuse, one must first acknowledge the victimization.

Thus, therapists must not collude with powerful culturally embedded rape myths (Burt, 1978, 1980) which blame the victim. Without this basic affirming context, the therapist is very likely to be perceived as, or, in fact, be a participant in, a process predicated on denial of the reality of the victimization. Flatly stated, it is not the task of the therapist to determine if a rape "really" occurred, and if a therapist does this, therapy ceases to be therapeutic.

Moreover, if denial of victimization is a block to therapeutic engagement, then so is a therapeutic engagement which does not affirm the effects of victimization. For example, much of the early treatment work with rape victims was focused on overcoming symptoms of fear and depression through the use of behavioral techniques. Clearly, managing symptomatic presentation is a key step in the treatment of rape victims. However, if the management of fear, depressive symptoms, or anxiety becomes the only focus of therapy, particularly if these feelings are defined as "irrational" or "unnatural" responses, then, in effect, the victim is being denied the power and the legitimacy of her affective distress. Axiomatic to a genuine acknowledgement of the centrality and reality of victimization is an affirmation of her emotional responses as real, rational, and appropriate. Symptoms are to be managed, not denied.

Perhaps the clearest and most perceptive summary of the centrality of trauma and the consequences of denial-mediated accommodation to one's victimization was published by Eugene O'Neill (1956):

> None of us can help the things that life has done to us . . . They're done before you realize it, and once they're done they make you do other things until at last everything comes between you and what you would like to be, and you've lost your true self forever.
>
> *A Long Day's Journey into Night*

Our analysis of the victimization process in acquaintance rape implicates the need for therapeutic interventions to be framed by an appreciation of the cognitive and interpersonal complexities of the trauma. When the stage is set by such appreciation, therapy becomes possible. For this possibility to become realized, a relationship must be forged between two people, one of whom has good cause to be wary of any closeness. Thus, considerable attention must be paid to the development of an effective therapeutic alliance, a task we will consider next.

THERAPEUTIC ENGAGEMENT AND ALLIANCE

An increasingly important focus of attention in the treatment of survivors of sexual aggression is the relationship between the therapist and the client and the development of a working therapeutic alliance. In the area of child sexual abuse, a number of authors have noted that the therapeutic process and therapeutic relationship may parallel the victimization process (Briere, 1989; Courtois, 1988). Although perhaps not as encompassing an issue as with child sexual abuse, a similar parallel can be drawn with acquaintance rape. In acquaintance rape, just as the victim trusted her rapist, she is now expected to trust her therapist, who is likely also to be a male. The anger, mistrust, and feelings of betrayal may be misdirected at the therapist. The fee for the therapy may be perceived as verification that the victim is only "paid attention to" when someone gets something from her.

In addition to transference issues, there exists the possibility of countertransference responses. Again, the parallel literature on child sexual abuse might be helpful to review. Frenken and Van Stolk (1990) found that 58% of the professionals "felt that their anger towards the perpetrator put them out of balance" (p. 258). Over 40% reported experiencing embarrassment and disgust, and over 40% reported identification with the victim. Finally, approximately one quarter reported feelings of powerlessness. Clearly, these are reactions that have parallels in the field of acquaintance rape. The anger may not only be directed at the rapist but, at times, at the institutions that fail to validate or, at times, even investigate the charges of acquaintance rape.

The identification for a female therapist may arise from not only her own possible history of sexual victimization but also the realization of her own vulnerability to rape by men she trusts. At times, these countertransference issues may be so strong that the therapist avoids discussing what happened, minimizes what happened, or focuses on figuring out "if it was really rape." All of these actions will be viewed as reconfirming the self-blame and guilt the victim experiences. The importance of the therapist's attitude is underscored by the results of a study of psychotherapists' attitudes toward victims of sexual assault. In this project, Dye and Roth (1990) found that psychotherapists who held more negative attitudes toward victims of sexual assault were "significantly more likely both to endorse treatment themes that blamed the victim and to employ treatment strategies that blamed the victim for the assault" (pp. 208-209).

Thus, there are significant problems standing in the way of creating a benevolent therapeutic environment. However, one of the cruel ironies of the experience of victimization is that recovery proceeds through relationships, not in isolation or withdrawal from relationships. Therapy is a crucible for a victim. Thus, to the same degree that a victim feels threatened by a trusting therapeutic relationship, such a relationship is necessary to recovery.

What makes this irony most cruel is the literature suggesting that women with sexual victimization histories are at higher risk to be sexually exploited by therapists. Finkelhor and Lewis (1988) have described the "sexualization of subordination" as one of the preconditions of perpetration of child sexual abuse. To the degree that male therapists sexualize the power granted by the context of therapy, victims who would be vulnerable by their history of traumatic sexual socialization are at risk. Revictimization of this sort strikes us as heinous almost beyond understanding. The therapist must become aware that the victim who sexualizes the therapeutic relationship is providing an opportunity for a "corrective emotional experience."

This opportunity is corrective only to the degree that the therapist does not confirm the earlier emotional experience. If the original sexual exploitation is recapitulated, during or after therapy, the victim's transformation into survivor has been crushed and the therapist has become another of her assailants. Typically, such an experience will make it even that much more difficult for her to trust a future therapist.

WORKING-THROUGH

If the therapist succeeds in creating a therapeutic "holding" environment that allows a victim who is easily threatened, ashamed, and insecure to feel safe, secure, and accepted, then the working-through process of therapy can begin. There are several essential therapeutic tasks of specific significance to acquaintance rape victims. In a recent theoretical review of the effects of rape victimization, Koss and Burkhart (1989) suggested that the critical process that should be incorporated into treatment of rape victims, particularly acquaintance rape victims, involves reappraisals in the cognitive process of the victim's coping. Examining the effects of rape victimization using a stress and coping model developed by Lazarus and Folkman (1984), Koss and Burkhart argued that the cognitive appraisals of a stressful event are critical to its long-term resolution. They argued that rape, like other traumatic events such as natural disasters or disease, destroys the present personal equilibrium of a victim by contradicting central beliefs through which people orient themselves in the world. These beliefs, such as personal invulnerability, the perception of the world as predictable and meaningful, and a sense of one's own value, are shaken badly by traumatic events.

However, as Koss and Burkhart (1989) point out

Despite these similarities, there are several critical differences between rape and natural disasters. Common to most of these differences are two factors that have profound implications for a psychological understanding of the stressful impact and consequent process of adaption involved in sexual victimization. These two factors are: (a) the interpersonal nature of the sexual victimization; and (b) the pervasive, malevolent social context of rape . . . Direct, focused, intentional harm involving the most intimate act -- that is the nature of rape. (p. 31)

Thus, the treatment of the rape becomes more than a process of restoration of equilibrium about the world. In addition, the victim has to come to terms with the personal and interpersonal meaning of her trauma. Moreover, if that meaning is defined by rape myths which attribute responsibility for rape to the victim, then the only resolutions available to the victim are self-blame and shame, or denial. Thus, part of treatment almost inevitably must involve the reappraisal of the rape and its meaning. It is the rare and lucky victim who is able to avoid the revictimization consequent to the meaning assigned by the "rape culture" (Burt, 1980) to her trauma.

Thus, there are two components of treatment for the acquaintance rape victim. The first component is focused on dealing with immediate post-trauma symptoms. This component is particularly important for the person who is seeking treatment immediately after victimization or whose earlier, but unresolved, victimization has reemerged in the context of symbolic cueing for memories of the trauma. In both contexts, the victim's initial symptom presentation often is characterized by an acute symptom constellation consisting of fear, anxiety, or phobic reactions often complicated by symptoms of depression. Several writers, including the authors of the immediately preceding chapter, have suggested that this symptom picture is indicative of a clinical syndrome, consistent with the *DSM-IV* (American Psychiatric Association, 1994), which includes features of depression, phobia, anxiety, and self-esteem and trust issues (Frank et al., 1988; Koss et al., 1994). Treatment response to this symptom picture thus must include a symptom management component. In fact, most treatment studies have utilized this component, usually in the form of a behavioral management of fear and anxiety. In general, these studies report only modest results. As Frank et al. (1988) state, "A comparison of the results from the assessment only studies with the assessment and treatment studies would suggest that active treatment does not have a powerful effect on the rate or extent of recovery" (p. 299). Our contention is that, though often necessary, acute symptom-focused treatment is insufficient. Given that the reaction to rape trauma includes responses involving cognitive appraisals and affective processing, treatment models require a second component, focused on the cognitive appraisals of the trauma, particularly the emotional meaning of the trauma. If the victim's subsequent development is driven by an accommodation to the meaning provided by pathogenic rape myths with their legacy of shame and self-blame, then recovery cannot be accomplished.

Treatment focused on trauma resolution involves several interrelated treatment components, all of which are connected by the need for the therapist to assist the client in understanding her victimization without contamination by the powerful misogynist myths of sexual violence. Thus, the tasks of therapy are to

1. connect symptoms to the reality of victimization
2. facilitate the understanding and resolution of negative affective responses
3. develop reappraisals of the trauma
4. use the new understanding to recover from the emotional and behavioral constriction which follows from the accommodation to rape myth-mediated coping

Though it would seem that victims should be well able to connect their symptoms to their victimization, such is not always the case. This is particularly evident in the delayed treatment seeker whose present distress may be the consequence of earlier victimization which she no longer is able to connect to her present circumstance. However, just as with child sexual abuse survivors, victims of acquaintance rape accommodate to their victimization by denial of its impact even though their subsequent adjustment is powerfully determined by how they

have had to cope with their trauma. For example, a woman
requested treatment because of her marital difficulties. Though
there were other complexities, the central issue was her sexual
difficulties, which had become an unresolvable problem in the
marriage. She basically described a dissociative response to
any sexual encounter with her husband which, despite her hopes,
had gotten worse during the first 2 years of her marriage. She
could define no etiological factor and simply did not understand
why she was so afflicted. During the initial phase of treatment,
she finally revealed that she had been raped at age 15 by her
first boyfriend. She had coped with this assault by becoming
dissociated, a defense response which thereafter characterized
all sexual encounters. Perhaps, not surprisingly, she had been
victimized on several other occasions when men interpreted her
dissociative passivity as consent.

In this situation, the client's initial coping with the trauma,
dissociation, became "stamped in" through her subsequent coping with sexual encounters. Such trauma-forged accommodations tend to become stereotyped, rigid, and unsuccessful. However, her denial of the reality of her trauma prevented her from
understanding and even examining the meaning of the symptom; thus, in her current distress, her behavior seemed alien,
maladaptive, and beyond her control. It was only when she was
able to connect her current symptoms to her past trauma that
she began to experience self-recognition through her coping and,
thus, was able to begin the process of recovery.

Being able to see the adaptiveness of her coping to the initial trauma allowed this woman to begin her recovery, that is,
to lay claim to parts of herself from which, as a consequence of
her trauma, she had been separated. This process allows for a
resolution of the negative and self-disparaging emotional responses to her traumatic accommodations. Briere (1989), in
reference to child sexual abuse, describes a similar therapeutic
tactic he has labeled "normalization," defined as "therapist interventions that help the survivor to understand that her current behavior is not abnormal but, rather, an entirely understandable reaction to her childhood experience" (p. 83). He
describes three specific techniques which might be helpful in
this process, including information about abuse, contact with

other survivors, and therapist clarification. Briere (1989) notes that information about child sexual abuse such as its frequency, typical effects, and so forth, can be shared in a variety of ways, such as direct education by the therapist or assigned readings on the topic. Contact with other survivors, he notes, may be accomplished by, for example, participating in formal therapy groups and in abuse organizations. Finally, Briere (1989) describes therapist clarification as cognitive therapy, in which the therapist first "asks the client to concretely describe those thoughts or interpretations of memories that cause her to feel as if she is intrinsically bad or different from others" (p. 84). The therapist then gently challenges these negative assumptions and calls forth emotional responses, such as anger, which provides the energy to empower the victim's reappraisals.

Clearly these processes can be adapted to treat acquaintance rape victims. With regard to information sharing, for example, we have been struck over the years with the reactions of students in class discussions of acquaintance rape. It is unusual to discuss the topic without at least one woman after class self-identifying and viewing the presentation as validation. Books on acquaintance rape are few, but Robin Warshaw's (1988) book *I Never Called It Rape* might be a helpful text for a client to read.

Such a process of recovery leads inevitably to the cognitive appraisals which have served to block the victims' recovery. In the dramatic example described in the second vignette opening this chapter, the victim was not able to begin this process of reappraisal until she could accept the legitimacy of her symptoms. For her, she did not deserve even to be able to be depressed and to grieve because what had happened to her was her fault. Worse yet, her assailants appraisal of her as a "screamer" became a malevolent feature of her accommodation to the trauma. She could not even have her memories because they brought so much shame mixed with the pain. Being unable to work-through these memories prevented her from the "realization" of what actually happened to her; thus, she could not begin to grieve, to become angry, or to recover in any fashion. She was blocked by the self-blaming appraisal of her victimization and the shame potentiated by this appraisal.

Once, however, symptoms are made human and the grip of these defensive accommodations to trauma is loosened, reappraisals are possible. The usual course of this phase of treatment is directed by the work of self-acceptance. As the victim begins to experience having been victimized and understands the boundaries of her responsibility, she is able to acknowledge her real pain and work-through the injury done to her. This is a painful process, involving coming to terms with new meanings about life. She may have to accept the malevolence of others, the reality of the world's dangerousness, and the unfairness of trauma. In addition, however, the victim should come to know an essential truth about herself: that facing her memories allows her to become stronger and surer about herself. Allowing herself to know what is real becomes a powerful prophylactic to prevent revictimization, a high risk consequence for untreated victims.

This part of recovery, wherein Burt and Katz (1988) have been able to identify growth-enhancing coping processes, is potentiated by the client's new ability to give voice to herself. No longer trapped by shame and self-blame in her silence, she may find herself able to reach for understanding from others. Davis and Friedman (1985) report that almost all crime victims talk about their victimization, and those who do talk about their experience rate this as a most important part of healing. Burt and Katz (1988) state explicitly, "We believe from our counseling experience with rape victims, that the ability to express feeling about the rape is *necessary* for most women if they are to achieve full-integrated recovery" (p. 354). We agree with this analysis and see it as part of the full recovery from the emotional and behavioral constriction which follows from rape-myth accommodation. As we have written elsewhere, "Clients who become free to tell their stories and own their feelings become free from them and are no longer trapped in the denial-shame feedback loop" (Burkhart, 1991, p. 299).

As the expressive confinement is broken, so too are the behavioral constraints challenged. The rape victim who has fallen into a restricted lifestyle can begin to experience her freedom to move through life as something other than trespassing on dangerous territory. Very often during this phase of treatment, previously undisclosed behavioral constrictions come to light and need to be worked-through. Though recovery from the emotional and behavioral constriction which resulted from the accommodation to the rape is a necessary component of treatment, the therapist must work from the understanding that the victim's defenses and symptoms once served a purpose and were adaptive to her appraisals. Thus, to change "naturally," the appraisals must be gently confronted. One way to do this is to identify how rigid and overused these defenses are and how, even when they work "successfully" (i.e., contain anxiety), they prevent a woman from living a full life. For example, a woman who copes with acquaintance rape by not dating is reducing her anxiety and increasing her sense of control but is also severely restricting her life.

Helping the victim to expand her coping repertoire is not an easy process and can be completed only when other therapeutic tasks have been at least partially addressed. The woman needs to understand as well as emotionally accept that her symptoms served a purpose and are understandable. Additionally, trust and hope are important and necessary tools for risk taking. The victim must be able to trust the therapist and her own abilities, as well as be able to envision a different life for herself. Unless the therapist has helped the victim work-through the negative emotional effects of the rape, such as self-blame, guilt, and powerlessness, the patient may not be willing to try to attain a better life or, even more likely, she may not feel that she is worthy of one. An apt analogy for this process is getting a novice on a trapeze to let go of one bar to catch another one. Unless the person has some belief that the task is within her reach and that there will be a safety net to catch her if she falls, the person will not let go. Instead, she will swing back and forth, not falling, but not going anywhere. In trying out the new behavior, the patient must have hope as well as the belief that the therapist, and later her own coping processes, will be available when having to venture into new territory.

With a strong therapeutic alliance, the therapy session is a safe haven to begin to practice these new emotional and behavioral styles. Indeed, working-through anger and trust issues with a male therapist could serve as a prototype of doing so with other relationships. Additionally, it is at this point in treatment that behavioral interventions and "homework" assignments may be productive. As always, however, patience and understanding need to be combined with hope and expectancy.

A very powerful procedure amplifying this process of recovery is the use of survivor support groups. In describing the treatment of child abuse survivors, Sgroi (1989) advocates such groups as the primary vehicle for abuse survivors to learn and rehearse new coping behaviors. Similarly, such groups for acquaintance rape victims should facilitate several of the critical therapeutic tasks. Of particular utility is the power of the group to validate the reality of the victimization experience. Such validation allows the victim/survivor to begin the work of examining her own accommodation to the experience. Additionally, the "helper" principle is a strong antidote to the toxic effects of attributional accommodation and self-blame. Having helped someone else see these processes as malignant accommodations provides a useful alternative to the helpers' tendencies to do the same.

Sgroi (1989), in discussing the last stage of recovery for child sexual abuse victims, notes the need for the woman to go beyond conceptualizing herself as a victim, or even a survivor, and instead view herself as a multidimensional person whose abuse constituted one part of her life. We believe this concept has considerable utility for the treatment of acquaintance rape victims. Thus, although treatment necessarily will increase the salience of the identity and, indeed, encourage a woman to define herself as a victim, effective treatment will also involve moving beyond this stage. As with child sexual abuse, the goal is for the rape to become a traumatic and important experience in one's past, as opposed to the defining feature and central identity of one's life. Thus, a new definition of the self will be incorporated into the survivor's self-schema via the cognitive restructuring component of treatment. This new self will not be controlled by the victimization experience nor organized around an identity as a victim. Instead, she will have found in herself a sturdy resilience and sureness which will allow for continued growth of the self.

REFERENCES

Ageton, S. S. (1983). *Sexual Assault Among Adolescents*. Lexington, MA: D. C. Heath.

American Psychiatric Association. (1994). *Diagnostic and Statistical Manual of Mental Disorders* (DSM-IV, 4th ed.). Washington, DC: Author.

Armsworth, M. W. (1989). Therapy of incest survivors: Abuse or support? *Child Abuse and Neglect, 13*, 549-562.

Briere, J. (1989). *Therapy for Adults Molested as Children: Beyond Survival*. New York: Springer.

Briere, J., & Runtz, M. (1987). Post sexual abuse trauma: Data and implications for clinical practice. *Journal of Interpersonal Violence, 2*, 367-379.

Burgess, A. W., & Holmstrom, L. L. (1976). Coping behavior of the rape victim. *American Journal of Psychiatry, 133*, 413-418.

Burkhart, B. R. (1991). Conceptual and practical analysis of therapy for acquaintance rape victims. In A. Parrot & L. Bechhofer (Eds.), *Acquaintance Rape: The Hidden Crime* (pp. 287-303). New York: Wiley.

Burkhart, B. R., & Fromuth, M. E. (1991). Individual psychological and social psychological understandings of sexual coercion. In E. Grauerholz & M. A. Koralewski (Eds.), *Sexual Coercion: A Sourcebook on Its Nature, Causes and Prevention* (pp. 75-89). Lexington, MA: Lexington.

Burkhart, B. R., & Sherry, A. (1993). Sexual victimization in adolescents. *Medical Psychotherapy: An International Journal, 6*, 171-183.

Burkhart, B. R., & Stanton, A. L. (1988). Acquaintance rape. In G. W. Russell (Ed.), *Violence in Intimate Relationships* (pp. 43-65). Englewood Cliffs, NJ: Spectrum.

Burt, M. R. (1978). Attitudes supportive of rape in the American culture. In House Committee on Science and Technology, Subcommittee on Domestic and International Scientific Planning, Analysis, and Corporation (Ed.), *Research into Violent Behavior: Sexual Assault* (Hearing, 95th Congress, Second Session, January 10-12, 1978, pp. 277-322). Washington, DC: U.S. Government Printing Office.

Burt, M. R. (1980). Cultural myths and supports for rape. *Journal of Personality and Social Psychology, 38*, 217-230.

Burt, M. R., & Katz, B. L. (1988). Coping strategies and recovery from rape. In R. A. Prentky & V. L. Quinsey (Eds.), *Human Sexual Aggression: Current Perspectives* (Vol. 528, pp. 345-358). New York: Annals of the New York Academy of Sciences.

Courtois, C. A. (1988). *Healing the Incest Wound: Adult Survivors in Therapy.* New York: Norton.

Courtois, C. A., & Sprei, J. E. (1988). Retrospective incest therapy for women. In L. E. Walker (Ed.), *Handbook on Sexual Abuse of Children: Assessment and Treatment Issues* (pp. 270-308). New York: Springer.

Davis, R. C., & Friedman, L. N. (1985). The emotional aftermath of crime and violence. In C. R. Figley (Ed.), *Trauma and Its Wake: The Study and Treatment of Post-Traumatic Stress Disorder* (pp. 90-111). New York: Brunner/Mazel.

Dye, E., & Roth, S. (1990). Psychotherapists' knowledge about and attitudes toward sexual assault victim clients. *Psychology of Women Quarterly, 14*, 191-212.

Ellis, E. M. (1983). A review of empirical rape research: Victim reactions and response to treatment. *Clinical Psychology Review, 3*, 473-490.

Finkelhor, D., & Browne, A. (1985). The traumatic impact of child sexual abuse: A conceptualization. *American Journal of Orthopsychiatry, 55*, 530-541.

Finkelhor, D., & Lewis, I. A. (1988). An epidemiologic approach to the study of child molestation. In R. A. Prentky & V. L. Quinsey (Eds.), *Human Sexual Aggression: Current Perspectives* (Vol. 528, pp. 64-78). New York: Annals of the New York Academy of Sciences.

Foa, E. B., Rothbaum, B. O., Riggs, D. S., & Murdock, T. B. (1991). Treatment of posttraumatic stress disorder in rape victims: A comparison between cognitive-behavioral procedures and counseling. *Journal of Consulting and Clinical Psychology, 59*, 715-723.

Frank, E., Anderson, B., Stewart, B. D., Dancer, C., Hughes, C., & West, D. (1988). Immediate and delayed treatment of rape victims. In R. A. Prentky & V. L. Quinsey (Eds.), *Human*

Sexual Aggression: Current Perspectives (Vol. 528, pp. 296-309). New York: Annals of the New York Academy of Sciences.

Frank, E., & Stewart, B. D. (1983). Treating depression in victims of rape. *The Clinical Psychologist, 36,* 95-98.

Frenken, J., & Van Stolk, B. (1990). Incest victims: Inadequate help by professionals. *Child Abuse and Neglect, 14,* 253-263.

Fromuth, M., & Burkhart, B. (1992). Recovery or recapitulation: An analysis of the impact of psychiatric hospitalization on the childhood sexual abuse survivor. *Women and Therapy, 12,* 81-95.

Holmes, M. R., & St. Lawrence, J. S. (1983). Treatment of rape-induced trauma: Proposed behavioral conceptualization and review of the literature. *Clinical Psychology Review, 3,* 417-433.

Jackson, T. L., Quevillon, R. P., & Petretic-Jackson, P. A. (1985). Assessment and treatment of sexual assault victims. In P. A. Keller & L. G. Ritt (Eds.), *Innovations in Clinical Practice: A Source Book* (Vol. 4, pp. 51-78). Sarasota, FL: Professional Resource Exchange.

Jacobson, A., Koehler, J., & Jones-Brown, C. (1987). The failure of routine assessment to detect histories of assault experienced by psychiatric patients. *Hospital and Community Psychiatry, 38,* 386-389.

Josephson, G. S., & Fong-Beyette, M. L. (1987). Factors assisting female clients' disclosure of incest during counseling. *Journal of Counseling and Development, 65,* 475-478.

Kilpatrick, D. G., Best, C. L., Saunders, B. E., & Veronen, L. J. (1988). Rape in marriage and dating relationships: How bad is it for mental health? In R. A. Prentky & V. L. Quinsey (Eds.), *Human Sexual Aggression: Current Perspectives* (Vol. 528, pp. 335-344.) New York: Annals of the New York Academy of Sciences.

Kilpatrick, D. G., & Veronen, L. J. (1982). Treatment for rape-related problems: Crisis intervention is not enough. In L. H. Cohen, W. Clairborn, & G. Specter (Eds.), *Crisis Intervention* (pp. 165-185). New York: Human Science Press.

Kilpatrick, D. G., Veronen, L. J., & Resick, P. A. (1979). The aftermath of rape: Recent empirical findings. *American Journal of Orthopsychiatry, 49*, 658-669.

Koss, M. P. (1985). The hidden rape victim: Personality, attitudinal and situational characteristics. *Psychology of Women Quarterly, 9*, 193-212.

Koss, M. P. (1990). The women's mental health research agenda: Violence against women. *American Psychologist, 45*, 374-380.

Koss, M. P., & Burkhart, B. R. (1989). A conceptual analysis of rape victimization: Long-term effects and implications for treatment. *Psychology of Women Quarterly, 13*, 27-40.

Koss, M. P., & Dinero, T. E. (1989). Discriminant analysis of risk factors for sexual victimization among a national sample of college women. *Journal of Consulting and Clinical Psychology, 57*, 242-250.

Koss, M. P., Dinero, T. E., Seibel, C. A., & Cox, S. L. (1988). Stranger and acquaintance rape: Are there differences in the victim's experience? *Psychology of Women Quarterly, 12*(1), 1-24.

Koss, M. P., Goodman, L. A., Browne, A., Fitzgerald, L. F., Keita, G. P., & Russo, N. F. (1994). *No Safe Haven: Male Violence Against Women At Home, At Work, and In The Community.* Washington, DC: American Psychological Asociation.

Koss, M. P., & Harvey, M. R. (1987). *Rape: Clinical and Community Approaches to Treatment.* Lexington, MA: Stephen Greene Press.

Lazarus, R., & Folkman, S. (1984). *Stress, Appraisal, and Coping.* New York: Springer.

Mandoki, C. A., & Burkhart, B. R. (1989, August). *Coping and Adjustment to Rape.* Paper presented at the 97th Annual Meeting of the American Psychological Association, New Orleans, LA.

Mandoki, C. A., & Burkhart, B. R. (1991). Women as victims: Antecedents and consequences. In A. Parrot & L. Bechhofer (Eds.), *Acquaintance Rape: The Hidden Crime* (pp. 176-191). New York: Wiley.

McCann, L., Pearlman, L. A., Sakheim, D. K., & Abrahamson, D. J. (1988). Assessment and treatment of the adult survivor of childhood sexual abuse within a schema framework. In S. M. Sgroi (Ed.), *Vulnerable Populations Vol. 1: Evaluation and Treatment of Sexually Abused Children and Adult Survivors* (pp. 77-101). Lexington, MA: Lexington.

O'Neill, E. (1956). *Long Day's Journey into Night.* New Haven, CT: Yale University Press.

Resick, P. A. (1983). The rape reaction: Research findings and implications for intervention. *Behavior Therapist, 6,* 129-132.

Resick, P. A., & Schnicke, M. K. (1992). Cognitive processing for sexual assault victims. *Journal of Consulting and Clinical Psychology, 60,* 748-756.

Rose, D. (1991). A model for psychodynamic therapy with the rape victim. *Psychotherapy, 28,* 85-94.

Rowan, E. L., & Rowan, J. B. (1984). Rape and the college student: Multiple crisis in late adolescence. In I. R. Stuart & J. G. Greer (Eds.), *Victims of Sexual Aggression: Treatment of Children, Women, and Men* (pp. 234-250). New York: Van Nostrand Reinhold.

Sgroi, S. M. (1978). Introduction: A national needs assessment for protecting child victims of sexual assault. In A. W. Burgess, A. N. Groth, L. L. Holmstrom, & S. Sgroi (Eds.), *Sexual Assault of Children and Adolescents* (pp. xv-xxii). Lexington, MA: Lexington.

Sgroi, S. M. (1989). Stages of recovery for adult survivors of child sexual abuse. In S. M. Sgroi (Ed.), *Vulnerable Populations Vol 2: Sexual Abuse Treatment for Children, Adult Survivors, Offenders, and Persons with Mental Retardation* (pp. 111-130). Lexington, MA: Lexington.

Sommerfeldt, T., Burkhart, B. R., & Mandoki, C. A. (1989, August). *In Her Own Words: Victim's Descriptions of Hidden Rape Effects.* Poster presented at the 97th Annual Meeting of the American Psychological Association, New Orleans, LA.

Stewart, B., Hughes, C., Frank, E., Anderson, B., Kendall, K., & West, D. (1987). The aftermath of rape: Profiles of immediate and delayed treatment seekers. *Journal of Nervous and Mental Disorders*, *175*, 90-94.

Summit, R. C. (1983). The child sexual abuse accommodation syndrome. *Child Abuse and Neglect*, 7, 177-193.

Warshaw, R. (1988). *I Never Called It Rape: The Ms. Report on Recognizing, Fighting and Surviving Date and Acquaintance Rape.* New York: Harper and Row.

6

Rape Education and Prevention Training

Kelly Carroll
and
Thomas L. Jackson

This chapter is designed to give practitioners the basic information they need to develop and present an accurate and sensitive rape education/training program. The aim of this chapter is to provide individuals who are already fairly knowledgeable about the topic of rape with the outline of a basic community education program, which can be modified for use with various target groups within the community, as well as for individual therapy clients. Thus, it is highly recommended that the novice in this area first develop a basic mastery of the topic, referring to basic reference material provided in the other chapters in this book as well as to other relevant materials as needed, before attempting to provide rape education/prevention programming to a community group.

The authors have delivered the presentations outlined in this chapter to over 175 diverse groups, including men's civic organizations; women's political organizations; junior and senior high school students; university students via fraternity, sorority, residence hall, classroom, and university-wide presentations; National Collegiate Athletic Association Division I and II member institutions' Athletic Departments; rape crisis volunteer training groups; police and medical in-service training groups; a national television audience on a popular talk show; and state superior and supreme court justices from across the country. The authors have collected the information for these presentations from a variety of sources. References for general statements can be derived from other chapters in this book. Only a few citations are provided in this chapter. These represent nonoverlapping issues when compared to the other works in this volume.

Presentations similar to the ones discussed in this chapter have been found to increase factual knowledge in the audience and to modify attitudes and attributions of blame toward rape victims and offenders (Holcomb et al., 1993; Jackson et al., 1989), and to decrease dating behaviors that have been associated with acquaintance and date rape and sexual assault (Hanson & Gidycz, 1993).

The chapter is organized like a handbook, in two parts followed by Appendices 6-A and 6-B (pp. 208-211). The first part discusses issues which should be considered prior to beginning the process of program development. It includes a discussion of the general philosophical framework on which the materials presented in this chapter are based. It also suggests the personal qualities which are desirable in a good presenter. Additionally, available sources of statistical, legal, and victim assistance/support information relevant to one's community, region, and state to which the practitioner may turn are discussed. The second part discusses both program content and process, beginning with the preparatory steps to be taken before making a presentation. It provides an outline of the general format for a rape education/prevention presentation. This general presentation format is followed by information on five specific topic areas: rape trauma, rape prevention in dating situations, general rape prevention, victim support strategies, and one example of an in-service presentation - an educational program for college athletes. The section ends with suggestions for program evaluation. Finally, tables and appendices detailing various aspects of the presentations end the chapter.*

BEFORE YOU BEGIN

PHILOSOPHY

Before we go any further, a major issue that needs to be addressed is the personal/professional philosophy regarding rape which is espoused by the presenter. The presenter must be able to approach the topic of rape from a nonblaming, pro-victim viewpoint. In order for a presentation to be both sensitive and successful, the presenter must be comfortable taking a feminist viewpoint. The presenter should be knowledgeable about the history of rape and other forms of sexual assault (refer to Chapters 1 and 2 in this book) and should have an understanding of the role that traditional sex role stereotypes play in the issues surrounding rape. By necessity, such traditional stereotypes, which blame victims, can neither be promoted by the speaker in the content of her or his presentation nor tacitly approved of in the audience by a speaker's failure to address directly the problems inherent in such stereotypes.

Implicit in a feminist philosophy is the conceptualization of rape, in the overwhelming majority of cases, as a crime against women committed by men. Oftentimes it is a crime in which the rapist walks away without any resulting negative consequences and in which the victim suffers the negative consequences for the rest of her life (refer to Petretic-Jackson and Tobin, Chapter 4 in this book). Petretic-Jackson and Tobin note "Rape in any context is a very real trauma. [It] violates not only the body, but the spirit as well, bringing in its wake a sense that any control over one's physical safety is now gone" (p. 102). The trauma of the situation is particularly exacerbated

---

*The safety tips and preventive steps presented in the tables and appendices in this chapter represent a compilation of useful information derived from public domain sources.

for the victim of sexual assault perpetrated by an acquaintance. The "unique malevolent social psychological context" in which rape by an acquaintance is viewed - not only by the woman's perpetrator, but oftentimes by the community at large and her friends and family - redefines the event to make it a "dirty little secret" shared only by the woman and her rapist, something "other than rape" and, basically, something that was, for all intents and purposes, "her fault."

A feminist viewpoint concerning rape is essential, requiring the typical pattern of victim blaming prevalent in society today to be challenged. Blame attributed to the female victim must be reassigned; concomitantly, blame should be assigned to the offender for his actions. Feminists also argue that some level of blame should be ascribed to society for the sanctioning of patriarchal attitudes which serve to promote the sexual victimization of women. Thus, the philosophy promoted in rape education/prevention programming is that the status quo concerning the common conceptualization and treatment of rape and its victims must change. Victims must no longer be blamed for their own victimization. Men must be responsible for their assaultive actions. The predominant social values which promote victimization must be changed. This change can occur only through educational efforts.

CHARACTERISTICS
OF A GOOD PRESENTER

Given the subject matter, it is not uncommon for the audience in a rape education/prevention program to present unique challenges for the speaker. Thus, we have found that certain traits are highly desirable in an effective rape education/prevention speaker. Presenters must necessarily feel comfortable with open discussions of sex and other sensitive topics. They must also be comfortable speaking in front of large, and occasionally hostile, groups. Lastly, presenters will be much more successful if they know how to "work" an audience. This means presenters must demonstrate the ability to draw the audience into discussions and be able to "play" one part of the audience against the other to allow for the most effective exchange of ideas. The ability to keep the participants focused on active discussion of the issues is often the most effective strategy for controlling "hecklers" and keeping the presentation on the correct footing. Rape is never an easy topic to discuss, and an audience's reactions - oftentimes hostile and defensive - are part of the challenge. Keeping calm and nondefensive as a speaker is critical, as is the ability to defuse angry interchanges between audience members expressing conflicting values and ideas.

The final qualities characteristic of a good rape education speaker are also those which characterize a good therapist - sensitivity and compassion. A presenter must never lose sight of the seriousness of the topic - the profound impact rape has on a woman's life. Given the statistic that 1 out of every 4 women will be raped in her lifetime, a presenter must always be attuned to the fact that, in all likelihood, rape victims and/or their partners, friends, and family are present in the audience. Such individuals are highly sensitive to the speaker's words and expressed attitude.

FINDING COMMUNITY-RELEVANT INFORMATION REGARDING RAPE: ASSESSING COMMUNITY RESOURCES

In the following, we will discuss the need to bring the experience of rape down to a more personal level for your audience. One way of doing that is to provide factual information about rape - such as state and community statistics, available services for victims, and state statutes defining rape - for your audience. If you do not currently have such information, where might you turn?

A community Rape Crisis Center is an excellent resource for basic material used to present the "facts and figures" of rape for the community. These centers generally have a large amount of literature, at both technical and popular levels. They also have access to statistical and legal information. Most important, however, they are an excellent resource for adjunctive victim services. Their major mission is to provide confidential advocacy services to rape victims. These services generally consist of a hotline, medical and legal escort services, follow-up counseling, and survivor groups. It may be possible to coordinate your presentations with rape crisis representatives. Before independently beginning your own rape education program development, it is advisable to contact such a center, if one is available in your community, to avoid duplication of services. You may find it more expedient to offer your speaking services as a member of the center's speaker's bureau. Alternately, practitioners can be instrumental in assisting in the establishment of a volunteer rape crisis center if one does not already exist.

The prosecuting/state attorney's office in your city or county should also be able to assist you in finding relevant information. They should be able to provide a copy of the rape statutes and are a source of local and state crime statistics. Cities often have Victim's of Crime Act (VOCA) workers. Victims of Crime Act workers go by different titles but generally work out of the prosecuting attorney's office. They offer victim assistance throughout legal proceedings and should have access to both statistical and legal information. They may also provide counseling or other services for victims.

Community Mental Health Centers (CMHCs) may also provide emergency and other services for victims. Occasionally CMHCs offer a speaker's bureau, which provides a variety of presentation topics, including rape, to the community.

Finally, local universities often have a Rape Task Force or similar programs. Such programs may be administratively housed under Student Service programs or be run as an independent, volunteer student service. These programs can offer useful statistical and legal information along with relevant literature. There may also be a victim service component, most often medical referral, to these programs as well.

THE PRESENTATION

The second part of this chapter will describe the process and content of a rape education/prevention program. To ensure that the presentation is meaningful and well received, preparatory steps that should be considered will be discussed first. Next, a description of both general and topic specific rape presentation formats, termed "formulas," will be provided. Presenters generally use a formula when creating a presentation, and this chapter will prepare speakers by providing both general and specific rape presentation formulas. The specific formulas include rape trauma, prevention of rape in dating situations, general rape prevention, victim support strategies, and examples of an in-service presentation to collegiate athletes.

The formulas are designed to be used either individually or in combination. Although established formulas are presented, to be most effective as a presenter you will need to use some ingenuity and keep the overall goal of the presentation and your specific target audience in mind. After preparing, giving, and evaluating several rape presentations, keep the best, toss the rest, and create new formulas. Let these formulas serve as guidelines, not limitations.

PREPARING FOR
THE PRESENTATION

Assessing Your Personal Values and Biases. This topic has been discussed previously. As a presenter, you must have a positive attitude toward both women and the role of women as victims in the crime of rape. You want to show, through your posture, gestures, and attitude, as well as by your words, that (a) you take the crime of rape seriously and (b) you are a sincere person whom the audience feels free to question and disclose to. Even though the aim of rape presentations is to educate the community, not to provide direct service to victims, your manner should be confident and sensitive enough for victims or their significant others to feel comfortable approaching you for more information - or to share their experience with you.

Personal experience has taught us that some individuals will wait until the presentation has concluded to talk to you individually. Our suggestion is to be approachable and to allow yourself some time after any presentation to permit individuals to talk with you. Often we ask the sponsors to give us this time explicitly rather than be "whisked away" before someone has a chance to ask questions or make comments. Consider this time spent with your audience post-presentation as a compliment to your skills as an effective presenter.

Along with a general attitude, you must spend some time in self-exploration - examining your own views concerning women and rape before ever giving a public presentation. If you think that women can avoid rape by "not going out unescorted late at night" or "not drinking to excess" or if you hold any of the rape myths presented in the table on page 192, then you should engage in continued values clarification and reorientation before you speak. Your audience will pick up on such attitudes even if you never state them explicitly. Such attitudes are contradictory to your role as a rape educator. If you believe any of the rape myths then you are implying victim blame. Although more subtle, if you believe that "Men should always protect women," you may be inadvertently supporting restriction of a woman's movements and adding to her sense of fear and lack of control over her environment. Women are, and always have been, easy targets and victims of random violence due to power and status inequities in patriarchal societies. We should all respect and look out for others - and ourselves, regardless of gender.

Knowing the Facts About Rape and Your Audience.
You should make yourself familiar with both local and national assault statistics and local (mental health, general community, law enforcement, judicial, health personnel) attitudes. The numbers are relatively easy to find (see previous section and Table 6-1, p. 185) from a number of sources. Additionally, a knowledge of community attitudes can be garnered from the media and by talking to people; be particularly cognizant of the views held by your prospective audience. You need to determine the attitudes of your particular audience early on, before the talk if possible, so that you can tailor your presentation accordingly. For instance, if you are speaking to a women's civic organization that contributes to women's programs, your approach will be more loose and relaxed than if you are speaking to a fraternity whose members have just been charged with gang rape and are mandated to attend your program. In the latter case, you will approach the topic directly, but in a manner designed to decrease audience defensiveness.

You should also assess what specific information your audience is most interested in hearing about. This will allow you to

TABLE 6-1: STATISTICS

Federal Bureau of Investigation estimated number of rapes in 1994	102,000
National Crime Victimization Survey annual reports of rapes and sexual assaults	500,000
It is estimated that there are 2.5 to 10 times more rapes than are reported	1,000,000
Percentage of women who will be raped in their lifetime	1 out of 4
Percentage of women who report being raped in college surveys	20%-35%
Percentage of women who report being raped on dates	20%
Percentage of U.S. households that have experienced incest	10%
Percentage of women who are physically assaulted on dates	10%
Percentage of men who report that a date said "No when she meant Yes"	75%
Percentage of rapists who are repeat offenders	60%
Percentage of victims who know their rapists	75%+
Percentage of college men who said they would rape if they wouldn't be caught	34%
Percentage of men in a college survey who admitted to raping	5%

select specific content to supplement the general introduction component to your rape education/prevention programs. Ask your group representatives what aspects of rape they wish to be informed about. Don't let them guess what information you might provide if they really don't have specific topics in mind. Give them a list of possible specific subtopics: your formulas.

They may be able to poll their group members for suggestions. In some circumstances, the group sponsor may have specific topics in mind for inclusion. Obviously, this individualizing is also critical if you have an audience of one: your therapy client. The presented information and formulas may be tailored to meet the needs of clients with specific histories and backgrounds.

Attaining and Documenting Expert Status. You need to establish your expertise in the area. A speaker recognized as an expert is attended to more and has a better chance of changing attitudes than a speaker perceived by the audience as a nonexpert. Although advanced degrees and educational experiences are often used to establish expertise, experiences relevant to rape intervention are more useful in terms of the acceptability of a speaker's expert status by the audience. This background could be provided by research participation, direct work with victims or offenders, expert witness status (providing testimony in court), or prior experience as a speaker/educator. As consumers, your audience has a right to know what credentials qualify you as an "expert" on this topic. Provide them with this information, briefly and nondefensively.

Creating an Atmosphere. Give your audience permission to ask questions or make comments from the onset of the presentation. Then work on establishing an open atmosphere, which fosters additional questions and comments. Often, novice presenters feel more comfortable if their audience either is not given the time or does not have the inclination to ask questions. Although time constraints may limit the extent of discussion, an open atmosphere which endorses the person's "right" and provides the "opportunity" to ask questions is essential in successful rape education programming. The audience must believe that the presenter cares about what it thinks as an audience, is giving information but not talking "at them," and expresses a willingness to answer any of their questions. If you feel comfortable having some flexibility in your presentations over time, you may want to adapt the presentation format to permit the inclusion of audience-generated foci. If you prefer more structured presentations, with less audience participation, this typically necessitates providing the opportunity for individual postpresentation contacts. If you want to encourage this, identify at the beginning of the presentation what approach you prefer (e.g., "Just feel free to ask any questions as they arise" or "I will also be available after the presentation to answer any additional individual questions").

Presenting the Introductory Content: A General Formula

Step 1. Showing Your Respect for the Audience. After introducing yourself and establishing your credibility/expert status, it is very helpful to reinforce or compliment the audience for the invitation to speak and for attending a presentation on rape. Remember, rape is a topic that most people would prefer never to think about, let alone hear a presentation on. Acknowledge the difficulty of the topic and applaud the audience for attending a presentation on such a difficult topic.

Step 2. Sharing Information on Available Services for Victims. Apprise the audience of the local services available to rape victims. Have a list of such services. (Be sure to have obtained prior permission from all agencies listed to provide their names and services provided.) Keep this information current and accurate. List agency contact persons when available and identify services within the context of the talk. Also provide flyers for distribution to your audience, listing all pertinent agency/provider services when they are available. Make these available to your audience after the presentation. It is also a good idea to give this list to the coordinator/contact person of the group sponsoring your presentation to post or make available to the group. Stress that these services are important to all of the members of the audience. Even if they are not women, they all have wives, mothers, sisters, daughters, friends, or colleagues who might need the services or know of others who do.

Step 3. Emphasizing the Seriousness of Rape. The tone for the next topic, the seriousness of the rape offense, is now set.

Most audiences realize that rape is a serious crime, but they do not realize just how prevalent rape is or how serious it is in terms of consequences to the victim and her significant others. Stress *why* rape is an important issue. There are three ways in which to emphasize the seriousness of the issue:

1. ***Provide Statistics.*** Statistics are very useful. Quoting a few statistics from credible sources brings the issue home (see Table 6-1, p. 185). Do not, however, get caught up in statistics. It is very difficult to comprehend the meaning of numbers when dozens of them are thrown out in a series during a talk. If you use overhead transparencies to illustrate your presentation, restrict the information on any one overhead to a maximum of seven or eight lines. More information is not legible, and tabular presentation of data cannot always be fully comprehended. Select the most powerful statistics. Even better, use one overhead for each point to be made.

2. ***Personalize the Statistics.*** This may be done by asking the members of the audience to raise their hands if they know anyone who has been raped or by counting the women off in groups of four (It is estimated that 1 out of every 4 women will be raped in her lifetime). A single woman is a more powerful statistic than a myriad of tables listing facts and figures. Also provide local (i.e., community and state) statistics.

3. ***Document the Serious Consequences of Rape to the Victim.*** It is preferable to simply mention consequences at this point, perhaps with a listing of major symptoms, and then to expound on the consequences in more detail later (see below).

Step 4. Defining the Crime of Rape. Given that you have now established the importance of the issues, the act of rape needs to be clearly defined. Although most people believe that they can correctly define rape, their definitions vary a great deal. During your presentation, provide the state definitions, if they are available, as well as the behavioral definition based on research (e.g., Koss, 1985; Petretic-Jackson & Tobin, Chapter 4 of this book).

It is best to avoid listing or defining all forms of sexual contact crimes by defining lesser crimes, such as felony sexual assault or sexual harassment, for example. Defining these terms may serve to confuse the audience and cloud the major issue. However, you should *know* the major statutory categories of sexual assaults for your state in case someone asks (e.g., age of consent; criteria for forcible rape; is it "rape" if the woman is drunk? the man? etc.).

Step 5. Debunking the Myths: Defining the Victim and the Rapist. Following a discussion of definitional issues, a description of the "participants" is necessary. This is a perfect opportunity to solicit audience participation and to begin demythologizing your audience about rape. If a chalkboard is handy, list three categories: "rapist," "victim," and "rape." Have the audience give stereotypical characteristics for each category. Using stereotypical characteristics will increase audience participation because they are asked to list "general" stereotypes, not their own views.

Once the characteristics have been listed, add any major ones that were missed. Then go through each category and discuss the correctness of each characteristic. Table 6-2 (pp. 190-191) includes specific examples. For instance, if *young* is listed under "victim," you would point out that victims are often young; statistically, the 16 to 24 year age range is the most prevalent age group for being raped. However, there have been reported victims ranging in age from a few months to 90 years.

You may also want to contrast the legal and psychological definitions of a rape victim (refer to Jackson, Quevillon, & Petretic-Jackson, 1985). If someone did not technically meet the "qualification of being an FBI rape statistic," might she still be a victim if she is showing signs of posttraumatic stress disorder?

Step 6. Debunking Other Common Rape Myths. The audience is now ready to discuss other common rape myths. Com-

TABLE 6-2: COMMON CHARACTERISTICS AND FACTS

CHARACTERISTICS OF THE RAPIST

1. The overwhelming majority of rapists are male. There are cases in which the rapist is female, but they are very rare.
2. Rapists come from every socioeconomic status level and every walk of life. Rapists are not only unemployed or blue-collar workers, but also professionals.
3. Less than 5% of rapists were considered mentally unstable when they were arrested.
4. The majority of rapists know their victim and the victim knows them. They are the victim's neighbor, friend, date, banker, and so forth.
5. Rapists can be any age from 12 to 80 years of age. Statistically, rapists between the ages of 17 and 28 are most prevalent.
6. Rapists can be from any minority or majority group. In general, black men rape black women and white men rape white women.
7. Rapists can be dirty and smelly, but they are just as likely to be clean-cut, Big-Man-On-Campus types.
8. Most rapists have at least one consenting sexual partner. They are not raping because they are hard up.
9. Rapists are repeat offenders.

CHARACTERISTICS OF THE VICTIM

1. The victim is almost always female. Male rape is, however, on an increase and does occur in settings other than prisons.
2. Victims can be from every walk of life and every socioeconomic class. They are from all races and religions and range in age from a few months to 90 years. Statistically, the age range that is most prone to be raped is 16 to 24.
3. Attractive, unattractive, slender, and overweight women are all raped. The rapist isn't looking for an attractive woman to have sex with but for an available, easy target.
4. Victims are never to blame for the rape. A report for the Federal Commission on Crimes of Violence states that only 4% of reported rapes involved any precipitative behavior on the part of the victim. That includes how they dress.

CHARACTERISTICS OF THE RAPE

1. The majority of rapes do occur at night and on weekends, but there is also a high incidence of rape throughout the day and the rest of the week.
2. Rapes do occur in deserted areas such as parking lots and parks, but the majority of rapes occur in the victim's own home.
3. Rape is, by definition, a violent crime. Fortunately, however, few victims suffer severe injury or death.
4. Weapons such as guns and knives are used, but rapists more commonly use physical force and threats.

---

mon myths and accompanying facts are listed in Table 6-3 (p. 192) and are readily available in other publications/brochures (e.g., refer to Warshaw, 1988). You can develop a series of overhead transparencies or slides which list both the common myth and the fact related to rape stereotypes. Deal with this topic directly; just start listing the myths, followed by the facts. The audience may find some of these very hard to take. Softening them with humor or pointing out the seriousness of believing them is helpful. For instance, pointing out that a man would have no trouble controlling his passion if the woman's father walked in, gets the "Men can control their sexual arousal" fact across in a humorous way. Pointing out that not listening to "No" means that you could go to jail or cause someone else a great deal of pain points out the seriousness of believing the "No means Yes" myth.

Note that material in the two previous sections could be integrated into a single component of the presentation as well as be discussed sequentially. Experiment to see which format works better for you.

Providing Specific Information: Specific Formulas. The formulas that are outlined below do not cover every possible presentation request. They do, however, give a basic outline of the most frequently requested presentations. All of these formulas can and should be modified to meet the needs of different audiences.

TABLE 6-3: COMMON MYTHS AND FACTS ABOUT RAPE

1. *There is no such thing as rape.* This myth goes along with the "It's impossible to rape a woman" myth. It is incorrect. Rapists are generally stronger and meaner than victims. They also often have weapons. If a woman is in shock or fears for her life, she is not likely to put up an effective fight and be able to avoid rape.
2. *Women "cry rape."* Rape shares the same false report rate as other serious violent crimes such as assault and kidnaping.
3. *It is easy to prosecute.* Rape is not easy to prosecute. It is difficult to find the rapist, let alone convict him. The court proceedings are very difficult and the conviction rate is quite low.
4. *She says "No" but she means "Yes."* When a woman says "No," believe that it *means* "No." As the statistics from Table 6-1 (p. 185) point out, 75% of the men acted on the belief that when a woman said no she meant yes. At the very least this is poor communication, and at the worst it is rape.
5. *After sex starts, men cannot stop.* Physiologically, there is no reason for a man to not be able to stop his sexual behavior. There may be a certain degree of discomfort that accompanies coitus interruptus, but it is not lethal. Furthermore, if a woman's father walked in while she and her boyfriend were in the "act," there is not a question that he would be able to stop. Men just need to realize that they can stop as long as they want to.
6. *Women like a "real man."* This means that men think that women like a "take charge" kind of guy who is persistent and perhaps even rough. This is the 1990s. A few, a very few, women may like "real men" but the majority of women want to make their own decisions and have those decisions respected, especially their decisions about matters as intimate as sex.
7. *Prior sex? Then you cannot say "No."* Whether you have had sex with a person before or have dated her for 3 years or are even married to her, does not mean that you have an inalienable right to have sex with her when she does not want to.
8. *If a woman is too drunk to say "No," it is not rape.* It is legally rape if a woman is too drunk to give informed consent.
9. *Pain of rape ends with the assault.* The victim's suffering only begins with the act itself. She now has the rest of her life to live with the fact that someone could take away every bit of control she felt she had over her life.
10. *Women do stupid things and therefore ask to be raped.* A woman may dress suggestively, drink too much, walk in unsafe places, or even flirt with the wrong people, but her punishment for not using good judgment should never be rape.

Specific Formula 1: Rape Trauma

Step 1:   Ending the "Debunking the Myths - Part II" section of the general formula with the myth "The Pain of Rape Ends with the Assault" provides a nice transition to this topic.

Step 2:   Review the statistics and general information on how common it is for rape victims to suffer after an assault. Pointing out that sometimes victims don't tell anyone that they have been raped until 5 to 20 years after the fact effectively stresses the seriousness of the consequences of rape.

Step 3:   Outline the stages and characteristics of Rape Trauma Syndrome (see Petretic-Jackson & Tobin, this book).

Step 4:   Provide information on the recovery process and rate (see Petretic-Jackson & Tobin, this book).

Step 5:   Provide basic information on how to help the victim (see Table 6-4, p. 194).

Step 6:   End the presentation by providing the audience a list of community resources.

Specific Formula 2: Preventing Rape
in the Context of a Dating Situation

Step 1:   End the general formula with the "No means Yes" myth.

Step 2:   Stress the incidence and prevalence of date rape again. Do this by listing the most common age of victims and the specific statistics on date rape and rape in colleges.

Step 3:   Stress that, by definition, date rape is illegal.

Step 4:   Identify the things women can do to help prevent date rape from happening to them. Also stress to the audience that while they can take all of these precautions, it could still happen to them.

Step 5:   First, define their expectations. Ask them what it is that they want out of a date. Tell them to examine their expectations and then to decide on

TABLE 6-4: HOW TO HELP A VICTIM

1. Just do your best. That is all anyone can ask of you. Remember, she must trust you a great deal to have even told you that she was raped.
2. Just be there for the victim. Ask her what it is you can do for her.
3. Listen to the victim and support her. Do not discount her feelings or experience.
4. Don't blame her in any way. This includes asking her how much she drank, how long she had known the man she dated, and whether she went back to his apartment. If you cannot refrain from blaming the victim, don't be with her.
5. Don't rescue the victim. She has already had control taken out of her hands. Help her get control back by letting her make the decisions.
6. Help the victim make decisions by helping her to redefine problems, by giving her information, and by backing off so that she can think.
7. Help her to utilize other resources. This includes talking to other friends or family members and calling a rape crisis center.
8. Recognize your own limitations. You can only be there for her for so long. It is okay to take a break. Try to have other resources available to her when you cannot be there.
9. Don't get angry. It is all right to be angry, but don't blow up in front of the victim. She has seen enough aggression.
10. Don't swear vengeance on the man who did this to her. You may dream about killing the guy, but don't take any steps in that direction. You will just succeed in reducing the number of people who are around to help the victim and increase her self-blame. In other words, you will end up in jail, and she will blame herself for it.

their own limitations before they go out on a date. Once these limitations have been established, stick to them. This step includes the practice of sexually assertive communication and is presented in detail by Andrea Parrot in the next chapter. Use a "drinking" example to explain and demonstrate this process. For instance, people generally consider how much they are going to drink before they go out to a party. If they have to work the next day, they may plan to limit themselves to two drinks. The person who sets his or her limit in advance will have an easier time staying within it than the person who does not set a limit and gets "smashed." People who date should do the same thing: define their sexual limits before the date. These limits then need to be shared with the dating partner. Role-play assertive communication regarding limits with the audience. Again, for solid examples of this process see Chapter 7 of this book or refer to Parrot's previous work (Parrot, 1990).

Step 6: Second, they need to know their rights. Explain to them that they have the right to say "No" at any point. These are other dating rights: You have the right to change your mind about sex at any time; you have the right to talk about sex; you have the right to have your feelings and wishes respected; and you have the right to negotiate about anything.

Step 7: Stress the need to be assertive. Point out that although women in our society are taught to be passive, there is nothing wrong with being assertive. Give the definition of assertive behavior. Provide examples of passive, aggressive, and assertive behavior using both dating and nondating situations. Identify the benefits of assertive behavior and how to use assertive communication successfully (see Chapter 7). A group exercise on assertive behavior might be used.

Step 8: Stress the importance of communicating openly. People have no trouble discussing movie and food preferences, but they typically do not discuss intimacy preferences. Accede the difficulty in talking about sex, but note that it is necessary. The topic can be approached either subtly or more directly. There are benefits to both approaches (see Chapter 7).

Step 9: Review the list of general dating safety tips (see Table 6-5, p. 196). Be aware that the audience

TABLE 6-5: DATING SAFETY TIPS

1. Check your date out before you go out with him. You already
    check to see if men are attached; go ahead and find out if he has a
    reputation.
2. Notice your prospective date's verbal and nonverbal behavior. Does
    he always make the decisions, always say he knows best, or always
    interrupt you? Does he get in your personal body space, ignore
    your nonverbal cues, and just go right ahead with what he wants
    to do even though you have dissented? If so, beware. If he wants
    to take charge of everything and does not pay attention to what
    you want, he may not pay attention to you when you say "No."
3. Date in groups. It is safer and usually more fun for the first couple
    of dates. That way, when you run out of clever things to say such
    as "What is your major?" and "Isn't the weather nice?" you have
    other people around to help you out.
4. Date in public. It is far safer to go to the movies, a party, a sport-
    ing event, or out to eat than to go on a hike, canoeing, to his
    apartment, and so forth.
5. Take separate cars. This may seem paranoid, but a car is a dan-
    gerous place. If he is driving, you have to go where he wants to go.
    Besides, if he ends up being a "loser," you can just leave and go
    join your friends somewhere else.
6. Pay for your own date. This is the 1990s, after all. That way you
    don't have to play any "you owe me" games.
7. Give a friend your timetable and the name of the man you are
    going out with. (Be sure to know his last name.)

will be defensive and might feel that the presenter
is trying to make them "paranoid." Point out other
benefits in using these safety tips.

Specific Formula 3: General Rape Prevention

Step 1: End the general formula with the myth "Rape only
happens to young women who are walking alone
late at night." Over 75% of rapes are committed
by people you know, and over 60% happen in your
own home.

Step 2: Several aspects of prevention will need to be included. Divide the prevention information into six categories: (a) assertive behavior, (b) home prevention, (c) moving car prevention, (d) parked car prevention, (e) walking alone, and (f) passive and active resistance strategies (see Tables 6-5, p. 196; 6-6, pp. 198-199; 6-7, pp. 200-201; and 6-8, p. 201; and Appendices 6-A and 6-B, pp. 208-211). (Note - audience members must believe that it could happen to them in order to take the following precautions seriously.)

a. Stress the need to be assertive. Point out that women are taught to be passive, that women are told they should never be assertive because it looks aggressive, and that they should always be nice. Stress that believing these things is dangerous. Women need to be assertive and need to stop being nice to everyone.

b. List some basic home precautions. Mention that some local police departments will do security checks for local residents. See Table 6-6 (pp. 198-199) for home safety hints. Add to the list. The main point to get across is to "use common sense." Even the best home security system won't work unless it is turned on. The major safety tip to stress is to keep outside doors locked at all times and not to let anyone in unless a voice or visual identification check is done first.

c. The audience should know the local emergency numbers and where emergency service buildings are located. Point out the need to know the name, address, and phone number of people you visit so that if you need to call emergency services, you can tell them where to come. List basic safety tips. The major safety measure to mention is to keep car doors locked at all times,

TABLE 6-6: HOME SAFETY TIPS

HOME SECURITY

1. **Safe Doors:**

   For more information on how to reinforce your home, check with a local police department, security consultant, or hardware store.

   - Keep all of your doors locked at all times.
   - All outside doors (including doors from the garage into your home) should have solid core construction or be metal clad.
   - All of the door frames to outside doors should be solid and firmly attached to the house frame.
   - All outside doors should have internal hinges.
   - All outside doors should have deadbolt locks with 1-inch throws.
   - Do not use door chains as a precautionary measure. They are easily broken and only give you a false sense of security.
   - Install a wide-angle peephole to view visitors.
   - If you have a sliding glass door, make sure that the door that slides does not slide on an outside runner. If it does, reverse it.
   - Use a "charlie bar," swinging metal rod, or broomstick as a wedge in the bottom rack of the sliding door.
   - Have your locks re-keyed or a new lock added when you move into a new house or apartment.
   - If you live in an apartment that has a locked foyer door which requires a key or the visitor to be buzzed up, never prop the door open and always find out who you are buzzing up.

2. **Safe Windows:**
   - Keep your windows locked.
   - Double-hung windows are easy to break in. Drill a downward hole through the top of the bottom sash into, but not through, the top sash. Then insert a pin or nail.
   - Secure sliding windows in the same manner as sliding doors.
   - If your windows don't have good locks, you can get better locks or removable safety catches at a hardware store.
   - Place knick-knacks and other things on your window sills. You will be likely to hear someone coming through the window if there are items on the sill that can be knocked down.

3. *Outside Safety:*

- Keep all entrances well-lit. You can obtain heat- or motion-sensitive lights or timed lights at local hardware stores. There are also remote control light units that can be activated from your car.
- Don't have trees or shrubbery around doors and windows.
- Keep your front and back lights on, even when you are home.
- Keep your garage and garage to house doors locked.
- Be a good neighbor and watch for unusual activity. Get to know your neighbors so that they will do the same.
- Form or participate in the local Neighborhood Watch program.

BASIC TIPS

1. Know the numbers to your local emergency services.
2. Keep your doors locked at all times. Even if you expect your room-mate to be back any minute, lock the door.
3. Always ask before letting people into your home. Make sure they answer and that you know who they are before you let them in. It is quite appropriate to have a repair person show his credentials or to call the main office to make sure he is legitimate.
4. If someone asks to use your phone, don't let him in. Make the call for him.
5. If you live alone, only use your initials or last name on your mail-box and telephone listing.
6. If you come home and find a door or window open or if you think someone has broken into your home, don't go inside. Go to a telephone and call the police.

when you are in the car as well as when you are out. One safety tip that should be stressed because of its prevalence is the ruse of some-one flashing car lights to feign car trouble. The driver should not pull over to the side of the road just because someone flashes lights at her or points at her tire. Many women have been fooled by this. It is best to drive to the next exit and check it out at a service station.

    d. List the parked car safety tips (see Table 6-7, pp. 200-201).

    e. List the walking alone safety tips (see Table 6-8, p. 201).

TABLE 6-7: CAR SAFETY TIPS

<u>MOVING CAR SAFETY TIPS</u>

1. Keep the doors of your car locked at all times. Keep your purse under your seat and away from the passenger's window. Smash-and-grab crime is prevalent in cities. This is smashing your car window while you are at a stop and grabbing your purse.
2. Stay out of untraveled areas if possible.
3. Pick out safe spots on your daily travel routes. These include 24-hour stores or gas stations and police and fire stations. Go to one of these if you have trouble.
4. When you are driving and you feel someone is following you, take it seriously and drive to a police or fire station or other previously determined safe spot. Flash your lights and sound your horn to draw attention to yourself if necessary. Never drive to your home and don't get out of the car until they have stopped following you. Don't feel foolish; you have intuition for a reason. Use it.
5. Keep up the maintenance on your car so that you are less likely to break down.
6. When you have your car worked on, don't give the repair person all of your keys, just your car key.
7. If your car breaks down, open your hood and attach a white flag to your antenna. Then get back in your car and lock the doors. When someone stops, crack the window and ask them to call a garage or the police for you.
8. If someone else breaks down, be a good samaritan and call the police for him or her.
9. Don't hitchhike. If you have to, stay away from deserted areas, only go with women or older couples, ask the destination before getting in, observe the driver's behavior, and always sit next to the door.

<u>PARKED CAR SAFETY TIPS</u>

1. Park in well-lit, heavily traveled areas. Try to get a friend or coworker to escort you to your car. Where it is available, have a security guard or an escort (lots of campuses have recognized escort systems) walk you to your car.
2. Make a fuss at your worksite for better security in the parking lots. This includes better lighting, more secure parking lots (fenced

and guarded), allowing employees who work late to park near the doors, and having someone escort you to your car.

3. As you approach your car, check around and under the car and in the back seat before you get in.
4. Try not to be battened down with lots of unwieldy packages that would greatly decrease your ability to escape. Carry your keys so that you don't have to waste time finding the correct one.
5. Keep the doors and windows of your car locked at all times.

TABLE 6-8: SAFETY TIPS FOR WALKING ALONE

1. Stay in well-lit areas when possible and try to do recreational walking with a friend or during daylight hours.
2. If possible, wear clothing that allows you freedom of movement. Wearing lots of expensive-looking jewelry (even if it is only costume) may also attract a mugger. Finally, try to leave your hands free. Lots of unwieldy packages greatly decrease your freedom of movement.
3. Walk confidently and at a steady pace. Have the "don't mess with me" attitude. Rapists look for women who appear vulnerable.
4. Walk on the side of the street that faces oncoming traffic.
5. Walk close to the curb and away from alleyway entrances or doorways.
6. If you think you are being followed, walk to a well-lit, populated area. You may also want to walk down the middle of the street. If all else fails, you may want to turn and confront your follower. Ask him point blank what he wants. This may intimidate him.
7. If a car appears to be following you, walk in the opposite direction and go toward a well-lit and populated area.
8. Be careful when people in cars ask you directions. Stay well away from the car.
9. If you believe you are in danger, run, scream, and/or blow a whistle for help. It is better to look a little silly and be safe than to ignore your intuition and get hurt.
10. If you need to get help, try calling "Fire" or "Call 911" or "Help, someone call the police!" Unfortunately, just yelling or crying help may be ignored by passers-by who think you are just having a fight with your boyfriend or who are not sure there really is a problem.

f. Discuss passive and active resistance. The most important thing to stress to an audience is that whatever they decide to do in a situation, that is the best thing to do. They are in a life-threatening situation and only they can decide what to do. Tell them to keep their head, think, and do whatever they need to do in order to survive. (Victims should obtain help following an assault.) Remind them that no one else can tell them what they should have done . . . they were not there (see Appendix 6-A, pp. 208-209).

The best way to deal with this issue is to explain both the passive and active resistance views to the audience and let them make an informed decision. Repeat that whatever a person chooses to do at the time is the right thing. That does not mean that she should not fight; it just means that every aspect of the issue should be considered, now, when she can think calmly. Appendix 6-B (pp. 210-211) outlines some relevant points. There are also several good books and programs on the topic.

Specific Formula 4: What You Can Do for a Friend

Step 1: Introduce this topic after any of the general formula myths, and add it to any of the other specific formula talks, particularly the rape trauma and prevention talks.

Step 2: The most important point to get across to the audience is that they should in no way blame their friend for the rape. This may seem to be a "given," but it is often ignored. This means they should *not* ask questions that may imply victim blame. Examples include "What were you wearing?" "How well did you know him?" "How much did you drink?" Stress that it is better to say nothing than to blame the victim.

Step 3: Stress the importance of providing emotional support to the victim. Comment that it is not always easy to know what to do. Audiences are often concerned that they will not say the "right" thing. Just being there and listening is usually enough. Tell the audience that if they are not sure what to do for the victim to simply ask the victim what they can do.

Step 4: Stress that although it is important to support the victim, no one should attempt to "rescue" her. This means that no one should make her decisions for her, and no one should insist that she do anything. Point out that the victim has just had every bit of control that she ever thought she had over her life taken away. Do not continue this pattern. Identify things the members of the audience might do or say to help her regain control and facilitate her informed decision making.

Step 5: Stress to the audience that they should not insist that the victim do anything. It is fine to give the victim information regarding a local rape crisis center, regarding the hospital or a doctor's office, or on reporting the crime. They can even say that they think she should do one of the preceding, but what they have to make sure to say and mean is that it is her decision. Stress the bottom line, which is that the victim is an adult and that no one should make her do something that she does not want to do. The victim has already had one person make her do something against her will; she does not need a friend to continue this victimization. Forcing the victim to do something will probably only result in further upsetting her and turning her away from you.

Step 6: Stress, especially to a male audience, that they should not get angry in front of the victim. Point out that getting angry in front of the victim and threatening or actually doing something to the rapist is the last thing the victim needs. First, being an angry male in front of a woman who has just been violently victimized does nothing to help calm her down. Second, the angry man is just taking care of his own feelings; he is not doing anything for the victim. Third, not only is his tantrum not helping the victim, it is hurting her. She now feels even worse because she has upset him, or she feels that she has to put her own trauma aside to take care of this man who cannot get it under control. The victim needs to be taking care of herself. The male friend needs to be taking care of her, or he needs to be somewhere else. Finally, if he harms the rapist he will probably end up in jail, and with a conviction much faster than the rapist. Then who is going to take care of the victim? Now how does he feel? How does the victim feel? Even worse.

Step 7: Finally, the audience needs to recognize their own limitations. A friend can be supportive, nonjudgmental, nonthreatening, and wonderful; but a friend has limitations. Friends can only do so much and can only be there for so long before they need a break. This is normal. Even professional therapists need and take breaks. The victim needs to know that you still care but that you need some time. Help the victim find other support so that you can take that time. You will do her and yourself a disservice if you do not recognize your limitations.

Specific Formula 5: A Prevention Program Designed for Athletes. One population that has only recently been dealt with regarding rape and assault is college student-athletes. The following formula was designed specifically for college and university athletic departments. It has been used for the past 6 years, with generally good success with a variety of NCAA Division I and II athletic departments. Prior to presenting any program within an athletic department, it is critically important to have the support of the athletic director and coaches (Jackson, 1992, 1994).

Step 1: Present the general incidence, prevalence, attitudes, and rape myth components of the previous general rape prevention program.

Step 2: Present the student-athletes with information regarding their special place in society. It is pointed out that athletes are viewed as public figures. With or without their consent, athletes are viewed as role models and held to strict standards with regard to their public and private behavior.

Step 3: Following the presentation of their special roles, the athletes are told that their public figure status, while providing additional privileges, also requires additional responsibilities. These include volunteer activities, appropriate manners and social skills in public, and the general obligation of "giving back" to the community that holds them in such high esteem.

Step 4: Next, data are presented dealing with athletes' perpetration and victimization rates involving sexual crimes (Jackson, 1991). Although these data indicate perpetration rates for male student-athletes in general that are not significantly different from nonathlete students, there are significant differences among the different sports represented in an athletic department. Specifically, the revenue-generating team sports of football and basketball, especially in highly ranked NCAA Division I schools seem to have the potential for greater allegations regarding sexual assault perpetration. These differences are detailed and discussion takes place. Interestingly, victimization rates for female student-athletes are significantly less than for nonathlete females. Discussion regarding this finding tends to sensitize male athletes to power imbalances in their relationships. The bottom line for athletes, be they student or professional, is that they *must* learn to distinguish appropriate on-field and off-field behaviors. The domination, aggression, and win-at-all-costs mentality, which is not only appropriate but a critical component of winning on-field behavior, must be separated from respectful, sensitive, communication-oriented behavior that is needed off-field.

Step 5: The final athlete-specific topic involves the cost of rape to the perpetrator and his associates. Although this topic is presented in more generic prevention programs, it takes on a somewhat more relevant air as history indicates that an entire athletic department can be implicated and held responsible for the actions of a single individual. During this step, examples are given of past transgressions by athletes at various universities and the resulting impact on that athletic department. It is also stressed here that serious negative consequences occur to athletes and departments regardless of whether criminal charges are filed. When athletes complain regarding the perceived injustice of this, the fallacy of the "just world hypothesis" is presented. It is typically stated that the higher the rank in the NCAA, the harder the fall in the media.

Step 6: Information is next presented involving disturbing experiences suggesting that male athletes may actually be more vulnerable than nonathlete males to perpetration as well as victimization. This increased vulnerability may stem from athletes' single-mindedness regarding winning and competition. This extreme focus on one aspect of life may exclude other, broader, life experiences that serve to mature an individual. Secondly, many athletes have coaches as their only male role models. Coaches tend to stress discipline and a general repression of emotions and feelings. This focus may also serve to constrict the athletes' interpersonal repertoire and make them more vulnerable to potential warm "father figures" who may or may not have their best interests at heart. A constricted interpersonal repertoire also likely means relative insensitivity to the subtleties and complexities of heterosocial interactions. Stated simply, athletes may simply miss cues that would warn more sensitive individuals that they are (a) about to be taken advantage of, or (b) about to cross a boundary and take advantage of someone else.

Step 7: Safe dating skills, sexually assertive communication, and relationship rights are then presented. With an athlete sample, role-playing "appropriate" language and behavior with regard to off-the-field interpersonal interactions is especially important.

PROGRAM EVALUATION

Having each audience member or the coordinator fill out an evaluation form after the presentation is extremely helpful to the speaker. These allow the speaker to improve his or her presentation and find out what topics needed to be covered better. Evaluation forms can be simple or more complex. The evaluation should ask for overall rating, specific evaluation of content (amount, level, comprehensiveness), specific presenter characteristics (sensitivity, knowledge base, interaction style), and a rating of how helpful the presentation components were. Only through feedback can the presenter or therapist refine the presentation and increase its utility.

SUMMARY

We feel that these types of presentations, whether they are presented to groups or individuals, can be extraordinarily powerful and useful. Care must be taken, however, to ensure presenter sensitivity and appropriateness of content. With the other chapters in this volume serving as reference material, the authors feel strongly that the goals of rape education and prevention programs can be accomplished in many communities.

APPENDIX 6-A:
PASSIVE OR
ACTIVE RESISTANCE?

There are basically two views on how to react if someone is trying to rape you. Should a victim use passive or active resistance? Passive resistance means not yelling or fighting back physically but keeping your head and trying to calm the attacker or talk your way out of the situation. Active resistance means screaming, fighting, and using whatever is at hand to get away from the rapist.

Those who stand on the active resistance side of the issue cite data from the 1960s suggesting that of the women who reported an attempted rape, only one-fourth of those were completed if the victim used active resistance. In order to make women better active resisters, the carrying of weapons (mace, guns, keys, etc.) and the participation in self-defense classes are recommended. Even if a self-defense class is not taken, lectures that stress the active resistance approach give demonstrations on how to use kidney punches, eye gouges, testicle grabs, and instep stomps. What this approach stresses the most, however, is that women stop being passive and take an active role in their own defenses.

Those who stand on the passive resistance side of the issue point out that the studies so often cited to support active resistance have methodological flaws. Do these studies accurately poll those women who fought back and were raped anyway? The passive resistance approach also points out the dangers involved in active resistance. Basically, active resistance is fine as long as you are fully aware of all the possible consequences of your behavior. These consequences include increasing the violence of the assault and having your weapons used against you. Remember that you have to live with what you start. If you scream, the rapist may just want to shut you up. Also remember that if you escalate the violence, you now have an even more violent and belligerent assailant than you did before. If you fight, you may just anger the rapist and increase the aggression. If you pull out a weapon - mace, a gun, a knife, a club, keys - be sure that you are willing to use them to inflict severe damage or even death, be sure that you know how to use them well enough to do that, and be aware that if they are taken away from you, they will probably be used on you. It is always your call, but remember that men are almost always stronger than you and that unless you are very willing and well-trained you may do nothing more than anger him. Finally, the passive resistance proponents point out that if too much stress is put on fighting, all of those victims who did not fight, or feel that they should have fought more, just have that much more guilt to deal with.

Passive resistance proponents stress the need for the victim to stay calm and to think. This may include persuading the rapist to leave you alone because you are on your period, you have AIDS, or you are a religious. Some women have gotten away from their attackers by pretending to be insane, or mentally retarded. Going along with your attacker but asking him to get you cigarettes or something to drink at a local store may give you the chance to get away.

The best way to deal with the active versus passive resistance issue is to explain both positions to the audience and let them make an informed decision. As already mentioned, whatever a person chooses to do is the right thing. That does not mean that they should not fight; it just means that every aspect of the issue should be considered, now, when you can think calmly. Appendix 6-B (pp. 210-211) outlines some of the finer points. There are also several good books and programs on the topic.

APPENDIX 6-B:
PASSIVE AND
ACTIVE RESISTANCE TIPS

PASSIVE RESISTANCE

1. Remember, it can happen to you.
2. The largest part of passive resistance is thought and preparation so that you don't get into a dangerous situation.
3. Be vigilant. Realize that one of your best defenses is to be aware of your surroundings and to pinpoint possible danger spots.
4. Think about what you would or could do if caught in a threatening situation. Set up likely scenarios and come up with a variety of solutions. Practice the solutions so that they will come naturally if you ever have to use them.
5. If you do get in a threatening situation, stay as calm as possible and think. As long as you can keep thinking, you may find a way out of the situation.
6. If you do get in a threatening situation, try to keep your options open.

ACTIVE RESISTANCE

1. Never fight unless your life depends on it because it is extremely dangerous.
2. Be willing to use physical resistance. This means being truly willing to strike out at someone as hard as you can. It is better to not even attempt to fight if you are not willing to fight to the best of your ability. In other words, if you only halfheartedly fight, you will simply succeed in making your attacker angrier.
3. Overcome your natural resistance to being aggressive. Most women in our society are taught to be passive observers. You will need to get over this inclination and become an active and aggressive actor. Don't be afraid that you will hurt your attacker; be afraid that you won't hurt him badly enough.

4. Be willing to strike first and strike to incapacitate. Remember that many rapists are under the influence of sensation inhibitors such as alcohol, drugs, and adrenalin. This will mean that they are less sensitive to pain.

5. Take preliminary precautions. These could include carrying mace or a weapon or taking a self-defense class. If you use basic self-defense techniques, remember that the goal of these techniques is to debilitate your attacker long enough for you to escape.

6. The thing to keep in mind for all of these tactics is that once you start fighting, the rapist may just fight harder and hurt you more than he otherwise would have.

REFERENCES

Hanson, K. A., & Gidycz, C. A. (1993). Evaluation of a sexual assault prevention program. *Journal of Consulting and Clinical Psychology, 61,* 1046-1052.

Holcomb, D. R., Sarvela, P. D., Sondag, K. A., & Hatton Holcomb, L. C. (1993). An evaluation of a mixed-gender date rape prevention workshop. *College Health, 41,* 159-164.

Jackson, T. L. (1990). An acquaintance rape education program. In L. G. Ritt & P. A. Keller (Eds.), *Innovations in Clinical Practice: A Source Book* (Vol. 9, pp. 325-339). Sarasota, FL: Professional Resource Exchange.

Jackson, T. L. (1991). A university athletic department's rape and assault experiences. *Journal of College Student Development, 32,* 77-78.

Jackson, T. L. (1992, October). *Rape Education and Prevention Programs for Athletic Departments.* International Conference on Sexual Assault on Campus, Orlando, FL.

Jackson, T. L. (1994, July). *Sexual Responsibility: Assault Prevention and Safe Dating.* NCAA Life Skills Program, Kansas City, MO.

Jackson, T. L., Petretic-Jackson, P. A., Ostrowski, M., & Keller, J. (1989, August). *Acquaintance Rape Attitude and Information Change Through Education and Empathy.* Paper presented at the American Psychological Association Convention, New Orleans, LA.

Jackson, T. L., Quevillon, R. P., & Petretic-Jackson, P. A. (1985). Assessment and treatment of sexual assault victims. In P. A. Keller & L. G. Ritt (Eds.), *Innovations in Clinical Practice: A Source Book* (Vol. 4, pp. 51-79). Sarasota, FL: Professional Resource Exchange.

Koss, M. P. (1985). The hidden rape victim: Personality, attitudinal and situational characteristics. *Psychology of Women Quarterly, 9,* 193-212.

Parrot, A. (1990). *Acquaintance Rape and Sexual Assault Prevention Training Manual.* Ithaca, NY: Cornell University.

Petretic-Jackson, P. A., & Jackson, T. L. (1990). Crisis intervention with sexual assault victims. In A. R. Roberts (Ed.), *Crisis Intervention: Techniques and Issues* (pp. 124-152). Pacific Grove, CA: Wadsworth Publishing.

Sandberg, G., Jackson, T. L., & Petretic-Jackson, P. A. (1987). College students' attitudes regarding sexual coercion and aggression: Developing educational and preventive strategies. *American Journal of College Student Personnel, 28,* 302-311.

Warshaw, R. (1988). *I Never Called It Rape.* New York: Harper & Row.

7

Sexually Assertive Communication Training

Andrea Parrot

Lack of assertiveness in sexual situations may contribute to sexual assault. Because women have not historically been taught assertiveness skills, women have most often been victims* of sexual assaults, and males usually have been the assailants.**

---

*The term victim will be used to indicate someone who has been forced to have sexual experiences against his or her will or without his or her consent. Some professionals working with sexual assault victims prefer to use the term "survivor." However, although victims may have survived physically, the victimization experience is likely to interrupt their psychological state and interfere with interpersonal relationships. Therefore, they are still being emotionally victimized by the sexual assault. Until victims are able to place the blame for their victimization with the assailants (where it belongs) and put the assault in perspective in their lives, they are still being victimized by the assault. Because many victims of sexual assault do not seek help, and because all victims experience some level of trauma after the assault, the term "victim," rather than "survivor," will be used.

**Not all acquaintance rape victims are female. The Federal Bureau of Investigation estimates that 10% of sexual assault victims are male. However, because most victims are female, the pronoun "she" will be used in this chapter to refer to victims.

This is due, in part, to the socialization practices employed when raising children in this culture. Males have traditionally been socialized to be aggressive, and females have traditionally been socialized to be passive, but generally neither sex has been socialized to be assertive. Sexual assaults do not only occur in heterosexual relationships, but because sexual assault is less frequent in homosexual relationships, the examples presented will be heterosexual. This chapter will focus on the relationship between assertiveness and sexual assault, reasons for lack of assertiveness, and ways in which therapists may help clients improve their assertiveness skills.

INTRODUCTION

In her *Assertion Skills for Young Women* training manual, McCarthy (1981) defines assertion, aggression, submission, and passivity.

Assertion is asking for what you want, stating your opinion, expressing your feelings in direct and honest ways that show respect for yourself and the people you're communicating with. Assertion is a way of standing up for your rights, yet not violating the rights of others.

Aggression is standing up for your rights, but expressing yourself in a way that violates the rights of others or shows them no respect. It may include sarcasm, humiliation, insults or overpowering the other person in order to win or dominate.

Submission is giving in to the other people's requests, demands or feelings, without regard to what you want or how you feel. Submission is based in the belief that other people's feelings, desires and opinions are more important and more correct than yours, or that you'll be punished if you express your own feelings and ideas. (The fear of punishment is often valid.) Submissiveness is often expressed by silence.

Passivity is letting people and events take their course, without attempting to control or modify their effect on you. Often this is done by not even *noticing* their effect. Often, the effect is that you're placed in a submissive position. (pp. 2-3)

Consider the situation of a nonsmoker on an elevator when a smoker gets on with a lit cigarette. A *passive* response would be for the nonsmoker to say nothing, to hold his or her breath, or to get off. A *submissive* response would be to say "I guess it's okay if you smoke since it is only for a few floors." An *aggressive* response would be for the nonsmoker to push the smoker out of the elevator, to grab the cigarette out of his or her mouth, or to yell at the smoker. An *assertive* response would be for the nonsmoker to say "When you smoke on the elevator, I feel frustrated because I am having trouble breathing, and I would like you to not smoke on the elevator."

In the passive and submissive responses the nonsmoker gave up his or her rights. In the aggressive example, the smoker's rights were being violated. However, in the assertive response, if the smoker put the cigarette out at the request of the nonsmoker, neither of them was forced to do anything.

Adults who are not assertive have usually not been taught assertiveness skills as children. Children need to be taught these skills, and they must know that they have a right to their own bodies and needs. One way that parents can teach these skills is to allow children to reject undesired social situations. For example, if Aunt Marge wants to kiss little Melanie, but Melanie does not want to kiss Aunt Marge, she should not be forced. By forcing her, the parents are teaching Melanie to ignore her instinctual feeling of discomfort and to allow her body to be touched in a way that makes her uncomfortable. She learns that she does not have the right to control her own body (Parrot, 1991).

All people are endowed with sexual rights. If people are aware of these rights, they may be more likely to assert for them; however, many people are both unaware of their sexual rights and lack the assertive skills to insist on those rights. Fifteen of those rights identified by Powell (1991) follow:

A person has the right to

- refuse any type of sexual contact any time or place, regardless of how aroused the partner may be
- express frustration and disappointment if sexual behavior is refused
- request any type of sexual activity in a sexual relationship, as long as it does not violate anyone else's rights
- any sexual feeling, fantasy, or thought
- expect his or her partner to share expenses which result from their sexual involvement
- know if a potential sexual partner has a contagious disease of any kind, or could possibly have been exposed to one
- know if a sexual partner is using a contraceptive or other protective device
- be free from becoming the object of unwanted sexual remarks or unwanted sexual gestures
- be free from physical contact of any kind unless he or she clearly indicates a desire for it
- be free from any sexual advances, suggestions, or pressures in a relationship with a helping professional
- work at his or her place of employment free from sexual communication or solicitation of sexual contact of any nature when submission to or rejection of such contact is intended to impose favorable or adverse working conditions
- wear clothing of choice, providing it is within the law
- (as a child) know what will happen to his or her body at puberty, and the implications of these changes
- be protected from any contact or experience with an adult which is for the purpose of that adult's sexual arousal or satisfaction; this is especially true for children
- know of the intentions of a partner before having sexual intercourse

Some of these rights are guaranteed by criminal and civil law. All of them are based on ethical and moral interactions with others. We often hear of cases of sexual assault or sexual harassment resulting because victims do not feel they have the skills or power to assert for their rights. In the case of University of Oklahoma Law Professor Anita Hill, she alleged that she was the victim of sexual harassment at the hands of now Supreme Court Justice Clarence Thomas, but did not feel that she could speak out against him at the time the harassment took place. Professor Hill was an attorney at the time, working for an agency which was established to eliminate sexual harassment, and still she did not feel that she could insist the harassment stop. Most victims of sexual assault and harassment lack the knowledge, training, and power which Professor Hill possessed when she was allegedly experiencing sexual harassment. Therefore, it is not surprising that most people find it very difficult to assert for their rights in a sexual situation.

ASSERTIVENESS AND ACQUAINTANCE RAPE

Sexual aggression among acquaintances is a result of violation of sexual rights, an abuse of power and control, and male's feelings of sexual entitlement (Rozee, Bateman, & Gilmore, 1991). American dating customs legitimize the use of force, power, and control by males when making sexual advances toward females (Burt, 1980; Check & Malamuth, 1983; Lewin, 1985). This situation is exacerbated by the female's subordinate position in our society, as well as males feeling that their needs are more important (Lewin, 1985). Traditional attitudes enhance this power differential (Farrell, 1986; Koss et al., 1985; Koss et al., 1994; Russell, 1984).

American culture devalues females, values males, and produces aggressive males (Jackson, 1994; Lott, 1987). Rozee et al. (1991) believe that this ideology is reflected in media portrayals of objectification of women, women as sexual victims, and the sexualizing of violence against women. This produces sexually coercive adolescent males (Kanin, 1967; Koss, 1985; Malamuth, 1981). Socialization, child-rearing practices, and media messages inform successive generations of males that aggressive, sexually coercive behavior is acceptable and even desirable (Rozee et al., 1991). This can be exacerbated in cases involving hypermasculine males, such as athletes (Jackson, 1994; Parrot, Cummings, & Jackson, 1994). Often the result is sexual assault.

The greatest risk women face as potential victims of sexual assault is the risk of acquaintance rape. Therefore, women should understand the patterns in acquaintance rape to be better able to alter a situation and avoid becoming a victim. Bateman (1982) reported a general pattern in acquaintance rapist's behavior. First, the man will invade the woman's personal space in a public area, like a bar or at a party. If the victim does not object, clearly and consistently, the rapist desensitizes the victim to the intrusive behavior by continuing the behavior and acting as if it is acceptable. The victim may feel uncomfortable but may not feel that she is in danger because other people are present; therefore, she does not give the rapist a clear message to stop the behavior. In the third stage the rapist moves the victim to an isolated place where the rape occurs.

One of the more dysfunctional and dangerous behaviors females are socialized to exhibit in this culture which may contribute to confusion in a relationship is token resistance. Token resistance is when the woman says "No" when she means "Maybe" or "Yes" (Muehlenhard & Hollabaugh, 1988). Many men believe that women never really mean "No" in a sexual situation. Therefore, those men feel entitled to continue pushing the woman to have sex. Although some women do engage in token resistance, many do not. But because men (especially if they are under the influence of alcohol) are often not able to distinguish between the two types of messages, their socialization encourages them to treat every woman as if she does engage in token resistance. Therefore, women should say what they mean and mean what they say in a sexual situation, and men should respect women's wishes. But clearly stating her wishes may not protect a woman from sexual assault. In some situations where acquaintance rape occurs, many women are assertive and do emphatically state their wishes, but they are not taken seriously (Kanin, 1984). Date rapists frequently ignore women's protests (Rapaport & Burkhart, 1984).

The lack of assertiveness may contribute to sexual assault involvement for both victims and perpetrators. It is unusual that assertiveness is ever taught to victims or assailants. Females are traditionally taught to be passive, while males are socialized to be aggressive (Tavris & Wade, 1984). It is very difficult for a victim who has been socialized to be passive to make her wishes clearly known if they are in conflict with her partner's. Male assailants may not know how to ask (especially in a date situation) for what they want sexually and may, therefore, use force or become aggressive if they become frustrated when they do not get what they want (Parrot, 1991).

SOCIALIZATION

Women have traditionally been socialized to think that sex should be saved for those they love, that if they "give in" too early they are "sluts," that they must say "No" even if they want to have sex with their partners to protect their reputations, and that sex should be a reward to a male partner in return for protection and love. Females are also socialized to please others and not embarrass themselves or others, which may cause them to ignore instincts that indicate a situation is dangerous (Lewin, 1985). For example, if a woman is in a situation in which she is feeling uncomfortable with her partner because he is drinking too much at a party and showing off for his friends, she is likely to minimize her negative feelings and give him the benefit of the doubt. She may think to herself "I've known him for years, and he is my brother's best friend; he surely wouldn't do anything to hurt me." By minimizing her fears, she is putting herself at risk. Women need to identify instinctual or "gut level" reactions and feelings and act on them appropriately.

Women have had a good deal of experience with intrusions into privacy and personal space and have developed a number of ways of dealing with those intrusions (Rozee et al., 1991), but not all of these methods are effective. Examples of such intrusions may include unwanted conversations, uncomfortable touching during conversations, crowding, and the use of overly familiar names and caricatures. Women may view these intrusions as harmless and may therefore not take them seriously. However, these intrusions may desensitize women to more serious intrusions that could be dangerous. The response patterns and defense mechanisms that women have developed to deal with these intrusions tend to be subtle and indirect (Bateman, 1982), such as stiffening the body or not returning an unwanted hug. However, if these responses are ambiguous, they do not provide the male with a clear indication of the woman's wishes.

Female behavior, however, is not a major contributor to the problem. The victim, by definition, is blameless. This chapter provides discussion regarding behaviors that are associated with the crime of acquaintance rape from both the perpetrator's as well as the victim's perspective. Male behavior that objectifies women is a major contributor leading to acquaintance rape. Farrell (1986) has identified three male sexual defenses against feelings of having been rejected by females:

1. Men often turn women into sex objects. It hurts less to be rejected by an object than a real person.
2. Men often suppress sexual feelings and replace them with dishonesty - politics works better than honesty.
3. Men often practice railroad sex; that is, they do not stop at friendship.

The longer the period of friendship, the longer the period of potential rejection. One of the difficulties in attempting to find the danger signals in everyday male behavior is that socially approved, even lauded, male behavior may contain many of the

elements common to sexual assault, such as "scoring" with females or telling sexist jokes (Rozee et al., 1991). Women who
are looking for danger signals may not see them as dangerous
because they are such an integral part of the American culture.
It is important for women to be able to recognize this behavior
and avoid the men who exhibit it. But the responsibility should
really be on men to stop objectifying women.

INABILITY TO USE HER BODY

If a woman is feeling threatened and has tried to get out of
a dangerous situation by acting assertively and asking for what
she wants, and the situation becomes more dangerous, she may
need to use physical self-defense. Unfortunately, most women
do not have the physical training to execute effectively a physical self-defense maneuver. In addition, because many girls do
not have the experiences early in life to understand that they
will probably not be seriously harmed if they are hit or knocked
down, they are often reluctant to physically defend themselves
because they are afraid of the consequences of physical reprisal.
If young girls were encouraged to play a contact sport such as
soccer or football, they might gain the valuable knowledge that
they are not *extremely* fragile, that they can be knocked down
without permanent damage, and that their bodies can be used
to effectively defend themselves. Therefore, parents may be
helping their daughters by encouraging them to play physical
sports to learn the limitations and strengths of their bodies.
These daughters may then be more willing to use their physical
strength and bodies to defend themselves in a potential rape
situation. This notion was supported by Jackson (1991), who
found that a sample of female student-athletes reported significantly less sexual victimization than their nonathlete student
peers.

A related issue regarding a woman's inability to use her
body involves the degree of familiarity she has with the assailant. In the event of a rape attempt, women are less likely to
defend themselves when the assailant is an acquaintance rather

than a stranger (Quinsey & Upfold, 1985). This may be due to a number of factors, including not wanting to hurt the man's feelings, fear of reprisal, fear of embarrassment, disbelief that someone she knows would attack her, or guilt for having gone with him in the first place (Rozee et al., 1991). Each of these reactions can keep a woman from effectively defending herself against an acquaintance rapist.

Gordon and Riger (1989) compared the rate of completed rapes to attempted rapes according to police reports (1:4), victimization studies (4:1), and media reports (1:13). Although attempted rapes are more likely to happen, the police and media are more likely to hear of and report on completed rapes. Therefore, women are likely to believe that most rapes are completed and that a woman's chances of fighting off a rapist are slim. This misinformation is likely to keep women from attempting to assert their rights or from fighting back in a rape situation. In a study of women who had been accosted by strangers and were able to avoid rape, avoiders usually employed more than one avoidance strategy or self-defense technique (Bart & O'Brien, 1985). Successful avoidance strategies included fleeing, screaming or yelling, using physical force (from pushing to self-defense techniques), employing "affective verbal" techniques (such as begging and pleading), and experiencing environmental intervention (such as someone else calling the police). The most effective combination was physical force and yelling (Bart & O'Brien, 1985). In general, the most effective avoidance techniques were those which are in direct conflict with traditional female socialization. Women are most likely to be willing to employ self-defense techniques when they are in danger if they have good self-esteem and a strong sense of self. It may be best for victims to employ assertiveness techniques first, before they attempt physical self-defense, because once a situation has escalated to violence it is difficult to decelerate it. However, even if a woman does not employ any of these prevention strategies and the result is rape, it is never the fault of the victim. The person who commits a crime is responsible for the crime, not the victim.

LOW SELF-ESTEEM
AND PEER PRESSURE

Low self-esteem is likely to contribute to victimization. People tend to behave according to how they view themselves and their sense of self-esteem (Clark, Clemes, & Bean, 1983). Negative self-evaluation leads to negative self-image, which, in turn, leads to behavior consistent with the self-evaluation. For example, if a young woman has given in to peer pressure to drink alcohol, she is likely to say "I have given in again to peer pressure" (negative self-evaluation). Therefore, she may feel that she cannot ever stand up for what she wants because she is weak willed (negative self-image). The next time she faces peer pressure, she may give in and drink when she does not want to (behavior).

Women who do not feel good about themselves may not feel that they have a right to defend themselves, especially if it means hurting someone else. They may spend time with people who treat them poorly, especially if they think that is the way they deserve to be treated (Parrot, 1984). If a popular person treats a potential victim poorly, the victim may stay with that person hoping to improve her social status through association with the popular person. People with low self-esteem, as compared to those with high self-esteem, are more likely to be influenced by peer pressure. Potential victims may go along to an unsafe environment because they are being pressured by the peer group. Potential assailants may become involved in situations like gang rape as a result of friends' pressure to be "one of the boys."

The four conditions necessary for high self-esteem are connectiveness, uniqueness, power, and models (Clark et al., 1983). *Connectiveness* is the feeling resulting from satisfaction from associations that are significant to her, and those associations are affirmed by others. *Uniqueness* is the special sense of self resulting from acknowledgement and respect for the attributes that make her special and different and when she receives respect and approval from others for those qualities. *Power* is a sense that comes from having the resources, opportunity, and capability to influence the circumstances of her life in important ways. Finally, *models* are reference points that provide human, philosophical, and operational examples that help her establish meaningful goals, values, ideals, and personal standards. These elements are necessary in a woman's life if she is to be willing to employ assertiveness techniques. In other words, she has to feel worthy of standing up for her own rights.

ASSERTIVE SKILLS POTENTIAL VICTIMS NEED TO KNOW

Teaching assertive skills may help prevent sexual assault involvement if the potential victim feels she can stand up for her rights. However, if she suffers from low self-esteem, she may not be willing to assert for her needs even if she knows how. Therefore, before teaching assertiveness skills, the therapist must make sure the potential victim feels good enough about herself to use these skills.

Women need to learn how to become less vulnerable so that they can avoid situations which may result in date rape. They must learn to assess potentially dangerous situations and exercise assertive behavior to get out of them or avoid them completely. For example, a woman may use her voice as a weapon by yelling, "Stop it! What you are doing is rape!" when threatened. She may also defend herself verbally in an assertive way against a date who tries to exploit her (Parrot, 1990b).

The assertive formula which all young people should be taught is "When you do 'x,' I feel 'y,' and I want you to do 'z.'" An application of this formula is "When you kiss me after I have said stop, I feel ignored and frustrated, and I want you to stop when I ask you to." In this example, the speaker is rejecting the behavior, not the person. She has not said "You are so damned inconsiderate," which would be verbally attacking the person rather than his behavior. The speaker is clearly tying her desires to her feelings. She is being behaviorally specific. When making an assertive request it is important to state it in a strong, firm voice without whining or begging. The request should sound as if the woman making the request has a right to it and knows that she has that right.

Women also need to learn that they have a right to defend themselves. This means not only standing up for their rights in an assertive way, but also using physical self-defense techniques if the assertive requests have been ignored.

ASSERTIVE SKILLS POTENTIAL ASSAILANTS NEED TO KNOW

Potential male assailants also need to change their behaviors to keep acquaintance rape from occurring. When working with males, the experiential, rather than the didactic, approach has been much more successful in changing male attitudes (Lee, 1987). Men's first incentive to change comes with redefining power; it comes from understanding the experience of powerlessness (while not denying the female her experience of powerlessness; Farrell, 1986). Therefore, male education about male privilege, aggressiveness, and assertiveness should allow men to attempt to feel how women feel in this culture. Appendix 7-A (pp. 230-232) addresses this issue. Males need to learn how to ask for what they want by taking both people's needs into account, his and his partner's. They must realize that having "notches" on their belts does not make them good lovers and that men do not always have to be ready and willing for sex.

However, males are socialized to think about and want sex often. Men between the ages of 12 and 40 think of sex on an average of six times per hour, and those between the ages of 12 and 19 think of sex 20 times per hour, or every 5 minutes (Shanor, 1978). Men fear being rejected by women, especially beautiful women (Farrell, 1986). It is that fear that contributes to adversarial relationships between men and women. If sex becomes less important to men, acquaintance rape will probably be less frequent. Therefore, parents, educators, and therapists must work to deemphasize the importance and mystique of sex and to encourage men and women to get to know each other as people, not sex objects.

WHAT THE
PRACTITIONER CAN DO

In a therapeutic setting it is important for practitioners to model assertive behavior. In addition, therapists should teach assertiveness skills to the client. Several assertiveness training activities from the *Acquaintance Rape and Sexual Assault Prevention Training Manual* (Parrot, 1990a) are provided in the Appendices at the end of this chapter to aid therapists and educators in this goal (see pp. 230-239). However, until the client feels good about herself and has good self-esteem, she will not be able to employ assertiveness behaviors because she will not feel that she has a right to put her needs before those of others.

Practitioners can provide assertiveness skills and training to clients in both individual and group settings. Discussion of how the therapist may provide this information in the individual therapeutic setting has already been discussed. Appendix 7-B (pp. 233-234) provides a model for assertiveness training in a group setting, and the preceding chapter on acquaintance rape education programs incorporates many of these concepts and suggestions. It would be best to provide this training prophylactically, rather than remedially, so that the client may be able to avoid an acquaintance rape, rather than learning them after she has already been raped.

There are a number of advantages to providing assertiveness training on a one-to-one basis. Role-playing on a one-to-one basis in a counseling situation may be appropriate. Appendices 7-C and 7-D (pp. 235-236 and 237-239) offer suggestions for this approach. This type of role-play is less frightening than performing it in front of a group, and the client will not feel "on stage." Individual counseling also allows for as much repetitive practice as necessary without the client feeling embarrassed for taking up too much group time or feeling "dumb" for having to rehearse many times (McCarthy, 1981).

McCarthy (1981) believes that groups are the preferred method of teaching assertiveness skills. This mode allows for participants to realize that there are many others who have the same needs and problems. A heterogenous group allows participants to learn from each other. In addition, feedback from more than one person allows for greater reinforcement of ideas.

CONCLUSION

These skills should be made available both to potential victims and to assailants. Potential victims may most appropriately employ assertiveness instead of passivity when attempting to make their wishes known and honored. Potential assailants may only know how to be aggressive regarding their wishes and may therefore be able to keep a situation from turning into a rape by exercising assertiveness rather than aggression.

Although many of the suggestions in this chapter focus on how women can change their behavior to be more assertive, we must not lose sight of the fact that men are generally responsible for committing sexual assaults. So, no matter how women change their behavior, they will not stop sexual assault, but they may prevent themselves from becoming victims. However, men prone to sexual assault are likely to simply seek out other nonassertive women as victims. Therefore, our societal efforts should be focused more heavily on resocializing men to stop committing sexual assault. Even if women do use assertive behaviors, they may be ignored, and a sexual assault may result.

Therapists also need to inform victims and potential victims that, regardless of what types of attempts they used to prevent or avoid sexual assault, that the one to blame for the victimization is the assailant, not the victim, no matter what the circumstances.

APPENDIX 7-A:
ROLE REVERSAL EXPERIENCE*

<u>CAUTION</u> - This activity will only work well with those groups in which

- there has been some trust established between the participants and the leader.
- not all participants know each other.
- there are nearly equal numbers of males and females.
- there is at least 1 hour remaining to allow participants to experience the feelings elicited by the activity and to process the activity.
- the group is fairly talkative and willing to risk.
- there are some "hams" in the group.
- the facilitator is experienced in working with groups.
- there are at least 20 participants.

OBJECTIVES

1. To provide the participants with the experience of feeling how difficult it is from the opposite perspective in a dating interaction
2. To enable the participants to gain insight into how they may make the dating interaction less difficult
3. To have participants learn from their feelings and each other, rather than from the facilitator

DIRECTIONS

Participants are told that they will have an opportunity to experience the dating interaction from the opposite perspective or role which is usual for them (e.g., if one is usually the aggressor, then he or she will behave passively, and vice versa).

***Note:** From *Acquaintance Rape and Sexual Assault Prevention Training Manual* by A. Parrot, 1990, Ithica, NY: Cornell University. Reprinted with permission.

They are told that the goal for the new aggressors is to end up with a partner at the end of the 15-minute experience. In addition, they are to establish a long-range goal mentally (such as getting coffee, obtaining a good night kiss, engaging in petting, having intercourse, etc.), and do whatever they consider most effective in attaining the long-range goal.

TELL PARTICIPANTS

Please do not select someone who you know. Remember, if you do not know anything about your potential partner, the only criterion you can use for assessment or interest is the initial appearance of the individual. What type of strategy will you use to attract the person in which you are interested?

The passive participants are to wait until they are approached. The reputation of the passive participants is at stake if they consent to too much too fast. Once people's reputations are destroyed, they may have a difficult time finding someone to take care of them and support them forever. Therefore, the passive person must attract a potential partner, but not give him or her "too much too soon." On the other hand, if the passive person appears too prudish, the aggressor may find another possible partner.

If there is an uneven number of aggressors and passive participants, there will be some without partners. Therefore, individuals in each group should decide what they will do to end up with a partner.

The participants are next provided with the opportunity to interact with each other for 15 minutes to end up with a partner. Some will ask what to do if they do not consistently behave in one way or the other, but are in the middle. Tell them that on the continuum of behaviors it is unlikely that they are *exactly* in the middle, so they should behave in the manner which is least common for them; if they are truly *exactly* in the middle, they may choose either behavior.

It is important not to assume that all people in your group are heterosexual. Therefore, do not refer to aggression as a traditionally male behavior and passivity as a female behavior. Approximately 10% of the population is gay (homosexual), and that group will not gain any insights from this activity if they are forced to behave heterosexually.

The facilitator should not participate but should observe the interactions.

PROCESSING

1. Ask participants how it felt to be in the opposite role.
2. Discuss objectifying (it is easier to be rejected by someone you do not know well and are not "invested in"; therefore, it is less ego deflating to be rejected by a sex object rather than a person).
3. Ask which strategies were effective.
4. Ask how they felt when someone did to them what they usually do to others in a similar situation.
5. Ask what they learned about having to assume the opposite role.
6. If they had a choice, which role would they assume in real life?
7. Will their behavior change as a result of this activity? If so, how?
8. If they chose not to participate, what was the rationalization used for the refusal?

Good luck . . . this is an extremely difficult activity to facilitate, but one which provides participants with tremendous insights if done properly.

APPENDIX 7-B:
ASSERTIVENESS IN OUR LIVES*

INTRODUCTION

Introduce the session by using a nonthreatening example which relates to assertiveness but does not reduce discomfort associated with a discussion of sexuality. This is an example which relates to smoking in an elevator. Tell participants the following:

Imagine you are all nonsmokers who hate cigarette smoke. You are waiting for an elevator on the first floor, and you must ride to the third floor. When it arrives, you get on it - and so does someone with a lit cigarette.

- *What do you do?* (Try to elicit as many different responses as possible from the participants.)
- *Would your response be different if there were a "No Smoking" sign in the elevator?*
- *Would your response be different if this person were your supervisor or teacher?*
- *Would your response be different if the smoker were someone you wanted to date?*

PROCESSING

The responses probably ranged from very nonassertive (such as "I would hold my breath," or "I would get off the elevator and walk"), to aggressive (such as "cigarettes are disgusting," or "I would put it out for him or her"), to lying (such as "I am allergic to cigarette smoke"). Did the types of responses differ by gender? If so, why?

---

*Note: From *Acquaintance Rape and Sexual Assault Prevention Training Manual* by A. Parrot, 1990, Ithica, NY: Cornell University. Reprinted with permission.

Most likely, very few answers were assertive and would not fit into the formula of "When you do 'x,' I feel 'y,' and I want you to do 'z.'" Assertions are difficult with people we do not know but may be even more difficult with people we know.

There are several reasons that it is even more difficult to be assertive in a sexual interaction:

1. You must put your desires over those of someone you care about when you are asserting for something contrary to the desires of others.
2. You are not usually taught or encouraged to talk about sex or use sexual words in normal conversation.
3. Communication about sex often takes place in the context of "game playing," not honest communication about feelings.
4. We are not generally expected to share our feelings with others, especially if that sharing may make us vulnerable.
5. We may not be absolutely sure about what we want sexually.
6. We have been receiving conflicting messages from many different sources in our lives about what is correct and how we should behave sexually.
7. We can use the law or our health as reasons to be assertive about smoking because smoking may be hazardous to health and is illegal in some nonventilated public areas. It is not always illegal or unhealthy to engage in behaviors such as "petting."
8. Either men or women are allowed to dislike smoking, but neither sex is supposed to dislike sex, and each sex is bound by certain restrictive sex roles.

APPENDIX 7-C:
SEXUAL ASSERTIVENESS
DRAMATIZATION*

Consider the difference between the reactions elicited by each of these two situations in which assertiveness skills are applied in a dating situation where a woman initiates a conversation with a man (while shaking his hand):

SCENARIO 1

How do you do? I am _____ (insert a female's name), and I would like to invite you to have dinner with me. How does that sound to you?

(He will probably give an affirmative response.)

I just want you to know that I am only interested in petting above the waist for at least the first five dates, but after that I may consider sexual intercourse. Is that okay with you?

(He will probably think you are crazy.)

Ask the group what they think about that kind of assertiveness. Why does it sound so bizarre?

SCENARIO 2

How do you do? I am _____ (insert a female's name), and I would like to invite you to have dinner with me. How does that sound to you?

(He will probably give an affirmative response.)

I really love Chinese food, but I am not so hot on Mexican food. Would it be alright with you if we went to the little Chinese restaurant down the street?

(Wait for his response, negotiate if necessary.)

If we are in the mood after dinner and feel like a movie, since I am a real Michael J. Fox fan and I don't like Clint Eastwood, could we go see *Back to the Future III*?

(Wait for his response, negotiate if necessary.)

---

*Note:** From *Acquaintance Rape and Sexual Assault Prevention Training Manual* by A. Parrot, 1990, Ithica, NY: Cornell University. Reprinted with permission.

Ask the group how the second scenario sounded compared to the first. Why is it not acceptable for us to be assertive in sexual situations, while it is more acceptable to be assertive in nonsexual situations?

Would the reaction have been different if the man were asking the question? Why?

APPENDIX 7-D:
SEXUAL ASSERTIVENESS
USING "I" STATEMENTS*

INTRODUCTION

There are probably many things you like about your partner interpersonally and sexually. There are also some things you would like to change. If you don't have a partner right now, you still probably have an idea of what you would like and dislike in an interpersonal and sexual relationship.

A very difficult communication task is to let your partner know what you don't like in a way that will not cause hard feelings or anger. One way to do this is to explain that you don't like the act, but you like the person and you like many other acts performed by your partner. In addition, if you can suggest what you would like instead, your partner may not feel helpless when you say what you don't like.

It is easier to hear criticism when

- positive feedback is given at the same time.
- the act, not the person is rejected.
- the criticism does not come at a time of "high emotional investment." (For example, tell your partner at breakfast, rather than when you are making love.)
- only one criticism is given in a sitting so the person doesn't feel like there is nothing he or she can do right.
- the message is clear, and the verbal message matches the nonverbal message.

DIRECTIONS

For short-term relationships (if this is your first sexual interaction with this partner). If you feel you can't tell your partner what you like and don't like before you begin to interact sexually, then tell him or her immediately when a behavior you don't like begins.

***Note:** From *Acquaintance Rape and Sexual Assault Prevention Training Manual* by A. Parrot, 1990, Ithica, NY: Cornell University. Reprinted with permission.

1. Use the formula "When you do 'x,' I feel 'y,' and I want you to do 'z.'" Be consistent with your verbal and non-verbal messages.

2. Reject the behavior, not the person (e.g., don't say "You are a terrible lover," or "Can't you do anything right?", but "When you kiss my neck in that way, I feel uncomfortable and I'd like you to stop kissing my neck." Make sure the feeling you indicate is clearly negative).

3. Do not allow the behavior to continue once you have clearly stated your displeasure with it.

4. If your partner does not stop that behavior, ask him or her to explain what he or she thinks you said. If your partner does not understand, explain again using different words, and check to make sure your verbal and non-verbal messages are consistent. If he or she understands, but still will not stop, *get out of the situation*; your wishes are being ignored.

For long-term relationships (to be done in the session). Make a list of the things you like and dislike about what your partner does sexually. Now circle those things in the dislike column which you really want changed, and leave the items which you could live with. Now number the circled items in the order of most important to least important ("1" being the most important).

To be done at home with your partner. When you talk with your partner about this, have him or her make a list for you, too. Then set aside a time when you will not be interrupted to discuss these issues. Tell your partner one thing from your like list, then one from your dislike list, and then finally another from your like list. When you are discussing the item from the dislike list, be specific, provide an alternate or substitute behavior, and put the dislike item in the formula of "When you do 'x,' I feel 'y'" (e.g., "When you ask me to give you a massage, but you won't give me one afterwards, I feel exploited or unimportant; I wouldn't feel that way if you would give me a back massage, too"). Then ask your partner to repeat back to you the positives, the negatives, the feelings you stated, and the suggestions you made. Once your partner has clearly heard all of what you have said, then switch roles, and your partner will tell you what he or she does not like.

Work on only one item at a time, and when you have mastered that, then go on to another one on your dislike list. Continue to revise your lists, and keep moving the improved behaviors over to your like side. This process could take months, but the results will be worth it.

REFERENCES

Bart, P. B., & O'Brien, P. H. (1985). *Stopping Rape: Successful Survival Strategies*. New York: Pergamon.

Bateman, P. (1982). *Acquaintance Rape: Awareness and Prevention*. Seattle: Alternatives to Fear.

Burt, M. R. (1980). Cultural myths and supports of rape. *Journal of Personality and Social Psychology, 38*, 217-230.

Check, J. V. P., & Malamuth, N. M. (1983). Sex role stereotyping and reactions to depictions of stranger versus acquaintance rape. *Journal of Personality and Social Psychology, 45*, 344-356.

Clark, A., Clemes, H., & Bean, R. (1983). *How to Raise Teenagers' Self-Esteem*. San Jose, CA: Ohaus.

Farrell, W. (1986). *Why Men Are the Way They Are*. New York: McGraw Hill.

Gordon, M. T., & Riger, S. (1989). *The Female Fear*. New York: The Free Press.

Jackson, T. L. (1991). A university athletic department's rape and assault experiences. *Journal of College Student Development, 32*, 77-78.

Jackson, T. L. (1994, July). *Sexual Responsibility: Assault Prevention and Safe Dating*. NCAA Life Skills Program, Kansas City, MO.

Kanin, E. (1967). Reference groups and sex conduct: Normal variations. *Sociology Quarterly, 8*, 495-504.

Kanin, E. (1984). Date rape: Unofficial criminals and victims. *Victimology: An International Journal, 9*, 95-108.

Koss, M. P. (1985). The hidden rape victims: Personality, attitudinal, and situational characteristics. *Psychology of Women Quarterly, 9*, 193-212.

Koss, M. P., Goodman, L. A., Browne, A., Fitzgerald, L. F., Keita, G. P., & Russo, N. F. (1994). *No Safe Haven: Male Violence Against Women at Home, at Work, and in the Community*. Washington, DC: American Psychological Association.

Koss, M. P., Leonard, K. E., Beezley, D. A., & Oros, C. J. (1985). Nonstranger sexual aggression: A discriminant analysis of the psychological characteristics of the undetected offenders. *Sex Roles, 12*, 981-992.

Lee, L. (1987). Rape prevention: Experiential training for men. *Journal of Counseling and Development, 66,* 100-101.

Lewin, M. (1985). Unwanted intercourse: The difficulty in saying no. *Psychology of Women Quarterly, 9,* 184-192.

Lott, B. (1987). *Women's Lives: Themes and Variations in Gender Living.* Monterey, CA: Brooks/Cole.

Malamuth, N. M. (1981). Rape proclivity among males. *Journal of Social Issues, 37,* 138-157.

McCarthy, G. (1981). *Assertion Skills for Young Women.* Tucson, AZ: The National Female Advocacy Project.

Muehlenhard, C., & Hollabaugh, L. C. (1988). Do women sometimes say no when they mean yes? The prevalence and correlates of women's token resistance to sex. *Journal of Personality and Social Psychology, 54,* 872-879.

Parrot, A. (1984, April). *How Locus of Control and Self-Esteem Contribute to Acquaintance Rape Prevention.* Paper presented at the Eastern Region meeting of the Society for the Scientific Study of Sex, Philadelphia, PA.

Parrot, A. (1990a). *Acquaintance Rape and Sexual Assault Prevention Training Manual.* Ithaca, NY: Cornell University.

Parrot, A. (1990b, April). Date rape. *Medical Aspects of Human Sexuality, 1,* 28-31.

Parrot, A. (1991). Vital childhood lessons: The role of parenting in the prevention of sexual coercion. In E. Grauerholz & M. A. Koralewski (Eds.), *Sexual Coercion: A Sourcebook on Its Nature, Causes, and Prevention* (pp. 45-73). Lexington, MA: Lexington Books.

Parrot, A., Cummings, N., & Jackson, T. (1994, October). *Playing the Game On and Off the Field.* Plenary session presented at the 4th International Conference on Sexual Assault and Harassment on Campus, Philadelphia, PA.

Powell, E. (1991). *Talking Back to Sexual Pressure.* Minneapolis, MN: CompCare.

Quinsey, V. L., & Upfold, D. (1985). Rape completion and victim injury as a function of female resistance strategy. *Canadian Journal of Behavioral Science, 17,* 40-49.

Rapaport, K., & Burkhart, B. (1984). Personality and attitudinal characteristics of sexually coercive college males. *Journal of Abnormal Psychology, 93,* 216-221.

Rozee, P., Bateman, P., & Gilmore, T. (1991). The personal per-
    spective: How to avoid acquaintance rape. In A. Parrot & L.
    Bechthofer (Eds.), *Acquaintance Rape: The Hidden Crime*
    (pp. 337-354). New York: Wiley.
Russell, D. H. (1984). *Sexual Exploitation: Rape, Child Sexual
    Abuse, and Workplace Harassment.* Beverly Hills: Sage.
Shanor, K. (1978). *The Shanor Study: The Sexual Sensitivity of
    the American Male.* New York: Dial.
Tavris, C., & Wade, C. (1984). *The Longest War: Sex Differ-
    ences in Perspective* (2nd ed.). San Diego: Harcourt, Brace,
    & Jovanovich.

Summary

Thomas L. Jackson

PURPOSES OF THIS BOOK

The preceding seven chapters were designed to provide the reader with a comprehensive background in the complex issue and traumatic consequences associated with the crime of acquaintance rape. As was stated in the introductory chapter, the intent was to present a wide range of topics involving acquaintance rape, while allowing the reader to consolidate this information in a clinically relevant fashion. The goal of the present chapter is to assist in this consolidation as well as provide the clinician with a philosophical rubric under which this information may be organized.

Three major goals were established for this book. We hoped the information provided in this book would (a) increase clinicians' sensitivity regarding the individual and societal contexts under which acquaintance rape occurs, (b) enhance clinicians' assessment and treatment knowledge and skills in working with victims and perpetrators of acquaintance rape, and (c) expand clinicians' fund of information and repertoire of techniques with regard to education and prevention strategies designed to prevent unwanted sexual contact in the context of both personal and professional relationships.

With regard to the first goal, this book was developed to provide clinicians with a more thorough understanding of the individual and societal contexts surrounding acquaintance rape. The material presented in the first two chapters was designed to help lift the veils of silence and ignorance surrounding acquaintance rape. The information presented in this book also suggests that the only effective approach to combating acquaintance rape requires attacking the problem on two fronts.

First, effective intervention approaches designed for individuals who are victims and perpetrators of acquaintance rape, as well as others within their social network, must be implemented. Chapters 3, 4, and 5 of this book addressed assessment and treatment issues with these groups. Second, through education and prevention programs such as those presented in Chapters 6 and 7, those individuals identified to be at risk for acquaintance rape victimization and perpetration must be disabused of rape myths, informed regarding the horrific costs of rape, and provided with effective communications and supportive strategies to prevent acquaintance rape's continuing occurrence. Ultimately such information must be communicated to society at large. None of the individuals associated with this book is naïve enough to believe that acquaintance rape can be totally eliminated. It is clear that as long as men and women interact, unwanted sexual contact will continue. However, if the information, techniques, and philosophy presented in the preceding seven chapters are widely enough disseminated and incorporated into clinical practice, it is believed that the costs of acquaintance rape to the individual could be substantially reduced, and the frequency of unwanted sexual contact between acquaintances could be lowered, at least among those with whom this information is shared.

With regard to the second goal, the clinician who is now finishing this book should be better prepared to approach rape and sexual assault victims and perpetrators with an increased armamentarium of assessment and therapeutic techniques. The information provided will assist clinicians in the early identification of both victims and perpetrators. This early identification will facilitate more accurate diagnoses and earlier interventions designed to insure the greatest chance of symptom amelioration and behavioral and lifestyle changes. The techniques and orientations presented will further allow the clinician to more effectively help victims through the healing process and modify perpetrators' attitudes and behaviors.

Finally and, in the editor's opinion, most importantly, the clinicians finishing this book will be more sensitive to the potential for unwanted sexual contact in all of the relationships they encounter, both in their practice and in their personal lives. In the context of clinical assessment, relationship assessment applies whether the clinician sees individuals or couples. This information is relevant to the counseling of couples in dating relationships, couples involved in premarital counseling, or married or cohabiting couples. In all of these relationships, the likelihood of sexual assault can be reduced by incorporating the education and communications material presented in Chapters 6 and 7 into the clinicians' treatment plans.

From a personal standpoint, readers of this book may become more sensitized to both verbal and nonverbal components of sexual communications in their own relationships. This may apply to the relationships of family members as well. Clearly, the educational component of dealing with sexual assault can lead to prevention of unwanted sexual contact in both professional and personal domains.

THE SCOPE OF RAPE REVISITED

A truism in presenting rape education and prevention programs is that, unless participation is made mandatory, those who can most benefit from this information are not in the audience. We can probably say with equal certainty that clinicians reading this book, being the caregivers, the sensitive, empathic clinicians who have dedicated their professional lives to providing symptomatic relief and helping individuals and couples lead more adaptive lifestyles, do not share the common social misconceptions and myths associated with acquaintance rape. At the risk of preaching to the choir, however, it must be stated that the public is far from recognizing the true scope of the problem of acquaintance rape in our society.

As evidence of our society's continuing ignorance of and insensitivity to the issues underlying acquaintance rape, consider the following three recent examples presented in the media. First, consider the public fanfare that accompanied the release from prison of convicted rapist Mike Tyson. The polarization that exists in our society regarding whether or not acquaintance rape involves "real rape" manifested itself with a vengeance following his release. There were groups who variously acclaimed Tyson as either a positive role model or a disgrace, as a wrongly accused celebrity whose status was taken advantage of, or as the epitome of what is worst about today's sports heroes.

Second, consider the state legislator who proclaimed, in his argument against the legalization of abortion for victims of rape and incest, that "everyone knows you can't get pregnant from a rape. The juices aren't flowing, and nothing can happen when it's really a rape." This statement reflects some of the most primitive and nonscientific views ever encountered regarding the aftermath of forced sex. Although hopefully not representing the sentiments and beliefs of the majority of the general public, this official nevertheless gave voice to a sample of the ignorance and prejudices that surround rape and sexual assault.

Finally, consider the public hue and cry over the proliferation of pornography on the Internet. Many civil libertarians are demanding full and complete access to all Internet-available topics and services. At the same time, several authors are expressing concern regarding the data, presented earlier, that demonstrate a linkage between sexually aggressive stimuli and subsequent sexual aggression. It seems troublesome that as technology advances, many long-standing societal problems are potentially magnified and proliferated. Only through a comprehensive understanding and acknowledgment of the scope of the problem can a better commitment to dealing with acquaintance rape be made.

Clearly, rape is not solely a "women's problem," although each year countless women must deal with the ultimate invasion of privacy that rape represents. Likewise, rape is not just a "men's problem," although men are clearly responsible for perpetrating most cases of rape. Likewise, rape is not just a gender problem, although the vast majority of rapes are heterosexual in nature and appear to stem from many gender-related issues (see Chapter 2). From a more global standpoint, rape must be seen as a cultural, societal, and, with the Bosnian war rapes serving as just one example, clearly an international problem as well.

With the above in mind, the first two chapters of this book present clinicians with information that should heighten our sense of societal urgency in dealing with the issues of acquaintance rape. It should be clear from these and subsequent chapters that rape is a rapidly growing, yet vastly underreported, crime that leaves trauma in its wake; not only for the victim, but also for family members, friends, and acquaintances. With the surety that the number of rapes in the United States in any 1-year period can be measured in the hundreds of thousands, it must be clear to the reader that many within their clinical caseload - and even among their family and friends - are at risk for this traumatic crime. The statistics presented each year by the FBI in its *Uniform Crime Reports* provide only a "tip of the iceberg" vantage. The frequency of unwanted sexual contact is difficult to put into context professionally until you begin sampling your clinical population. It is also next to impossible to fully grasp the enormous impact of acquaintance rape on a more personal level unless you have been exposed to sexual assault, whether as a direct or indirect victim, as a perpetrator, as someone accused of being a perpetrator, or as a friend or family member of a victim or perpetrator.

In order to better understand the personal salience of acquaintance rape and unwanted sexual contact from a victim's perspective, consider our most recent survey of unwanted sexual contact. In our latest sample of college women (Giles & Jackson, 1996) fully 75% reported unwanted sexual contact at some time in their lives. More significantly, one-third of this sample reported experiences that met the legal definition of rape. That is, fully one-third of a sample of college women whose average age was only 19½ years old reported that they had sex against their will because they had been either physically threatened or forced, or they had sex when they did not want to because they were too drunk or drugged to resist. These are devastating incidence figures and seem to contradict the FBI's reports of dramatic decreases in reported rapes over the last 2 years (FBI, 1995). In order to personalize these statistics, you need only list 10 women with whom you are acquainted. If they are over 18, then try to imagine which two have *not* been victims of unwanted sexual contact. The magnitude of the problem is overwhelming. Although not all women who experience such contact are clinically symptomatic, the many who experience distress face a wall of silence. The implicit message they receive is, "If you aren't asked, don't tell, or you might be blamed." Using the information provided in this and other resources, we as clinicians must work to alleviate this problem.

CHAPTER SUMMARIES
AND CONSOLIDATION

Each of the preceding chapters stands on its own merit. The purpose of this section is to highlight individual contributions from each chapter and draw together issues addressed in different chapters to provide the clinician with a coherent view of acquaintance rape.

The first chapter clarified the definition of acquaintance rape. The authors pointed out that, although all forms of rape are underreported, underreporting is more common in cases where the victim knew the perpetrator, which occurs in approximately 80% of rapes. This underreporting is related to the failure of many acquaintance rape victims to acknowledge their experiences as constituting rape and is further confounded by society's notions of what constitutes "real rape." Lending further credence to the concept of underreporting, the incidence figures for rape and sexual assault provided by the FBI and from clinical research were contrasted.

This review of definitional/statistical/incidence issues was followed by the second chapter which presented several theoretical and empirical assertions regarding the occurrence and continuation of the crime of acquaintance rape. Chapter 2 discussed such factors as society's adherence to rape myths, the proliferation of pornography, hidden victims, perpetrator insensitivity, ignorant or uncaring legal and health care professionals, and victim self-blame as contributing to the maintenance of a rape culture. This chapter then detailed the severe underreporting of rape. With regard to acquaintance rape victims, fewer than 50% tell anyone, even their closest friends, about the assault, and fewer than 10% report the rape to police. It was also reported that few rape victims seek treatment specifically for rape, despite the fact that exceedingly high percentages of most clinical samples of females have been raped. As is pointed out in Chapter 2, all of these issues/factors can lead to an increased risk of revictimization without appropriate identification, treatment, and client education.

Although clinicians are less likely to treat perpetrators than victims, Chapter 3 provides extraordinarily useful information regarding perpetrators of rape and acquaintance rape. The focus on personality and attitudinal variables associated with acquaintance rape perpetrators provides the clinician with strategies for assessing the potential for sexual assault perpetration in their client population. The comprehensive assessment and treatment review further provides the clinician with additional, empirically supported devices and techniques to use when working with this difficult-to-treat and not yet well-understood population. Perhaps most important of all is the discussion of sexual aggression proclivity, followed by practical and ethical issues involved in assessing and treating these potentially dangerous individuals.

Chapter 4 began the two-chapter sequence on victim identification, assessment, and treatment issues. This chapter provides an excellent, comprehensive review of the Rape Trauma Syndrome in its various forms, including acknowledged and hidden victims of both stranger and acquaintance rapes. The appendix, which details suggestions for assessment, will assist the clinician in specifying the constellation of symptoms experienced by individual victims. This chapter also prompts the clinician to consider the possibility of potential victimization experiences in those who have not yet reported victimization given the clinical presentation of comorbid problems.

Chapter 5, which addressed the treatment of victims, represents a unique contribution to the literature. This chapter clarifies that the use of manualized or problem-specific treatments alone is not necessarily sufficient to insure relevant and meaningful client improvements. Understanding, compassion, and building trust in a victim cannot be accomplished by problem-specific treatment regimes alone. Although structured treatment techniques are presented in this chapter, and discussed in Chapter 2, the focus of Chapter 5 rests more heavily on the constructs of identification, therapeutic alliance, and the working through of the victimization and consequent adaptation. These well-articulated processes, discussed in terms of validated techniques and orientations, provide the clinician with a wealth of understanding involving the healing process the victim must accomplish.

The distinction between immediate and delayed treatment-seekers, and the subsequent theoretical and therapeutic implications, represents another important contribution from Chapter 5. At least one recent program of research (Giles & Jackson, 1996) supports Chapter 5's reliance on the therapeutic alliance, increasing coping strategies, and enhancing self-esteem in acquaintance rape victims. The authors found that post-traumatic stress disorder symptomatology in a sample of over 200 victims of unwanted sexual contact was mediated by self-esteem levels of the victims. Causal modeling techniques indicated that victims' self-esteem was, in turn, directly affected by the degree and quality of social support the victim received and the level and types of self-blame in which the victim engaged. Finally, both of these constructs were directly affected by the severity, type, and frequency of sexual assault the victims suffered. Clearly, the Rape Trauma Syndrome represents a complex cluster of symptoms and attitudes that demands the combination of therapeutic interventions, including content and process considerations that Chapter 5 presents.

Chapter 6 presented rape education and prevention programs for various groups. Program content included safe dating tips, common statistics, rape myths, general and specific safety tips, and suggestions for how to help victims. The information presented in the appendices can also be used with individual clients or couples in the clinician's practice. These tips may also have applications for clinicians in their personal lives, as sons and daughters begin dating.

Finally, Chapter 7 provides basic sexually assertive communication skills that have been demonstrated to decrease miscommunication regarding sex in dating and increase self-esteem and self-confidence. Used in conjunction with chapters detailing the assessment, treatment, and education issues, information in this chapter should allow the clinician to assist victims or potential victims by providing proactive skills to communicate clear expectations of dates and acquaintances with regard to current and future physical interactions.

A FINAL NOTE

This book was intended to provide the clinician with a comprehensive background and understanding of acquaintance rape. It has presented definitions; incidence figures; individual, cultural, and societal reasons why acquaintance rape continues; identification, assessment, and treatment strategies for both perpetrators and victims of acquaintance rape; and education, prevention, and communications-training strategies that can be used by clinicians for treating individuals or couples, or for presentation to various community groups.

It is up to you, the reader, to first believe that the problem exists in its stated proportions, to next understand the maintaining variables and forces, and then, finally, perhaps using some of the material presented in this book, to do something about it, through individual and conjoint treatment as well as community interventions.

REFERENCES

Federal Bureau of Investigation. (1995). *Uniform Crime Reports: Preliminary Annual Release.* Washington, DC: U.S. Department of Justice.

Giles, M., & Jackson, T. (1996). *Long Term Consequences of Sexual Victimization and Their Mediators.* Manuscript submitted for publication.

Subject Index

A

Acceptance of Interpersonal Violence Scale, 82

Accommodation, 104, 117, 124, 126, 147, 148, 157, 160, 165-170

Acquaintance rape:

    acknowledged victim, 101-102

        symptoms, 105-115

    compared to stranger rape, 102-103, 118

    in context of ongoing relationship, 24

    definition, 100-101

    double bind of, 104

    "fit" with "typical" rape victim profile, 101

    gender inequality and, 19

    help seeking, 3

    hidden victim of, 102 (*see also* Acquaintance rape, unacknowl-

        edged victim)

    impact of, 12

    incidence statistics, 11-12, 17-18, 247-248

    influences/causal factors:

        situational variables, 24-28

        societal factors, 19-23

    invisibility of victims, 3

    as multidetermined crime, 19

    negative outcome, 25

    offender's vantage point, 25-26

    postassault factors, 28-30

    relabeling of, 3

    releasers of, 24-28

    reporting rate, 11, 30-31

    self-blame in victims, 29, 114, 120, 122, 123, 125, 126

        examples of, 153

If You Found This Book Useful . . .

You might want to know more about our other titles.

If you would like to receive our latest catalog, please return this form:

Name:_____
(Please Print)

Address:_____

Address:_____

City/State/Zip:_____

Telephone:(_____)_____

I am a:

_____ Psychologist
_____ Psychiatrist
_____ School Psychologist
_____ Clinical Social Worker

_____ Mental Health Counselor
_____ Marriage and Family Therapist
_____ Not in Mental Health Field
_____ Other:_____

◆   ◆   ◆

Professional Resource Press
P.O. Box 15560
Sarasota, FL 34277-1560

Telephone #941-366-7913
FAX #941-366-7971

AR/1/96

Add A Colleague To Our Mailing List . . .

If you would like us to send our latest catalog to one of your colleagues, please return this form.

Name:_____
(Please Print)

Address:_____

Address:_____

City/State/Zip:_____

Telephone:(_____)_____

I am a:

_____ Psychologist   _____ Mental Health Counselor
_____ Psychiatrist   _____ Marriage and Family Therapist
_____ School Psychologist   _____ Not in Mental Health Field
_____ Clinical Social Worker   _____ Other:_____

◆   ◆   ◆

Professional Resource Press
P.O. Box 15560
Sarasota, FL 34277-1560

Telephone #941-366-7913
FAX #941-366-7971

AR/1/96

Add A Colleague To Our Mailing List . . .

If you would like us to send our latest catalog to one of your colleagues, please return this form.

Name:_____
(Please Print)

Address:_____

Address:_____

City/State/Zip:_____

Telephone:(_____)_____

I am a:

_____ Psychologist   _____ Mental Health Counselor
_____ Psychiatrist   _____ Marriage and Family Therapist
_____ School Psychologist   _____ Not in Mental Health Field
_____ Clinical Social Worker   _____ Other:_____

◆   ◆   ◆

Professional Resource Press
P.O. Box 15560
Sarasota, FL 34277-1560

Telephone #941-366-7913
FAX #941-366-7971

AR/1/96

If You Found This Book Useful . . .

You might want to know more about our other titles.

If you would like to receive our latest catalog, please return this form:

Name:_____

(Please Print)

Address:_____

Address:_____

City/State/Zip:_____

Telephone:(_____)_____

I am a:

_____ Psychologist   _____ Mental Health Counselor
_____ Psychiatrist   _____ Marriage and Family Therapist
_____ School Psychologist   _____ Not in Mental Health Field
_____ Clinical Social Worker   _____ Other:_____

◆   ◆   ◆

Professional Resource Press
P.O. Box 15560
Sarasota, FL 34277-1560

Telephone #941-366-7913
FAX #941-366-7971

AR/1/96